Paul Kingsnorth was born in 1972. He studied history at Oxford University, and is a former deputy editor of the *Ecologist* magazine. www.paulkingsnorth.net

ONE NO, MANY YESES

a journey to the heart of the
global resistance movement

Paul Kingsnorth

PAUL KINGSNORTH

*f*P
FREE PRESS

First published in Great Britain by The Free Press in 2003
An imprint of Simon & Schuster UK Ltd
A Viacom company
This edition published, 2004

PICTURE CREDITS
Chapter 1: Antonio Turok; 2, 3, 5, 7: Paul Kingsnorth
4: Associated Press; 6: Eartha Melzer; 8: www.adbusters.org
9: AFP/Menahem Kahana

1 3 5 7 9 10 8 6 4 2

Simon & Schuster UK Ltd
Africa House
64–78 Kingsway
London WC2B 6AH

Simon & Schuster Australia
Sydney

www.simonsays.co.uk

A CIP catalogue for this book is available
from the British Library.

ISBN: 0-7432-2027-7

Typeset by M Rules
Printed and bound in Great Britain by
Cox & Wyman Ltd, Reading, Berks

For my parents

CONTENTS

ACKNOWLEDGEMENTS

This book could not have been written or published without the assistance of the many people all over the world who helped me through, kept me going, put me up, fed me information, inspired me and made my journey worth undertaking. If I have missed any of their names from this list, I can only plead information overload and offer an apology. They have my gratitude anyway.

In Mexico, José Maria Sbert took me to dinner without really knowing who I was, and Ryan Zinn and Ernesto Ledesma, of Global Exchange in Chiapas, were enormously helpful. Gustavo Esteva was kind and helpful; I am, as the first chapter makes clear, indebted to him for my title. Sophie Style, Mary Zacaroli and Mantina Garcia Lopez Loaeza pointed me in some important directions before I got to the country. Lucy Ginsburg made it all possible with her support and tireless translation, and also showed me how to drink tequila properly. It wouldn't have been so much fun without her.

In Bolivia, Jim and Lynn Schultz put me up in their house for a week, and their dog, Simone, woke me up every morning, whether I wanted her to or not. I am hugely grateful for their hospitality, and for Jim's help in steering me through the politics of the Cochabamba water war. In South Africa, Patrick Bond put me up, fed me food and information, ferried me around and let me drink his gin with never a murmur: his help was invaluable. Heinrich Bohmke housed me in his flat, took me to Chatsworth and introduced me to Durban's seedier nightlife, for which I nevertheless forgive him. With Ashwin Desai, he has my gratitude. George Dor was helpful and patient with my questions, and Trevor

Ngwane, Virginia Setshedi and Dudu Mphenyeke were similarly magnanimous.

In the USA, Bill Talen, Bill Brown, Al Decker, David Barsamian, Brian Drolet, Marty Durlin, David Solnit and the ever-elusive Mike took me through the complexities of cultural activism and the media wars, and showed me so much that I couldn't fit it all into the book. Jeff Milchen and Jennifer Rockne in Boulder, Colorado, showed me some kind hospitality on my first visit to the USA and introduced me to corporate paradigm-shifting and the Rocky Mountains. Mary Zepernick, Nancy Price and Lois Robins fed me and put me up without ever having met me before. Virginia Rasmussen, Jan Edwards, Bill Meyer, Doug Hammerstrom, Jeff Kaplan, Paul Cienfuegos and Kaitlin Sopoci-Belknap were friendly, generous with their time and unfailingly helpful.

In West Papua, many people who cannot be named showed me enormous hospitality and gave me vital help, often putting themselves at risk as they did so. I hope I have done their cause some good here in return. I am hugely grateful to Galile in particular, and to Steve; they both know who they are. In Brazil, Jan Rocha and Sue Branford gave me some vital pointers and Daniella Hart provided an essential translation service. Most of all, I am grateful to the many MST settlers who gave me their time.

Back at home, friends and family made a real difference. My brothers Neil and Simon Kingsnorth, provided me with vital research material and an excellent website, respectively. Colleagues at the *Ecologist*, particularly Stephanie Roth, Malcolm Tait and Zac Goldsmith, behaved like true (and truly patient) friends. My agent, Patrick Walsh, got me where I am today and my editor at Simon & Schuster, Andrew Gordon, sensitively nursed what you hold in your hands to fruition. Any mistakes or oddities that remain after all this are, naturally, mine.

Mark Lynas and Katharine Ainger bravely read through everything I cobbled together, offered up excellent advice, most of which I followed, and prevented me from burning the whole thing in my darkest hours. If it weren't for Katharine's love, advice and patience I might not have finished it at all. My parents, who have put up with my pig-headed political opinions for a decade, made me who I am today, by accident or design, and have been supportive throughout. A huge amount of love and gratitude goes out to them for everything they have done for me over the years.

Finally, this book stands on the shoulders of the hundreds of people I spoke to on my travels, in fields and farmland, in houses and studios, in forests and autonomous villages, in convention and convergence centres. Beyond them, it stands on the shoulders of the millions more who have built up the movement it attempts to describe, far beyond any spotlight and for no personal gain. Their bravery, commitment, vision and sheer hard work is hardly ever acknowledged. If the world turns for the better, it will be their doing.

1 'to open a crack in history'

'While Chiapas, in our opinion, does not pose a fundamental threat to Mexican political stability, it is perceived so by many in the investment community. The government will need to eliminate the Zapatistas to demonstrate effective control of the national territory and of security policy.'

CHASE MANHATTAN BANK EMERGING MARKETS GROUP, INTERNAL REPORT, 1995

'It is good for them to know, the gentlemen of money, that the times of yesterday will no longer be those of today nor those of tomorrow . . . They shall no longer humiliate those of us who are the colour of earth. We have always had a voice. But it shall no longer be a murmur which lowers its head. It shall now be a shout which lifts the gaze and which shall force them to see us as we are, and to accept us as we are.'

SUBCOMANDANTE MARCOS, ZAPATISTA ARMY OF NATIONAL LIBERATION, 2001

Mexico, January 1994

What may turn out to be the biggest political movement of the twenty-first century emerged from the rainforest remnants of southern Mexico on 1 January 1994, carried down darkened, cobbled colonial streets by 3,000 pairs of black leather boots at precisely thirty minutes past midnight. The owners of the boots carried rifles and the odd AK-47 or Uzi. Those who had drawn short straws carried fake wooden guns.

Three thousand faces, hidden by black woollen ski masks, bore the distinctive features of the Mayan Indians of Central America; a people outgunned, outcompeted, pillaged, slaughtered or simply passed over since the Spanish *conquistadores* first arrived on their shores in the sixteenth century. Now, half a millennium later, here in Chiapas, Mexico's poorest and southernmost state, 'the ones without faces, the ones without voices' had come to make the world listen.

The people of San Cristobal de las Casas, the old *conquistador* capital of Chiapas, were still groggy from their New Year celebrations when their town came alive with the sound of marching boots. They heard orders barked in Tzotzil, a local Mayan language, by the black-haired major, carbine in her hands, pistol strapped to her chest, who commanded this uninvited army. And from the picturesque central square, the Plaza 31 de Marzo, its ancient yellow cathedral and colonial government buildings framed by a clear white moon, they heard the sound of gunshots.

Those citizens brave or curious enough to venture out into the square were met with a sight they were unlikely to forget: dozens of masked guerrillas were swarming around the Plaza. Some were standing guard with their battered rifles, others were surrounding the police headquarters, while a third group, armed with sledgehammers, pounded on the great wooden doors of the Municipal

Palace. There could be little doubt in the minds of the people of San Cristobal about what they were witnessing. It was the first act of a revolution.

By the time the rebels began carrying furniture out of the Municipal Palace and using it to build barricades across the streets, to check the expected approach of the Mexican army, the Plaza was thronging with locals, drunks, tourists and curious spectators. Then, as they watched, a small group of guerrillas raised a flag in the middle of the elegant square – a black flag, printed with four red letters: EZLN.

As they did so, a masked figure emerged on to the balcony of the Municipal Palace. In his hand he held a piece of paper. It was a declaration of war against the Mexican government: one which, on that same morning, would be read aloud to the people of six other towns in Chiapas which this 'EZLN' had also claimed as its own.

'We are the product of five hundred years of struggle,' he read as, in the background, more gunfire and palls of smoke indicated that a rebel column was storming the police headquarters. 'We are the inheritors of the true builders of this nation . . . denied the most elemental preparation so they can use us as cannon-fodder and pillage the wealth of our country. They don't care that we have nothing, absolutely nothing . . . There is no peace or justice for ourselves and our children . . . But today we say: *Ya basta!* Enough is enough!'

Five hundred miles away, Mexico's president, Carlos Salinas, and his anointed heir, Luis Donaldo Colosio, were celebrating the New Year in an exclusive holiday resort on the Pacific coast. As the midnight bells rang, Salinas and Colosio raised glasses of champagne and toasted the official arrival of NAFTA – the North American Free Trade Agreement – which, at the stroke of midnight, officially came into operation. With the sound of those bells, NAFTA had created, for the first time in history, one great borderless free market between Mexico, Canada and the USA.

Mexico had officially entered the modern world, and Salinas was celebrating his legacy.

Two hours later he was on the telephone, listening to news of a development that would shatter not only that legacy, but his successor's presidency and his party's age-old iron grip on Mexican politics; and which, later – much later – would begin to shake the legitimacy of the global free-trade project itself. The Secretary of Defense was calling from Mexico City, and he had bad news. An armed insurgent force, calling itself the Zapatista Army of National Liberation – EZLN – had seized control of seven towns in Chiapas state and declared war on the army, the government – and NAFTA itself.

'Are you sure?' croaked the president.[1]

Back in San Cristobal, a journalist had collared the masked man who had led the assault on the police station. Unlike the other guerrillas, what could be seen of his face suggested not an Indian but a *ladino* – a Spanish Mexican. The man wore bandoliers across his chest, and a tattered green cap studded with red stars on top of his ski mask. A pipe protruded from his mouth. Ignoring Major Ana Maria, the Indian woman who had led the invasion of the city – which, as an Indian woman, was exactly what she had come to expect – the journalist asked this tall white man with the big nose who he was.

'Who am I?'

'Yes! Are you, perhaps, "Commander Tiger"? Or "Commander Lion?"'

The man with the pipe looked at the journalist with a mixture of weariness and amusement behind the black wool of his mask.

'No,' he said. 'I am Marcos. Subcomandante Marcos.'

It didn't last. That day, around 3,000 Zapatista soldiers took control of seven towns in Chiapas. The government responded swiftly and decisively: 15,000 troops poured into the state; helicopter gunships bombed Indian villages, killing 150 people; specialist assault teams hunted down the Zapatista units. The guerrillas retreated from San Cristobal barely twenty-four hours after they had arrived. Within twelve days the government, responding to an unexpected surge of national support for the masked rebels, declared a ceasefire, and the EZLN melted back into the rainforest from whence it had come.

As revolutions go it was, shall we say, unimpressive. In less than a fortnight, it seemed, the Zapatistas had been crushed, along with their insurgency. An ignominious end to yet another ignominious revolt: the latest in the long line of guerrilla uprisings that Latin America just couldn't seem to grow out of.

And yet. As the truth about these 'Zapatistas' – a grass-roots peasant army who named themselves after the followers of the slain hero of the original Mexican revolution of 1910, Emiliano Zapata – began to emerge, so did something curiously different. These, it seemed, were no ordinary *guerrilleros*. For one, they claimed that they had no desire to seize state power. Unlike so many Latin American revolutionaries before them, their aim, they said, was not to grab 'power' on behalf of 'the people', but to dissolve power down to the level of communities – to take back what they claimed had been rightly theirs, before governments and private economic interests stole it from them. 'Power is not taken,' they would later be heard to say. 'It is constructed.'

Their language, too, was new. Where was the talk of 'the proletariat', 'the bourgeoisie', Marx, Lenin, Mao, permanent revolution? Why, instead of appealing to 'the workers' to rise up and join them, were they calling on something called 'civil society' to stand between them and the soldiers of their government? Why did they speak not of a dictatorship of the proletariat but of a rebirth of democracy? Why was their uprising directed not just at a government, nor even simply at the usual capitalist stooges, but at an apparently innocuous regional trade treaty?

Why did this Marcos character, who spoke in poetry, stories and riddles, describe his homeland as 'an object of shame dressed in the colour of money'? And why were so many people beginning to describe what had happened that day in the green high-sided canyons of Chiapas as 'the first post-modern revolution'?

The answers to these questions would take a while for the world to figure out. When it did, this tiny indigenous rebellion in an overlooked part of Central America would provide the spark that lit a bigger rebellion all across the world. The Zapatistas would become the unwitting, but not unwilling, forgers of a truly global insurgency against history's first truly global system.

Like most of the rest of the world, I didn't notice the Zapatista uprising at the time. I was at university, writing essays and finding myself dragged into a mini-revolution of my own: the road protest movement which was then spreading like a rash over what was left of the British countryside. Up trees, down tunnels, in squatted factories, padlocked to bridges and balanced on top of digger arms I, like thousands of others, was politicised by the road protests, and began to make the links between what was happening in Newbury, Winchester, Bath and Leytonstone and what was happening to the wider world.

Over the next few years I got involved in what seemed to be a putative but growing mass movement, in Britain and beyond, which was taking those links to the streets. As it occupied motorways, holding street parties where previously there had been traffic jams; invaded the shareholder meetings of oil companies; lobbied parliament; refused to lobby parliament; marched, grandstanded and grew, it talked of the global forces behind the problems it was trying to tackle. It talked of 'neoliberalism' (whatever that was); of powerful, unaccountable corporations, of a grinding-down of democracy, of a global economic machine spinning out of control, eating up the things that people valued and spitting out share prices as it passed.

It began to talk, too, of these Zapatistas. I heard that the EZLN were something new, radical, remarkable. I heard that they had reinvented politics. I heard that Chiapas was the lodestone of a new revolution. I heard that they were anarchists, communists, reactionaries, fools, poets, warriors. I heard that they were none of the above. I heard that Subcomandante Marcos was the new Che Guevara. I heard that they did an extremely natty line in T-shirts.

In September 2000, I went to Prague, and, with 20,000 others, tried to shut down the annual meeting of the World Bank and the International Monetary Fund. There I saw something extraordinary. Protesters from all over Europe were joined by others from around the world in an unprecedented coalition of the most unlikely, and yet strangely united, forces. And on the streets, among the banners, the flags, the tear-gas, the batons and D-locks and stun grenades, the energy and the ideas, thousands shouted a slogan first heard in the San Cristobal Plaza on that January morning in 1994: '*Ya basta!*' Enough is enough.

Back home, after that, it was difficult not to be disillusioned with the way the world was going, and the people who were running it. The world was changing, further and faster than anyone could remember, and none of the old answers, from left or right or anywhere, seemed to fit the new questions. On the streets, meanwhile, something was massing. At the *Ecologist* magazine, where I was working, reports were coming in every day, from all over the world, of resistance, rebellion, uprisings against the system. If you added up the numbers involved, it totalled millions of people, in dozens of countries. Few of the stories ever made the mainstream media. Something big was happening out there, and nobody was listening.

I couldn't escape a growing conviction that what I was seeing was the fumbling birth of a genuinely new political movement – something international, something different and something potentially huge. But what exactly was it? Where had it come from? Was it really, as so many claimed, 'global', and if so, what did that mean? Did it have any substantial ideas beyond objecting to the status quo? Was it a flash in the pan or a bushfire across the political landscape? I felt a part of it, whatever it was. I wanted to know.

It took me eight months of travelling across five continents to get near to answering those questions. I knew that to really understand this movement I would have to go and see it at work – not simply in the cities where the highly publicised protests happen, but in the places where the movement was really born, where its strength and numbers lie and where its essence can be found – places which lie mainly in poor countries, away from the camera's eye. Choosing some of the places to visit was difficult, but one decision was easy to make. I knew I had to go to where so many said this whole thing had been born: I had to go to Chiapas.

I knew that whatever had happened, and was happening, in Chiapas, would tell me a lot about this movement, and about the hopes that kept it alive. Hopes expressed by the shadowy Subcomandante two months after he stormed the police station in San Cristobal, in words which, as well as any other, provided an explanation for the hard struggle into the light of something genuinely new: 'In our dreams, we have seen another world.'

Mexico, August 2001

My plane touched down in a Mexico that would have been almost unthinkable just a few years before. In July 2000, the country had finally shaken off the world's longest-ever period of rule by one political party: one which, more or less, had been in existence since Mexico became the stage for the first revolution of the twentieth century.

In 1910, sick of the corrupt, thirty-four-year rule of their dictator-president Porfirio Díaz, the people of Mexico rose up in revolution. Armies of peasants, led by the populist radicals Pancho Villa and Emiliano Zapata, called for *tierra y libertad* – land and freedom – in a seven-year skirmish of competing interests. When the dust settled, in 1917, nearly a million lives had been lost, and Mexico had emerged with a new constitution and a new political order.

For seventy-one years that constitution had been – so they claimed, anyway – safeguarded by its descendants, the deliciously named Institutional Revolutionary Party (PRI). Seventy-one years is a long time in politics, and in the intervening period the PRI, who remained in power throughout, had moved from being (at least in theory) a party of revolutionary redistributists to a party of laissez-faire corporate libertarians; from a party of democrats to a party of oligarchs; and from a party loved, or at least supported, by the majority, to a party loathed or at best tolerated by most of its people.

Mexico was, theoretically, a democracy under the PRI, and had been since the revolution. In reality, elections were rigged so heavily and blatantly that for seven decades, despite growing popular discontent, the PRI managed to stay on top. But in 2000, the complacent party unexpectedly lost the first presidential election in its history. Shell-shocked, the rightful rulers of Mexico cleared their desks to make way for the parvenu Vicente Fox, ex-head of Coca-Cola Mexico, leader of the conservative National Action Party (PAN), cowboy, political novice and showman. It was the start of something very new. Would it be something very different?

A year later it wasn't yet clear what, if anything, would be changed by Fox's shock defeat of the PRI. It was beginning, though, to be obvious what wouldn't. Fox's PAN, like the PRI and perhaps even more so, were enthusiastic free marketeers, committed to NAFTA, 'globalisation', open markets and everything else that had given birth to the Zapatista rebellion. Fox, on coming to power, had boasted that he could solve the Chiapas problem 'in fifteen minutes' – and unlike his PRI forerunners, he was talking about dialogue rather than military crackdowns. When I arrived in Mexico City, though, he had been in power for a year, and the Zapatistas were still where they had been since January 1994 – in the forests of Chiapas, holding out for a new nation.

The twenty-hour bus ride from Mexico City to San Cristobal de las Casas is painful. On cracked leather seats with dubbed

American films blasting out from four television screens, the bus takes us through valleys and forests and fields, along motorways and pitted tracks, from a modernising metropolis towards something much older. I am here with a friend, Lucy, who speaks Spanish and has been to Mexico before. We arrive, dazed, in San Cristobal, check into a hotel, grab some food, and then wander the gently undulating cobbled streets, taking in the sights.

The lanes and squares are full of tourists, come to gaze on the colonial beauty of the buildings: the grey and white Municipal Palace, from the balcony of which the declaration of war was read; the vast, curlicued gold and white cathedral, like a conqueror watching over its people; the trees decked with ropes of red, gold and white for forthcoming Independence Day, and all around, the rolling green mountains.

In the central Plaza where the Zapatistas announced themselves to the world, withered old men in cowboy hats lean on poles strung with bags of candyfloss. Men with wooden boxes strung around their necks roam the square offering sweets, *chiclets*, single cigarettes. Chaotic kids chase you for money, try to clean your shoes, sell you dolls, purses, belts – the deserved fate of the rich foreign tourist. In the centre of the Plaza stands an iron bandstand reminiscent of the Bournemouth Pleasure Gardens, surrounded by lawns and flowerbeds, newspaper stands and shoe-cleaning stalls, their shadows painted on to the paving stones by a deep white sunlight.

San Cristobal is a beautiful city, but it tells you little about Chiapas. The only indication that over a quarter of the state's inhabitants are pre-conquest people are the Indian women, their black hair flowing in ponytails down their backs, long blue or black skirts, delicate white tops, ruffled in pink and green and yellow, the traditional colours of their villages. The women are in San Cristobal trying to sell necklaces, beads and trinkets to the tourists. They will step off the pavement as you pass because, even now, despite all that has happened since 1994, they know their place.

But look beyond San Cristobal, at the state of Chiapas itself, and you begin to see why an uprising happened here. Chiapas is paradoxically the poorest and the richest state in Mexico. It is the top producer of coffee in the country, growing 36 per cent of Mexico's total coffee production.[2] It produces 55 per cent of Mexico's hydro-power (from a series of vast dams, many built on requisitioned Indian land) and almost 20 per cent of the country's total electricity.[3] It produces 13 per cent of the country's maize, 5 per cent of its oil, and 12 per cent of its natural gas.[4] What remains of the heavily deforested Lacandon jungle, in the south of the state, is trumped in terms of Latin American biological diversity only by the Amazon. Chiapas, by any standards, is extraordinarily resource-rich.

Meanwhile, its people are extraordinarily poor, even by the standards of a nation in which 40 per cent of people live below the poverty line. For the riches of Chiapas do not go to feed, pay, house or clothe the people from whose land they are extracted. They go to other states, to Mexico City, to the USA and to the world's export markets, courtesy of national and foreign corporations, corrupt landowners and deeply unjust land and property distribution.

Thus it is that in the state which produces almost 20 per cent of Mexico's electricity, more than a third of homes do not have electricity at all. Thirty per cent of the population is illiterate, rising to 49 per cent in some rural areas. Almost 40 per cent live on an income of less than US$3 a day; 19 per cent simply have no income. Diseases of poverty, from river blindness to malaria, are rife. Education is sparse, health services often non-existent.[5] 'There are seven hotel rooms for every thousand tourists,' noted Subcomandante Marcos, sharply, in 1992, 'while there are only 0.3 hospital beds per ten thousand Chiapaneco citizens.' Worse, he said, 1.5 million people in Chiapas had no medical services within reach and 54 per cent of the population suffered from malnutrition. 'The tribute that capitalism demands from Chiapas,' wrote Marcos, 'has no historical parallel.'[6]

Marcos wrote those words shortly after the government had set in motion a measure that tipped the putative EZLN over the edge – the measure that, more than any other, they were later to say, cemented their determination to go to war, even if it meant their deaths – better that, they would say, than the death which would come if they stayed silent: the death of their people.

It has been said that the Mexican Revolution never reached Chiapas – certainly it remains a land of corrupt landlords, racism and inequality. What did get there, even if slightly fitfully, was Article 27 of the post-revolutionary constitution of 1917. Article 27 set in motion a process of land reform dedicated to breaking up the corruption of Mexico's ancient *hacienda* system, under which vast tracts of land were owned by rich absentee landlords and thousands of peasants starved, or existed as *peons* – debt slaves, forced to work for their landed masters.

Article 27, one of many radical measures in the post-revolutionary constitution, allowed the government to expropriate land to provide each rural community with an *ejido* – a piece of communal land. Landowners had no right of recourse, and the size of land owned by an individual – or, crucially, a corporation – was limited. *Ejidos* could not be broken up or sold; they were to be passed on through families to ensure rural self-sufficiency and stability and fend off poverty. Mexico's 28,000 *ejidos* make up almost half of the national territory – and a huge difference in the lives of those who live on them.[7] They were the best and only hope for many rural families, in Chiapas as elsewhere, to achieve self-sufficiency – and with it a measure of pride and something to pass on to their children.

But Carlos Salinas, PRI president from 1988 to 1994, had plans for the *ejido* law. Salinas was the man at the helm of Mexico as the world emerged from the Cold War and George Bush Senior's 'new world order' came into operation. As elsewhere, this order turned out to be the order of a newly triumphant capitalism – 'neoliberalism', as it is widely known in Latin America – its authority and ideology finally unchallenged by any serious alternative. Salinas was going to modernise Mexico, seek a place for his nation near the top of that order – drag it into the twenty-first century, whether it liked it or not. He knew it wouldn't be easy.

The *ejido* law presented him with his first major obstacle. A quarter of his fellow Mexicans still worked on the land; largely on small farms, *ejidos* and family holdings. They were secure, they were rural and they were, in the government's view, hopelessly 'anti-modern'.[8] They needed 'restructuring', the ultimate aim of which was to destroy the peasant class in Mexico and replace it with the kind of rural landscape that was becoming the norm elsewhere in the world – intensive agribusiness farms focused on export. This was the progressive thing to do. It made economic sense. And it was a prerequisite for Salinas's dreams of a New Model Mexico.

And so it began. Article 27 was repealed in 1992. Privatisation of communal land was allowed for the first time since the revolution, and land redistribution was brought to a standstill to prevent any more land being given over to 'inefficient' peasant production. For the first time since 1919, land reform in Mexico was officially over. Latin American historian Eduardo Galeano called it 'the second death of Emiliano Zapata'.[9] But this low punch to Mexico's rural population was no isolated legal change. Article 27 was repealed to lay the ground for something much bigger; something that the Zapatistas would call the 'death blow' for their people: NAFTA.

When the North American Free Trade Agreement was dreamt up by the leaders of Mexico, Canada and the USA in the early 1990s, it was sold to their people as a treaty which, by removing unfair trade barriers, would bring jobs, development and growth to all three countries. The real impact was very different. Millions of jobs were lost as economic sectors collapsed, their government support removed. A steady stream of US and Canadian companies moved their operations to Mexico to take advantage of its cheap labour. NAFTA also allowed private corporations to sue governments if they felt they were getting in the way of their 'investor rights'; which they began to do. The US waste-management company Metalclad, for example, successfully sued the Mexican government for almost $17 million when it was prevented from siting a toxic waste dump in an ecological reserve.[10] But it was in agriculture that NAFTA caused the most devastation; and Mexican agriculture in particular.

NAFTA began to phase out government support for vulnerable crops and opened the country's markets to mass-produced imports from the USA and Canada. Within a year, Mexico's production of corn fell by half as cheap imports, many of them below market price, flooded the country. Meanwhile, the price of corn in the shops rose. Record profits were recorded by some agribusinesses in the USA as millions of peasants in Mexico lost their land – land that was no longer secure because of the repeal of the *ejido* law, and no longer economically viable because of NAFTA. The hundreds of varieties of the ancient maize plant, which originated in Central America, began to disappear, replaced by a handful of intensive chemically raised hybrid varieties grown on the vast prairie farms of the USA.[11]

For the Mayans of Chiapas, known since the dawn of time as 'the people of the corn', who lived by growing maize, the effect was devastating. Entire rural communities were decimated – a process that shows no sign of stopping. 'We, the indigenous people,' wrote Marcos in 1996, 'are not profitable. We are a bad investment . . . Power's money does not want to buy a merchandise that does not yield good profits . . . Today, the shopkeeper has to modernise his store and get rid of all the merchandise that is unattractive. And we, with our dark skin and our overwhelming need to stay close to the earth . . . are not attractive.'

The repeal of Article 27 and the signing of NAFTA meant that the last avenues for the Indians of Chiapas had been shut down. As far as they could see, they had two choices: they could rise up against what was being done to them by an unscrupulous alliance of their own government and foreign economic interests, or they could lay down and die.

And so, on 1 January 1994, they rose. Twelve days later, a cease-fire declared, the EZLN and the government of President Salinas began a game of cat-and-mouse that was to last for years, continuing through the governments of his successor, Ernesto Zedillo, and, later, Vicente Fox. While the Zapatistas declared an indefinite ceasefire, the governments of Salinas and Zedillo alternated dialogue with military incursions and bombing raids. National and international pressure on the government to reach a negotiated settlement grew and finally, in 1996, after months of talks, the EZLN and government negotiators agreed to a set of proposals known as the San Andres Accords, after the Zapatista village in which they were thrashed out.

The government said it would craft a new law on indigenous rights based on the Accords. Though what they contained was by no means all that the rebels had wanted (they had hoped to talk about bigger, national, non-Indian issues like democracy and development and the future of Mexico; the government was having none of it) they represented a big step forward for Mexico's 10 million indigenous people. The Accords called for Mexico's Indians to be granted 'autonomy as part of the Mexican state', giving them the right to choose their own forms of political and social organisation based on their customs and traditions, control their own land and resources and organise their own lives as communities. It would give them a degree of control over their own destinies which they had not enjoyed since the arrival of Hernán Cortés.

And for a brief moment, in 2001, it looked like the dream could come true. President Fox's first act on taking office in December 2000 was to send an indigenous rights bill based on the San Andres Accords to the Mexican Congress for approval. Buoyed up by possibilities, the Zapatista army, masks still on but guns left behind, undertook a historic 2,000-mile journey – quickly labelled the 'Zapatour' – from the jungles of Chiapas to Mexico City along routes lined with cheering crowds. When they got there, 100,000 people came out to meet the first rebels to come to the capital since Pancho Villa met with Emiliano Zapata in 1914, at the height of the revolution. Still masked, the Zapatistas were allowed to address the Congress, and plead with the legislators to pass the indigenous bill.

Within a few months, the dream was dead. Congress passed the bill in July 2001, but with so many amendments that the Zapatistas – and every other Indian group in Mexico – rejected it as worse than nothing. Where the San Andres Accords had promised autonomy, control of resources and indigenous rights, the 'gutted' law said that indigenous communities were subject to existing government structures, that any moves towards autonomy must be designed and approved by each state, and that Indian use and ownership of their own resources was subject to national laws governing resource extraction. In other words: no change. The Zapatistas issued a furious condemnation of the government's 'betrayal', claiming that Fox had always intended to hijack the bill, and retreated back to the forests of the Lacandon. They are still there.

I'm hoping Ryan Zinn is going to help me understand what might happen next. Ryan, a young, friendly Californian with ginger stubble and a limitless supply of patience, works for Global Exchange, a US-based human-rights group which has been working in Chiapas since the Zapatista uprising. Officially, like virtually everyone else who works on the issue, they don't take sides – the Mexican constitution gives the president the power to immediately expel any foreigners accused of meddling in Mexican politics, and that power has been used many times since 1994. Over 450 people, from aid workers to journalists to priests, have been ejected from the country for being, or looking like they might be, involved in the Zapatista struggle. It's the reason I'm keeping my notebook firmly in my pocket in public.

It's a few days into our stay in Chiapas, and Ryan has agreed to let Lucy and I tag along on one of Global Exchange's 'reality tours' of some of the Zapatista communities. These involve a group of a dozen or so people from the rich world, mostly the US, forking out a wad of cash in exchange for a week being escorted around rural Chiapas, talking to Zapatistas and others about what's happening here. The idea is to wake people up to the ongoing low-intensity war in Chiapas, to spread the word and to further some kind of mutual understanding. As an introduction to some of the realities of Chiapas, and of *Zapatismo*, it's just what I need.

Thus it is that we are piling into a cramped minibus with a dozen reality tourists, for an hour-long journey to Oventic, one of the key Zapatista bases in Chiapas. Our companions include an affable teacher from 'Noo Joisey', a twenty-something Californian witch, an Irish priest and an overweight neoliberal economics professor from the American midwest, whose reason for being here is unclear, but who appears to disagree with everything everybody says. It looks like being an interesting day.

The Zapatista revolution became an armed struggle when there was nowhere else for it to go. Long before 1994, though, it began as a process of grass-roots community resistance to what its people called *mal gobierno* – bad government. And *Zapatismo*'s success can be measured not in that short twelve-day war, not in the Mexican government's response to its demands – not even in the success it has had at inspiring something global. Its success can be measured in the fact that, on the ground, among hundreds of thousands of Mayan villagers in Chiapas, a revolution is still taking place.

Oventic is evidence for this. In December 1994, thirty-eight Zapatista-supporting villages in Chiapas declared themselves 'autonomous municipalities'. In a reaction to continued government stalling over their demands, the municipalities declared that their territory, totalling almost a third of Chiapas, was now under official Zapatista control. In these autonomous zones the villagers ejected local government officials from their territories and declared that they would run their own communities their own way.

This, they said, was what *they* meant by revolution: 'Not the same form of power with a new logo or wardrobe,' explained

Marcos, but 'a gust of fresh air'. 'The communities created the autonomous municipalities,' said a villager from one of the autonomous villages, 'so we could be free to create what our thoughts tell us, to create what we want according to our needs and our history. We are not asking for the government to hand us clothes, but rather the right to live with dignity.'[12]

Since 1994, the autonomous zones, against all the odds, have survived. They run their own local government, hire and fire their leaders, run their own services and train teachers and doctors. None of it has been easy. Despite support from charities and solidarity movements, abroad and at home, the autonomous communities are desperately short of money and basic necessities, from petrol to food. They refuse to accept any resources or help from central government until the San Andres Accords become law. They put up with attacks by paramilitary groups supported by landowners and PRI politicians and insistent pressure from a government that could well do without thousands of its own people effectively seceding from its control. Sometimes, that government's patience snaps. In 1999 in San Andres, the police, in a surprise operation, invaded the town hall, shut down the Zapatista government and reclaimed the town for the state. The next day, thousands of Zapatistas – not the guerrilla army, but ordinary, unarmed citizens from San Andres and surrounding villages – re-invaded, took back the town hall and re-declared their autonomous zone. The police never tried again.

The Zapatistas have managed to do this because community support has been virtually total. *Zapatismo* has survived not because of the few guns the guerrillas wield, and not even through international solidarity – though this has played a crucial part. It has survived, above all, because it has a seemingly unbreakable community base. 'The Zapatistas' are not just the few thousand guerrillas in the forests that the rest of world likes to focus on; they are the estimated quarter of a million people in the towns and villages from whence that army was drawn. The people who, in many cases, are living autonomy every day, and without whom the guerrillas would be nothing. *Zapatismo* is not just an armed rebellion – it is a whole region in daily resistance.

This powerful support base has created what may come to be the most lasting legacy of the Zapatistas – a legacy that has built on two crucial ideas. First, that power is not something to be concentrated at government level, changing hands between political elites every few years: it is something to be devolved down to community level, to be used by and for the people it affects. And secondly, that anyone who wants this to happen should not waste their time waiting for government to hand it down to them, but should rise up as a community and take it themselves.

After an hour's journey along twisting, mountainous roads, our minibus pulls up outside a makeshift gate, which gives way to a long dirt track leading down a hill with a collection of wooden buildings strung out along it. We squeeze out and stand by the side of the road, gazing at the surrounding forests, encircled in ribbons of mist. Next to the gate is a wooden building covered in murals. Murals, as I am to discover, are to be found in every Zapatista community, and this building is plastered with the faces of four icons that appear in almost all of them: Marcos, Emiliano Zapata, Che Guevara and the Virgin of Guadelupe, the ancient vision of a brown-skinned Virgin Mary which appeared to a shepherd boy near Mexico City in 1531, and laid the foundations for Mexican Catholicism. In Zapatista murals, the Virgin wears a ski mask.

Ernesto, Ryan's colleague at Global Exchange, is negotiating with a black-masked man who has arrived to greet us. He hands over our passports and a letter of introduction. The man disappears, then returns, and we are officially welcome to Oventic. We are ushered into the mural-swathed building, which turns out to be a shop and café. Inside, the cash-strapped Zapatistas are hoping we will open our wallets in exchange for the tempting array of goodies they have laid out before us: Marcos T-shirts, ski masks, bandanas, posters, keyrings, tape recordings of revolutionary songs, books, caps, even EZLN ashtrays. Down a few steps are two rows of rickety tables and a wooden serving hatch – the whole building looks to have been made by the villagers – behind which women are making tortillas, beans and rice. They are also doing a brisk trade in bottles of Coca-Cola.

'Ryan,' I say, 'they're selling Coke.'

'You're right,' says Ryan, 'they are selling Coke.'

'But they're Zapatistas . . . they, er, well, they don't like *neoliberalismo* or US colonialism, right? And they drink *Coke*?'

'Well, they like Coke. Comandante Tacho is supposed to have said that the only good thing to come out of capitalism was Coca-Cola.'

'Really? Ah.' I can't shake off a feeling of disappointment, which is followed immediately by a feeling of guilt about feeling disappointed. Why shouldn't they drink Coke? No, hang on, why *should* they?

'What you have to remember,' says Ryan, 'is that despite all the nice posters and cute dolls and all the rest, this is still an insurgency. Coke or no Coke, this is still a revolution.'

As we talk, the man who met us at the gate comes in, hands over a few pesos, and walks out with a bottle. He still wears his black ski mask. Perhaps this is *Zapatismo* sticking two fingers up at the Coca-Cola corporation of America. Or is it the other way round?

After a spot of lunch, we are given a tour. First stop is the clinic, a vast, concrete building covered in a stunning array of murals – Mayan dragons, masked faces, guns, fire, plants entwining themselves around windows, children holding hands. *Pueblos Unidos!* reads one wall. *Democracia, Justicia y Libertad* reads another. Inside, we gather round as the doctor, a young, dark-haired, white-coated man called Nastacio, tells us how short they are of supplies and how hard it is to work here. He grew up in a nearby village, and believes strongly, he tells us, in what *Zapatismo* stands for.

'We are training our own doctors and health professionals to work in the autonomous communities,' he says, 'because we want to be able to keep our people healthy. But it is very hard to attract people here. You can see that we have no money. We have some medicines, but not enough. And none of us are paid.' He says it not as a lament, simply as a fact.

'Sometimes,' he goes on, 'people bring us corn, tortillas or beans in exchange for treatment or medicines. Which at least means we can eat!' He smiles.

Further down the track is a school. We are led into a classroom, and sit down on small wooden desks, scratched, ink-stained, tatty, like any school anywhere. The room is dusty and lined with what look like home-made bookshelves, crammed with books about Latin American history, sociology, politics, revolutionary theory and practice. Some of the books are in Tzotzil, the local language. Overhead projectors, old computers, cardboard boxes and a dented metal globe are piled up in a corner on the concrete floor, and motes of dust hang in the sunlight that stutters through the dilapidated windows. Only the graffiti on the desktops give away where you are: instead of 'I love Ricky M', the scratched slogans say 'Zapata Vive!' and 'EZLN'.

At the end of the room, behind the teacher's desk, in a semi-circle, sit eight men who have been awaiting our arrival. They wear cowboy hats or baseball caps, cowboy boots or sandals, and every one of them, without exception, wears a mask. Some are bandanas, but others are the black woollen balaclava masks that have come, more than anything else, to represent Zapatismo. The ski masks perform two practical functions: in the case of the guerrillas in the forests, they keep the worst of Chiapas's cold mountain winters at bay; and in the case of the Zapatistas in villages like Oventic, they make it harder for the police, the state, the paramilitaries or unfriendly observers to identify the wearer.

But the masks have come to represent more than that. The Zapatistas – 'the ones without faces, the ones without voices'; the despised Indios – were ignored for centuries when they weren't actively repressed. It was only, paradoxically, when they hid their faces that Mexico noticed them. Now their masks, in their identical blankness, are a symbol of identity. 'The voice that arms itself to be heard' goes in tandem with 'the face that hides itself to be seen' – and upon those unseen faces, say the Zapatistas, can be sketched the features of anyone, anywhere, who rises up to resist oppression. Behind the masks, they say, they are us – we are all Zapatistas, and we are everywhere.

In the school, through one of those masks, we are being treated to a lecture by a representative of the EZLN Education Commission. He is explaining to us that this is one of the Zapatistas' first autonomous schools, in which they will be propounding a 'revolutionary, popular system of education'. It will focus on the real needs of children and communities, not those imposed from Mexico City, and it will be teaching children what the communities have decided they need to know. 'We want to construct an example for humanity,' says the man. 'A people without education is one without history; a dead people. We will not have these teachers who sit behind their desks with their minds in New York or Mexico City, educating our children to make money at the expense of their people. We will provide a revolutionary education for our own people. The government says we have weapons here, and they are not wrong. Education is a very dangerous weapon; it wakes up minds, and consciences.'

This is all rather interesting, but after two hours of it, most of the group are desperate to escape. The talk has become a political monologue, in monotone, and it has become clear that even the Zapatistas have their crashing bores. There are some inherently human problems that it seems no revolution can solve. It's a bit depressing. Ryan is virtually dead, having been translating, non-stop, for two hours. We file outside into the bright sunlight, blinking and exchanging looks.

'Well,' I say to Lucy, '*that* was fun.' She grimaces.

Before we pile back on to the bus we have an appointment at the women's co-op. A group of women have been waiting patiently all this time to introduce us to their work. The 'Society of Women for Dignity' is one of many projects in Zapatista communities run by and for women. It's a co-op, to which female artisans from different communities bring their wares to sell, and any money they make is divided up equally between all the members.

'It is important to us to organise as women,' says their spokes-woman. They are all lined up in front of us, beneath hanging weavings and before shelves of woodwork and pottery. She seems nervous, which is probably not surprising. 'For a long time, we had no way to do this. It has been hard work, but we have come together as women to assert our dignity and it has made us proud.'

The position of women in Zapatista communities is an example of how *Zapatismo* has striven to fuse traditional Mayan culture with newer ideas – and how they are prepared to reject aspects of that traditional culture which are no longer acceptable to them. The deeply male nature of traditional Chiapas is one such aspect, which was rejected in the EZLN's Women's Revolutionary Law. The law, drawn up by women, applies to all Zapatista communities and explicitly grants women the same rights as men in all things – including decision-making, marriage and armed combat (up to a third of the Zapatista guerrillas are said to be women). Talk to any woman in any Zapatista community, I found, and she will tell you that the law, though patchily enforced, has led to a marked improvement in their lives – and a new confidence in their dealings, as equals, with the traditionally dominant men.

Some habits are hard to change, though. Before the woman speaking can go on, a man in a cowboy hat interjects and summarises everything she has just said, in his own words, as she listens, silently, overshadowed.

'Which is why they need a women's co-op,' says Lucy. 'Men are the same everywhere.'

Outside again, a village leader has something to say to us before we go. He is an old man in a checked shirt, and he wears no mask. He bows slightly beneath the weight of his words. Tiny, peeping chicks scratch around his feet.

'You must know,' he says, simply, 'that we are suffering here. You have seen, now, how we are. Life is hard, but we struggle. We must struggle because there is nothing else. But we know that there are

Zapatistas elsewhere in Mexico – that there are Zapatistas all over the world. Like us, they struggle, and they will not give up. We are everywhere. All we ask of you, now, is that you take our word; that you speak it and sing it and breathe it wherever you go. That is all.'

'Thank you,' says Ryan, with a slight bow of his head. And then, we are gone.

Back in the minibus, accelerating down the hillside back towards San Cristobal, the neoliberal professor is unhappy. He has a kind of quixotic smile-frown on his face and is sweating gently through his stretched blue T-shirt.

'Now, you see,' he is saying to anyone who'll listen, 'that women's co-op is not going to survive if it goes on like that. It's not operating efficiently. Did you see what they do? Every woman contributes different amounts of work, different skill levels, different products and yet they divide up the remuneration equally. That means that the harder-working and more skilful women are subsidising the less talented ones.'

'I think that's the idea,' says his long-suffering wife, who seems to have made an art out of looking embarrassed.

'Well, they don't understand basic economics, that's all. It's not going to survive long-term. You can't subsidise under-achievers.' He is straight from central casting, and he's making me feel ill.

'Look,' I say, 'it's deliberate, isn't it? It's community support, small-scale industry, co-operation, mutual aid. I thought you economists liked private initiatives. What alternative do you suggest? Perhaps the faster workers could take the money and run? Or do they need to set up a benefits system to dole out cash to the ones left behind?'

'Well, I don't think that would be ideal,' he replies. 'If they were to ask me, I would say that what would really benefit them would be a nice, clean *maquiladora* just on their doorstep . . .'

'What's a *may-kee-adora*?' says the teacher from New Jersey.

'A sweatshop,' says a sharp old woman from New York, who has been eyeing the professor with increasing distaste. He looks pained.

'Well, that's a derogatory term, but in any case . . . they could work for a daily wage, perhaps making sneakers or shirts, or whatever, for export to the States. Under NAFTA they would get very favourable rates. They'd earn money from export, and that would allow them to develop and—'

'Who's got a cigarette?' demands the woman from New York. 'I need a cigarette.'

'I really don't like smoking,' says the professor, looking pained again, 'particularly not in enclosed spaces.'

'Yes,' says the woman from New York. 'I know.'

In a small plaza in the north of San Cristobal, overshadowed by a great, florid church, Lucy and I are wandering aimlessly through a sprawling Mayan market. The stallholders are indigenous people, mostly women, and they lay out their wares on the dusty ground and on old wooden tables, plastic sheeting always at the ready to throw over their stalls when the heavy tropical rains come. Much of what they sell is tourist trinkets – clothes, paintings, souvenirs – and among these, since 1994, most of the stallholders have been doing a nice line in souvenirs for the revolutionary tourist. For the Zapatistas sell.

Here you can pick up many of the things we saw in Oventic: ski masks, posters, flags, calendars, keyrings. One of the most popular buys for the discerning *Zapaturistica* is a mini EZLN soldier, made of black felt with matchsticks for guns. These are either hung from keyrings or stuffed by the half-dozen into crudely made but brightly painted little wooden lorries with 'CHIAPAS' written on the side. The best of them, in addition to the masks and guns, have little pipes sticking out of their mouths. You can also find, in the market and in every tourist shop in town, Zapatista T-shirts. They come in dozens of different locally printed designs, sizes and colours, but virtually all of them have one thing in common: a picture of Subcomandante Marcos.

Every political movement needs its icon and Marcos, whether he likes it or not, has become one – not simply for the Zapatistas of Chiapas, but also for the growing global movement they helped to spawn. Interestingly though, he is not, even to his most fervent worshippers, 'followed', because he refuses to be anyone's leader.

Partly this is a reflection of reality. In the official scheme of things, Marcos is not the leader of the Zapatistas because the Zapatistas have no leader. The Zapatista army is run by twenty-three *comandantes* who make up the 'Clandestine Revolutionary Indigenous Committee'. All of them are Indians and they are elected by, and take their orders from, the autonomous communities they come from. The decision to go to war in 1994, for example, was not made by the *comandantes* – they do not have the authority to make such significant decisions without the go-ahead from the Zapatistas in every autonomous village. Only after an exhaustive, months-long process of consultation and voting across Chiapas did the EZLN get the go-ahead for war; and only then did they act.

Marcos, meanwhile, is simply a *subcomandante*. In theory, this makes him a deputy, instructed by the *comandantes* to train and command the Zapatista troops. In reality, though he is not the leader of the Zapatistas, he is their voice, both in Mexico and internationally. He provides a vital bridge between the world of the Indians and the modern world. But he refuses to lead, to be followed, or to write anyone a manifesto, political or otherwise. Because to do so would be to make a nonsense of everything that *Zapatismo* stands for – local democracy, political and economic control at community level, and a very different way of looking at power.

Marcos is always writing, though. He can't seem to stop himself. 'Communiqués' have stuttered forth from his jungle redoubt ever since 1994, and are instantly recognisable both from their unique style and from their sign-off, which never varies – 'From the mountains of the Mexican Southeast, Subcomandante Insurgente Marcos'. All self-respecting guerrillas, of course, have to write acres of revolutionary cant about the evils of capitalism. It's in their job description. Marcos, while not immune to this tendency, is decidedly more poetic, and more unpredictable, in his approach. He writes elegant denunciations of political opponents: 'Health to you,' he closes one communiqué to former president Zedillo, 'and a parachute for the cliff which comes with your tomorrow.' He writes 'telegrams' to 'international civil society': 'THE GREYS HOPE TO WIN STOP RAINBOW NEEDED URGENTLY STOP'. He writes absurdist morality tales: 'The tale of the lime with an identity crisis'; 'The tale of the nonconformist little toad'. And he is surely the only guerrilla in history whose pet beetle, 'Don Durito of the Lacandon', writes his own stories, essays and economic critiques.

'This making of a new world,' says Marcos, by way of explanation, 'is a serious business. If we can't laugh, the world we make will be square, and we won't be able to turn it.'[13] One thing seems clear: this is no ordinary Latin American *guerrillero*. Che Guevara may have had the student beard and the martyr's death, but he never had Marcos's sense of the absurd. This is revolution with a twinkle in its eye, and you don't get much more post-modern than that.

Who Marcos really is remains a mystery. President Ernesto Zedillo, Fox's PRI predecessor, 'unmasked' him as an ex-philosophy professor from Mexico City. Marcos naturally denied it. What does seem clear is that the young Marcos, whoever he was, started his journey in Chiapas as a revolutionary steeped in the hard-left dogma of the twentieth century, and ended it as something very different. His journey from where he was then to where he is now has become one of the central legends of *Zapatismo*, and it makes a telling point about a growing political movement that rejects the rigid ideological certainties of both left and right.

The story goes that Marcos arrived in Chiapas in the early 1980s, with a now defunct bunch of Maoists from Mexico City. They wanted a revolution. Revolutions happened when the oppressed workers rose up against the capitalist classes, seizing the means of production for The People, and strangling the last Starbucks executive with the innards of the last World Bank consultant. The indigenous people of Chiapas, if they were anything, were certainly oppressed. They looked like fertile ground. All they needed was a proper education in the realities of their class position, and hey presto: a vanguard in the making.

Only it didn't work out like that. 'Rise up!' Marcos told them. 'Go away,' they said. 'We're not a proletariat, our land is not your means of production and we don't want to work in a tractor factory. All we want is to be listened to, and for you big-city smart-arses to stop telling us how to live. As for your dialectic – you can keep it. You never know when it might come in handy.'

For Marcos, Chiapas was a revelation. 'We thought we were the light of the world,' he once told a Mexican journalist, 'sent here to organise the Indians. Then we began to speak with the communities, and they had a very important lesson for us.'[14] The young revolutionary learned more than he taught – learned about grassroots democracy, about tradition, about working the land and closeness to nature, and about an entirely different, ancient, indigenous worldview, that could not be classified by any of the political rigidities of the modern world. He began to question his ideological certainties, and learned, through over a decade in mountain caves and forest redoubts, in villages and valleys and farms, that what *los indios* wanted, after 500 years with the white man's boot on their collective neck, was the freedom and power to live and grow their own way, untramelled by the ideals of those who would 'develop' them, from right or left or centre, and all for their own good.

Was this revolutionary? Was it conservative? Did it matter? Marcos didn't seem to think so, and has since taken to revelling in his and *Zapatismo's* quixotic position as a new, old, radical, traditional, local, global, romantic and practical political phenomenon, which no one has managed to cram into any existing ideological boxes. 'The communists accuse him of being anarchist,' he writes, autobiographically. 'Guilty. The anarchists accuse him of being orthodox. Guilty . . . The reformists accuse him of being an extremist, a radical. Guilty. The radicals accuse him of being reformist. Guilty. The "historical vanguard" accuse him of appealing to the civic society and not to the proletariat. Guilty. The civic society accuses him of disturbing their tranquillity. Guilty. The Stock Exchange accuses him of ruining their breakfast . . .'[15]

Marcos likes to insist that the answers the Zapatistas have found apply only to them. He will not tell anyone, anywhere, what they should do; only that, when they find their own answers, appropriate to their own situation, they should put them into practice. Out of the first post-modern revolution comes the first post-modern guerrilla: one who offers more questions than answers, to whom ideology is fluid, to whom power is to be redefined not seized, to whom mocking is more effective than preaching, to whom 'our word is our weapon'. Marcos's political identity crisis turned him into something new and unique: a kind of dissenting, faceless Everyman. And in him, more than any other one person, the thinking, and the workings, of a new, rising international movement are reflected.

Who is Marcos? He has answered that question himself. 'Marcos,' he wrote in 1994, 'is gay in San Francisco, a black person in South Africa, Asian in Europe . . . a Palestinian in Israel, a Jew in Germany . . . an artist without a gallery or a portfolio . . . a sexist in the feminist movement, a woman alone in a Metro station at 10 P.M. . . . a writer without books or readers, and a Zapatista in the Mexican Southeast . . . He is every minority who is now beginning to speak and every majority that must shut up and listen. He is every untolerated group searching for a way to speak, their way to speak. Everything that makes power and the good consciences of those in power uncomfortable – this is Marcos.'[16]

In other words, if Subcomandante Marcos did not exist, the international movement that is coalescing in opposition to 'globalisation' would have to invent him. *Todos Somos Marcos* reads a slogan chanted by crowds and printed on T-shirts from Mexico City to Seattle to Genoa: *We are all Marcos*. Who is Marcos? Who isn't?

I've been in San Cristobal almost a fortnight, interviewing people, trailing the Global Exchange crowd on a few other visits, organising interviews, being a tourist and trying to work out what I think about what I've seen so far. I was never sure exactly what to expect in Chiapas, but I am realising the complexity of the situation. The poetic guerrilla rebels that are sometimes romanticised by activists in the West are, in reality, determined peasant farmers, indigenous people fighting for their own lives and traditions. Nevertheless, I think I am beginning to grasp some, at least, of the essence of *Zapatismo*.

Autonomy is clearly a key part of it. Every Zapatista you talk to will tell you that autonomy – real, local control of their community, economically and politically – is a hard-fought-for principle, rather than an expedient political move. They will tell you, too, that autonomy for them doesn't mean independence, dropping out, isolation – it means control of their own destinies. Linked with that is the commitment to community democracy – real control, by all, at community level, however difficult it may be to implement.

Taken together, these seem to be at least the beginnings of a practical realisation of all Marcos's words about re-thinking what power is and how it should be used. In a world of centralised power blocs, 'the ones without voices' will always be trampled on. Challenge that by devolving as much power as possible down to ground level, and ensuring that the people really get their hands on it, and you have already begun a revolution in the way the world works – though it may not be one that any traditional revolutionary would recognise.

I was told I would find something in Chiapas which would inspire me. And this *is* inspiring, for it seems to me that, despite the hardship and the struggle these people are going through, they have hit on something which has, in principle at least, global potential. Something that is spreading. Later, on my travels, I will understand just how far.

But I need to see more – need to see where the Zapatistas are really coming from, literally and otherwise. So Lucy and I have arranged to spend some time living in one of the five Zapatista 'capitals' – all known as Aguascalientes. Oventic was one, but this one – La Garrucha – is much more remote. We will be there as peace observers. The Zapatistas, who are still harassed and occasionally attacked by the army and paramilitary gangs, are keen to have groups of 'internationals' living in their most vulnerable villages; a tradition that began in 1995, when the government's military assault against ordinary Zapatista villagers was at its height. The internationals both gather information on military comings and goings, and, theoretically, act as some sort of deterrent – a clear signal to the Mexican government that the world is still watching Chiapas. For the next ten days, this will be our job – in return, we get to live and work in the birthplace of *Zapatismo*.

Before I leave, I write a letter to Marcos and the General Command and deliver it, as instructed, to a contact somewhere in San Cristobal who has promised to get it to whatever lonely outpost the guerrillas are currently camped in.

'We will send it,' she promises me, 'but I don't think you will be lucky.' She's probably right. Since the success of the Zapatour and the consequent failure of Congress to honour the San Andres Accords, the EZLN General Command have been incommunicado, and the usually garrulous Marcos has been refusing all interviews. Still, it has to be worth a try.

Ocosingo is a frontier town. It has a lot of potholes, fume-spewing trucks, flyblown bars, a fair few drunks, no tourists and absolutely no Internet cafés. Two hours and a world away from San Cristobal, it guards the entrance to the *Cañadas* – canyons – great green valleys which run through the Lacandon rainforest down to the border with Guatemala, some seventy miles away. The Cañadas are the wild, forested, rebellious heart of Chiapas where the Zapatista rebellion was fomented, and where Marcos and his guerrilla band lived for years in caves and forest camps, and probably still do. In 1994, Ocosingo was one of the seven towns the Zapatistas invaded, and the scene of the worst disaster of the uprising, when the EZLN were ambushed and gunned down by the army and the air force, some shot in the back of the head after surrendering. Around 150 people – Zapatistas, soldiers and civilians – died in the bloodbath that was Ocosingo.

We're only here to get transport out again, and soon we find ourselves packed on to the back of a truck which staggers out of town and on to a road hardly worthy of the name. There are no buses east of Ocosingo – buses can't cope with the roads, so truck travel is the only way into the heart of Zapatista country. Lucy and I are shoehorned between piles of old tyres, boxes of beer, bags of corn and about ten other people. There are skinny old men hauling great sacks of maize; women on the way back to their villages from market; children hanging on to their skirts; a gang of grinning, shoeless wide boys perched on the roof and a couple of shaven-headed, slab-chested soldiers on leave from the military bases that squat near the Zapatista villages.

The journey to La Garrucha takes four hours, and we alternate between teetering on the end of wooden benches that are jolted up into the air by every rut, and standing on the wooden slats that make up the side of the truck. A ratty brown dog, lying under one of the benches, quietly and persistently ejects the contents of its stomach, which flows gently up and down the floor with the movement of the vehicle. The road is scatter-bombed with potholes the size of large ponds, and we have to get out and push several times.

But the Cañadas have a powerful beauty. They grow deeper as you drive south, away from the cities, passing small thatched villages, smoke rising through the wooden roofs. Women in traditional dress gaze shyly at you as you pass and children chase the truck for a few yards, yelling in Tzeltal. The branches of overhanging trees are smothered in brilliant red fungi, gentle white blossoms and tree orchids, and all around the green, misty hills close in, cutting you off from any other reality. Vultures collide with air currents overhead, insects whistle and whine and all around you, wherever you look, there are butterflies. Huge iridescent blue ones, with wingspans like palm leaves; tiny tiger-printed ones; white, red, purple, brown and bronze ones, with the fitful sun filtering through their litmus-like wings, circling and seething along the miles of fog-swollen road until it seems that a shimmering cloud of leaf-thin butterflies escorts our truck to the gates of La Garrucha.

La Garrucha bears little resemblance to Oventic: where that was buzzing with activity, this is almost silent, apart from the ever-present sound of insects. As we jump down from the back of the truck, hauling our rucksacks after us, we are virtually the only people around. We are deep in the Cañadas, and the tight green valley we were in has widened enough for dozens of thatched smallholdings, surrounded by *milpas* – tiny fields of maize – to dot the grasslands between the forested and still cloud-hung mountains. A man in a sombrero leans against a fence post chewing a blade of grass and a couple of dogs are sniffing about in the ditches at the side of the track. As the truck lumbers off down the valley, a line of pigs – a mother and three offspring – wander into view, trotting neatly down the side of the road in single file, going nowhere in particular.

The only sign that this is an 'Aguascalientes' is a huge mural on the side of a wooden building to the right of the road. We wander round it and tell the grass-chewing man who we are. He waves in the direction of some huts on the other side of a grassy area surrounded by haphazard buildings. There is a stone church on one side – the only building that looks new. Next to it is a crumbling school, painted with a huge mural of the magnificently mousta-chioed Emiliano Zapata. On another side is a long, slatted wooden building featuring a painted rendition of a famous photograph – lines of unarmed Zapatista women successfully, and peacefully, preventing armed soldiers from storming their village. *Resistencia!* says the red slogan painted next to it. On another side of the grassland is a long barn with a rusting blue bus sitting next to it, and completing the quadrangle is a small collection of huts. We knock on one of the doors.

Inside are four men, sitting in a circle on plastic chairs, chewing grass or smoking. These, it turns out, are the community leaders. One of them plonks himself behind an old desk which sits at an awkward angle on the dirt floor, and asks for our passports and letters of introduction. We hand them over. They are perused, then handed back to us.

'Welcome to La Garrucha,' says the man. 'We will show you where to sleep.'

The barn, it turns out, is our sleeping quarters. Its beams are strung with the mosquito nets and hammocks of the other peace observers who are already here. We dump our kit in a corner and go to find them. The sound of voices and the smell of smoke wafting from a small, mural-scrawled hut next to the barn identifies their likely hiding place. A grey, saddled horse is tethered next to the door. We push it open and go in.

'Hi,' we say, our eyes adjusting to the dimness. The hut is evidently a kitchen – it is hung with battered and blackened old pots, and on its wonky shelves are bags of beans, piles of tortillas and the odd vegetable. Six people are sitting around a shaky table, chatting. They look up.

'Hi,' they chorus.

We sit down and I hand out a chocolate bar I wisely brought with me.

'Chocolate!' says one girl, wide-eyed. 'Oh God, chocolate! It's been a week since I saw chocolate!' Instantly popular, Lucy and I are handed scratched plastic mugs full of coffee boiled mercilessly on the open fire in the corner.

'They grow it here,' says a Spanish guy with dreadlocks and a scraggy beard. 'Good, isn't it?' It is. The other peace observers turn out to be, like us, European. There are a couple of Spaniards, two Basque separatist women who say they identify with the Zapatistas, and a smart-looking, in relative terms, German man, here with his girlfriend.

'It's wonderful here,' says one of the Basque women. 'Very beautiful. But not much happens. It's good if you want to relax.'

'The soldiers aren't relaxing,' says the German. 'Three trucks of them came past today. Moving towards the military base a couple of miles up the road. We don't know why.'

'There's a big new military influx into all the bases, apparently,' I say. This is what we were told before we left San Cristobal by the civil rights organisation that had arranged our stay here. 'But nobody's sure why.'

'Then it is good we are here,' says the Spaniard. 'Is anybody yet hungry?'

Everyone pitches in to make dinner, and in an hour or so, our clothes smelling deliciously of woodsmoke, we all have plates of beans, rice and, naturally, tortillas, to go with our plastic cups of water. This is virtually all we will eat for the next ten days, and I will not tire of it in all that time.

'It's a bit . . . well – I mean it's a bit quiet here, isn't it?' I say to one of the Spaniards, who seems to have been here the longest. 'I was expecting a bit more . . . *life*.'

'I know what you mean,' he says. 'But they don't have much reason to use a lot of these buildings now. The school was built by the government, and hasn't really been used since autonomy. The teacher ran away. And a lot of the other buildings were put up for the Encuentro and haven't really been used since. It's a gathering place, and apart from the villagers there's no one really to gather here right now.'

The *Encuentro* – encounter – that the Spaniard is talking about has already become legendary. It created the key corridor down which the ideas and principles of *Zapatismo* began to inspire and create a global movement of political resistance.

In January 1996, the Zapatistas issued an invitation to 'rebels from all continents' to join them in Chiapas later that year for an 'Intercontinental Encuentro for Humanity and Against Neoliberalism'. The Zapatistas built the five Aguascalientes to accommodate their visitors, and anticipated the arrival of perhaps a few hundred people. But they had underestimated just how far the words of Marcos and the ideas he was communicating, facilitated by the newly spreading Internet, had travelled. Over 3,000 people from more than forty countries arrived in Chiapas in August 1996. They came from Europe, from the USA and Canada, from all over Latin America and from places that the Zapatistas could never have imagined their word being heard in: countries from Iran to Haiti, Japan to Kurdistan, Zaïre to the Philippines.

Groups of delegates shuttled between the five Aguascalientes, discussing every aspect of 'life under neoliberalism'. They shared experiences, argued, and above all, planned. Planned what they would do, together, internationally, about what was happening to the world. For they saw, as the Zapatistas intended them to see, and as I saw when I arrived in Chiapas, that the forces affecting south-east Mexico were the forces affecting the world.

The EZLN, meanwhile, sat and listened. They refused, despite requests, to provide any of their visitors with a blueprint for change or a plan for a global utopia, and when asked by people from other nations what they should do about the problems they faced, they told them to work it out for themselves. The Zapatistas, they told their visitors, were here to learn, not to teach. They had no one idea that could be universally applied, nor did they want one.

The Encuentro sent *Zapatismo* global. The 3,000 delegates returned to their countries with new ideas, new ways of thinking about the future, and above all, new links. The next year, another Encuentro was held, this time in Spain, which would cement those links even further. From it, more than any other single event before or since, would grow the 'anti-globalisation' movement as it exists today.

At the end of the Chiapas Encuentro, the Zapatistas issued a declaration, written, of course, by Marcos. Ever since, it has followed the movement wherever it goes. It followed me as I travelled the world and heard it quoted back to me from South Africa to California. It is as near as this movement has ever got to a statement of intent, a manifesto, and it still sends shivers down my spine.

On the one side is neoliberalism, with all its repressive power and all its machinery of death; on the other side is the human being. There are those who resign themselves to being one more number in the huge exchange of power . . . But there are those who do not resign themselves . . . In any place in the world, anytime, any man or woman rebels to the point of tearing off the clothes resignation has woven for them and cynicism has dyed grey. Any man or woman, of whatever colour, in whatever tongue, speaks and says to himself or to herself: Enough is enough! *Ya basta!*

A world made of many worlds found itself these days in the mountains of the Mexican southeast . . . Let it be an echo of our own smallness, of the local and particular, which reverberates in an echo of our own greatness . . . an echo that recognises the existence of the other and does not overpower or attempt to silence it. An echo that takes its place and speaks its own voice, yet speaks the voice of the other . . . Let it be a network of voices that resist the war Power wages on them.

*

For the first couple of days at La Garrucha it's almost possible to forget where we are, and why. To forget, among the butterflies and the banana palms, that we are in a war zone. Every day I hang in my hammock, drinking coffee and watching nothing much happen. Lucy and I make friends with the local children, who announce their presence by throwing crab apples at us from the bowing branches of low trees. We watch the La Garrucha football team training on a pitch in a jungle clearing; the goalposts are logs and the pitch is dotted with the pyramidal nests of leafcutter ants. I wait in vain for Marcos's summons to come from the hills. And every night, we are awakened by the local dog pack, howling their lungs out as they storm the kitchen door in pursuit of the food they can smell on the other side. We all take turns to get up and throw things at them.

It's only on the third day that we get a rude awakening. Lucy and I are on observation duty, sitting in a couple of hammocks by the roadside, chatting, when a low rumble fills the valley. It's a good two minutes before we see its source crest the hill from Ocosingo and move down the dirt track towards us. We scramble for our notebooks, pens and cameras and shout for the others, who come running from the kitchen and the barn.

'Give us a hand!' I yell. 'There are too many!' Twenty minutes later we have logged, between us, 31 military vehicles with around 650 soldiers, ammunition, explosives, guns and equipment, passing just feet away from us, moving towards one of the military bases that dot the Cañadas, surrounding the Zapatistas on every side. Some of the soldiers flash ironic peace signs at us. Others take our photos as we take theirs. Some smile, others just stare, coldly, through their mirrored sunglasses. They're just passing, for now, but they're a potent reminder of why we're here. Every day, for the rest of the week, we see similar scenes, though never as big or as unexpected. There is certainly a military build-up going on. If I needed an explanation for why the General Command are not answering my letter, this is probably as good as any.

For the villagers, though, life goes on much as normal; they have, as they tell us, seen worse than this since 1994. I have asked one of the village leaders if I can interview him and his colleagues, and ask them what life is like here, why they are Zapatistas, what they will do now. It takes him a day to come back to me with an answer: he has consulted all the members of the village council, and they have voted on it and they're sorry, but right now they don't want to talk.

They are in a bit of a quandary about their international visitors at the moment, they have told us; a week or so before my arrival, a woman peace observer from Spain accused one of the village men of sexually harassing her. The villagers voted to stick him in the village lockup for a few weeks as punishment; he is still there now. This has never happened before, say the village leaders, and they don't like it. This may be why they don't want to talk to me; whatever the reason, Zapatista democracy is thwarting my ambitions.

Instead, I talk to the villagers that I meet every day. I talk to the man who runs one of the small shops in the mural-swathed building, which he opens when he wants to. His name is Aurelio, and he is a *militante*; one of a number of people here charged with defending La Garrucha in case of attack. Somewhere, Aurelio and his colleagues probably have a cache of guns which, if the community agreed, they would use if necessary in self-defence. They have never used them yet, though, and Aurelio isn't talking about them.

He will talk about other things, though, sitting behind the counter of his shop. He will talk about 'resistance', a word I hear everywhere, and about how the villagers find it hard to live every day in rebellion.

'What can we do but keep struggling?' he asks. 'What we want is for the government to let us speak, and to let us live. But we have seen that only through joining together can we have a hope of this. They promised us an indigenous law, but the law they have passed treats us as objects, not subjects.' He is a big man, and he doesn't seem given to whimsy. But he knows what he wants, and what his community wants; and he knows they're not getting it.

'We have been here for five hundred years,' he says, almost plaintively. 'How long do they expect us to wait? Perhaps they would like us to go away, to be silent. But there are Zapatistas elsewhere. In other states in Mexico; perhaps in other places too. They struggle, like us, and like us they will not stop.'

Across the green, in the women's co-operative shop, which sells much the same stock as Aurelio's – old bags of crisps, soft drinks, rice, beans, staples – the woman behind the counter tells me the history of La Garrucha. Prior to 1994, she says, before the Zapatistas rose up, took over the land and declared it autonomous, it was a cattle ranch. The landlord sent in hired gunmen to drive them off the land, but they fought back and won.

'When we worked for the landlord,' she says, 'he paid people fifteen pesos a week [slightly more than £1]. Many times he would pay in drink, not money. Many people were *peons*. We felt like slaves. Today, most of us have land, animals, and crops. Life is still hard; we need some machinery to help us farm, and it is hard to sell anything. But life is also much better now.' Now, she said, they are in control of their own destinies, and the difference is immeasurable.

It is twilight, and I am standing in the meadow behind the barn, gazing across the spidery canyons to gardens of mango and banana beyond the darkening river. In a couple of days we will be leaving La Garrucha, and I will miss it. A villager saunters past me slowly, going nowhere in particular.

'Buenos dias,' I say, in bad Spanish.

'Buenos *tardes*,' he corrects me, smiling.

'How are you?'

'Fine.'

'Peaceful, isn't it?'

'Yes.' He stops and gazes slowly at everything and nothing. 'We have had a lot of rain, but it is beautiful rain.' He ambles off again, in the direction of the shop, which is lit by a hissing gas lamp.

Back in the barn, Lucy has been fiddling with her radio alarm clock.

'Hey, listen,' she says, emerging from the doorway and waving it in my face. Very faintly, through the crackle of a thousand miles of teeming air, comes a voice, speaking in English. A journalist and an economist are discussing 'the future of the IT sector in Mexico'. The faint breeze of words comes sweeping down into the valley like a Martian invasion.

And it suddenly seems to me that, yes, this is a war zone, and it is a war. A war against the real. Against the real places and real people that have been passed over in a great planetary rush towards something we don't even know that we want. A war waged by economists, sophists and calculators, IT experts, clean-shoed intellectuals, cut-and-paste politicians and bean-counting corporate buccaneers. A war waged against people like the Zapatistas – 'people the colour of earth', as they describe themselves. And the war is hard because those people, and everything they stand for, stubbornly refuse to die.

And perhaps, I think, as the fireflies begin to wink in the trees – perhaps, underneath, all of them, all of us, are the colour of earth. Perhaps no amount of growth and progress can wash away that colour. Perhaps it's too deep, too old, too ingrained. Perhaps what *Zapatismo* has to teach – perhaps the first thing it has to teach – is that the war against the real, however hard we try, can never be won.

And perhaps I am beginning to understand – beginning to *feel*, now – what this is really all about.

The Plaza in Oaxaca City is similar to the Plaza in San Cristobal, but its orange stone cloisters are lined with restaurant tables, where tourists and locals sit drinking beer and eating tacos in the much-needed shade, to the sound of an army of roving buskers. Oaxaca City is the capital of Oaxaca state, the next state up from Chiapas. I am on my way, with a lot of regret, back to Mexico City, my month in Chiapas over, and I have stopped in Oaxaca on the way to talk to a man I've been wanting to meet since I arrived in Mexico.

Gustavo Esteva is an old man, with wisps of grey hair remaining on his head and a kindly smile on his face. The author of over a dozen books, he describes himself as a 'deprofessionalised intellectual' and has been working for years with Indian communities in Oaxaca. He is buying me dinner at one of the Plaza cafés and explaining to me why the Zapatistas matter.

'The world is clearly shifting,' he says to me. 'I think that if you look at the wild reception the Zapatistas get in Mexico – well, we know that people have been disillusioned with the ballot box for a long time, here and all around the world. And yet they are disillusioned too with rebels who come with guns and say "give us the state, we will do it better". So what are we seeing in Chiapas? It is an alternative to both – a new notion of doing politics. You could call it radical democracy. People take their own destinies into their own hands – this is what autonomy is about in Chiapas. And it is legitimate.'

Esteva is getting at what I have experienced many times in the years I've been involved in radical politics, but have never quite been able to put my finger on: a new energy, a new idea of what politics is, and should be. But how does it work, I ask? What does he mean?

'Well,' he says, chewing slowly on a green enchilada, 'here is a new way of looking at the world. Take the Zapatistas. They call thousands of people down here to Mexico for the Encuentro, and when they get here, the EZLN say "don't follow us, we will not be your vanguard". Why? Because they say they don't have the truth, and they should not lead anyone else. Perhaps they have *a* truth – a truth for Chiapas, but not a universal truth, that can apply everywhere. All over the world, there are other truths. In other places, perhaps the principles can be applied – radical democracy, at the grass roots, claimed by people who are linked together worldwide. But the way it manifests itself can be different everywhere.'

A terrible busker who has been doing the rounds of the tables approaches us, bellowing '*Oaxaca! Oaxaca!*' to the sound of a tuneless guitar. Gustavo waves him away with a patient smile.

'I like to use the analogy of a telephone network,' he says. 'You can pick up a phone now and call anywhere in the world. This network is global and interlinked, but there is no centre – no controller, no one person or company that runs it. It is local and global, it has rules but no ruler. You see these "anti-globalisation" groups everywhere now and they operate like that. So do the Zapatistas.'

'For a long time,' he goes on, 'I have worked in Mexico with many other groups, opposing the system that we have today. And there have always been many different people with many different ideas, many different struggles, but one common objection. When the Zapatistas appeared and said "*Ya basta!*", millions of people, nationally and then globally, came together to support them. And we see all those people, from very different traditions and backgrounds and places, saying *basta* to the same thing. *Basta* to globalisation, *basta* to neoliberalism, *basta* to big corporations – *basta* to a specific set of global policies that are creating this world. *Basta!* We cannot wait any more!' He takes a sip of water and carries on.

'This *basta*,' he says, 'is a collective cry of *No!* from these many different people and groups, in many different places. And the people who shout it, the world over, have many of their own ideas about how to replace this system, or change it, how they want to be, their own alternatives. And they have perhaps learned from history that no one ideology can provide for all – no one system can integrate the needs of all the different people in the world, who all want different kinds of things. There is no one alternative to one bad system. So we ally to fight this system, and at the same time create our own, different worlds in opposition to it. And these worlds – they are different but connected, united but distinct. The *Basta* is the no, and the alternatives of the many different people are yeses. One no, and many yeses.'

One no, many yeses. 'A world made of many worlds.' This is it. This is what connects the movement I know to the people in Chiapas, the people the colour of earth. It is what links me to Marcos and Marcos to everyone; what draws together millions of dissidents from many different worlds. One no, to the homogenising power of an undemocratic market. Many yeses in its place – many different worlds, cultures, economic and political models, within a shared humanity.

And I can see, now, what this is about. It is about redistribution: not just of resources or wealth or land, but of the *power* from which all these flow. It is about democracy: real, local, participatory democracy – economic, as well as political; it is about different worlds within one world, the vitality of the human rainbow. And it is about resistance – resistance to a system that steps over, and steps on, people like the Zapatistas in the name of growth.

And I wonder, as I say my farewells to Gustavo and walk back to my hotel under a rising moon, whether this represents a new *kind* of politics. Could this really be the scattering of seeds that will grow into a new political idea: one that sees power as something to be exercised from the bottom, not the top; something which views all ideologies, all 'isms', with suspicion? Something that rejects all grand schemes, all big ideas, in favour of constructing something anew? Something that can't yet be pinned down by either left or right? A politics not of vanguards but, at last, of people?

I know I need to go and find out, and suddenly even leaving Chiapas seems worth it, because I am going to follow this idea, and the movement it colours, around the world, and find out what it means. I am going to look for the nos and the yeses, for the people who say and do them, from the ground up, and I am going to tell their stories. Gustavo could be wrong about all this; so could Marcos. But if they are right, what does it mean? Can the world be changed by a massing of diverse interests with a common grievance but no common programme?

'The problem of power,' Gustavo had said to me, over dinner, 'is not somewhere up there, to be taken. It is in everybody's hands – the hands of the people. The Zapatistas realise that. They took their power and they are using it to do something that no one would have thought they could do. This seems to me to be a lesson.'

The question for me, now, is how far that lesson is being learned. I know there is a global movement out there; I have seen at least part of it with my own eyes. But is this what unites it: this idea of diversity versus monoculture; one no, and many yeses? Is this increasingly global tide of defiance built upon an idea that, in the words of Marcos, explains what change really means?

'It is not necessary to conquer the world. It is sufficient to make it new.'

PART 1

one no

'If there is no struggle there is no progress. Those who profess to favour freedom and yet deprecate agitation are men who want crops without ploughing the ground. They want rain without thunder and lightning. They want the ocean without the awful roar of its many waters . . . Power concedes nothing without a demand. It never did and it never will.'

FREDERICK DOUGLASS, EX-SLAVE AND ABOLITIONIST, 1857

2 the belly of the beast

'The protesters are winning. They are winning on the streets. Before too long they will be winning the arguments. Globalisation is fast becoming a cause without credible champions.'

PHILIP STEPHENS, *FINANCIAL TIMES*, 17 AUGUST 2001

'You can't have a trade summit these days without tear-gas. It would be like having a cheeseburger without cheese.'

US GOVERNMENT OFFICIAL, SUMMIT OF THE AMERICAS, APRIL 2001

The weather is no harbinger of what is about to happen. The sky is a pure, cloudless blue and the white sun floods the domes and battlements of this most beautiful of Italian cities with a purity of light that only a Mediterranean summer can produce. It is July 2001 and here in the ancient port city of Genoa, 300,000 people have gathered to stake a claim to the future.

By the end of the day, everything will have changed. We don't know it yet, but we are about to undergo a baptism of fire. Fire and tear-gas and blood and bullets. And one of us is about to die.

Right now it is mid-morning, and we have no idea what's coming. A giant car park on the coast has been converted into an activists' 'convergence centre' in which vast crowds are gathering. The atmosphere is more like a festival than a revolution. A pink fairy with gauze wings is struggling with a bottle of factor-six suntan lotion. An old man in a green robe, silver shades and white beard is parading around in front of a red Fiat 'peace car' with a badly rendered plastic dove on its roof. A 'radical emancipative transformation dragon' with six pairs of human legs is stumbling over a dog carrying a revolutionary banner in its teeth. Streamers of rainbow balloons vie for airspace with Trotskyist placards denouncing the 'imperialism of capital' and heart-shaped signs that say, optimistically, 'love, respect and share the world'.

A unicycling clown playing an accordion weaves past a throng of twenty-somethings in Zapatista T-shirts: *Todos Somos Marcos*, reads one. They are adjusting their red bandanas and grinning at passing photographers. Behind a group of Riverdancing cheerleaders, putting themselves through a final practice routine, headscarves and dreadlocks, nose-rings and unfortunate beards gather round a notice board fluttering with A3 sheets of scribble and brown duct tape. 'Friday, July 20', says one; 'Siege of the

Summit'. 'WANTED', says another – 'write down what you have to give, and what you need'. The 'what you need' section is long but straightforward. 'Gas masks,' it says. 'Gas masks, gas masks, gas masks, gas masks . . .'

Then, from the pure blue of the sky, comes a sharp noise. Thousands of heads tilt upwards to see a steel-coloured aeroplane, a prominent stars and stripes bombasted across its tailfin, pass low overhead, the white ocean sunlight crackling across its wings. It is 11:20 A.M., George W. Bush is due to touch down at the city airport in ten minutes' time, for a get-together with his representatives on Earth.

'It's Air Force One!' someone shouts. A roar ripples through the crowd; a cheer, a jeer and a yell of defiance rolled into one. Hundreds of middle fingers shoot upwards in a mass salute. 'Hey, fuckwit!' a voice rings out. 'Welcome to Genoa!'

Barely a mile away, ringed with steel fences, armed police, soldiers, armoured cars and crates of tear-gas, the leaders of the eight most powerful countries in the world will soon be meeting, in closed session, to discuss everything from AIDS drugs to privatisation, climate change to biotechnology. The outcome of their private discussions will determine, to a great extent, the future of the global economy. In the medieval Ducal Palace, Tony Blair, George W. Bush, Vladimir Putin, Silvio Berlusconi, Jean Chrétien, Gerhard Schröder, Jacques Chirac and Junichiro Koizumi are gathering for what their official agenda cosily terms a 'fireside chat'. It is the annual meeting of the G8. It will not be allowed to chat in peace.

To ensure that none of their people get anywhere near them, the world's leading democracies have built themselves a one-day police state. Twenty thousand soldiers and police have been deployed, armed with live ammunition, rubber bullets, tear-gas launchers, water cannon and armoured personnel carriers. The city's airport has been fitted with surface-to-air missile launchers. 'Anti-terrorist scuba divers' patrol the harbour.

Meanwhile, the whole of the city centre has been designated a *Zona Rossa* – a 'Red Zone' – which only residents, journalists and politicos are allowed to enter. A ten-kilometre-long security fence, five metres high, has been installed, shops have been boarded up and manhole covers welded down. Trains and planes into Genoa have been cancelled and motorways are being patrolled. Italy has temporarily suspended its membership of the Schengen Agreement, which grants free movement to all EU citizens across national boundaries, and has turned a reported 2,000 people away at the border. The cost of all this to the city has been reckoned by the authorities at 250 billion lire – about $110 million. For all this, nobody knows quite what is going to happen, or who will be doing it. We are about to find out.

Big international anti-summit demonstrations like this, whether they are against the World Trade Organization, World Bank, International Monetary Fund, Summit of the Americas, Asian Development Bank or G8, have only been around in their current form for a few years, but already they have developed common ways of organising. Genoa is no different. The makeup of the participants is hugely diverse: unions, environmentalists, church representatives, middle-aged anti-debt campaigners, teenage anarchists, party politicians and many thousands upon thousands of non-aligned but passionate people. No one person or organisation is 'in charge' of this sea of humanity; it will move as it sees fit. Nevertheless, there is a shape to it.

Most people have got themselves into small 'affinity groups' with like-minded others, for security and solidarity. Those groups then join up with larger groups that activists have divided themselves up into according to their beliefs and tactics. Some groups will be committed pacifists, to the extent of refusing even to defend themselves against police aggression. Others will be seeking non-violent but determined confrontation with the authorities. Others will be happy to instigate property damage; a few will even be prepared to attack the police. Some groups will try to scale the fence into the Red Zone, others won't want to take the risk. Some will dance around the streets, others march in formation with banners and leaders. Some groups will dress up, others won't; some will be silly, others serious; some single-issue, most multi-layered in their concerns. Nobody will tell anybody else what to do.

In Genoa, as in Seattle and Prague before, many of the groups are colour-coded: black, white, pink, green and more. The plan is for different groups to surround the Red Zone fences at various strategic points. What happens then depends on the approach of each group. And on luck.

I don't have an affinity group, but I do have a friend: Robin, a long-haired, affable English anarchist who I have bumped into a couple of times over the last few days. He has lost his friends in the heaving crowd and I am here alone, so for today, we're together, and together we've decided to join the pink-and-silver group. Pink fairies, pink dragons, tinselled cheerleaders in silver wigs and fishnets, blonde women with pink umbrellas, stubbly men in silver lamé trousers: the pink-and-silvers are deeply committed to what they call 'tactical frivolity' – a 'confrontational carnival', which aims to get through the fence if it can, but to do it in a way that will leave no one injured, and which people might even enjoy.

At about midday we break free of the car park, moving in a slow shuffle out of the convergence centre and into the streets. We're going to find the Red Zone. Police helicopters buzz overhead and a samba band strikes up. To shouts and waves from residents' rooftops we wind our way through the streets. The sun is still shining. Robin has a full pack of rolling tobacco. It looks like being a good day.

It's when we reach a huge central avenue that runs from the sea to the edge of the Red Zone that things start to get confusing. Other groups are moving in from side streets and mingling with us. The streets are throbbing with thousands of people. Robin and I are sidetracked by French cultural icon José Bové and his group of chanting cheese farmers, carrying a long banner, waving their fists and shouting 'No G8!' through their magnificent Asterix moustaches. When we try and find the pink-and-silvers again we're not sure which direction they've gone in.

We're standing in the middle of the road swapping tobacco and tossing coins to decide which street to head down when, from three or four side streets, masked figures in black begin flooding into the boulevard. Some of them have iron bars and none of them look pretty.

'Bollocks,' I say. 'It's the Black Bloc.'

The Black Bloc are a hardcore anarchist contingent. Their philosophy is fairly straightforward. They want to smash capitalism. They want to do it by smashing the symbols of capitalism. That means banks, McDonald's, Starbucks and anything else that looks big and filthy rich and exploitative and, well, symbolic. Or, in their own words: 'We believe private property is theft, state property is a tool for the protection of corporate interests and that both must be destroyed for the creation of a society based on mutual aid and individual liberty.'[1] And, though opinions are divided on the matter, plenty of Black Bloc-ers are also happy to smash police heads ('Since the police are the violent face of capitalism, in other words, the guard dogs for the rich, they are on the frontlines when the anarchists come to pursue our class war against the rich'[2]). You either love or hate the Black Bloc, but whichever it is, it's a bad idea to be in their way when they start getting down to work.

We head up the street, hastily. A few of our black-clad colleagues have already broken the windows of a bank and are joyfully lobbing the computer terminals on to the streets, to raucous cheers. There is a familiar whoosh, and a line of tear-gas canisters thuds on to the asphalt ten yards away, harmonised by the sound of shattering glass and boots on cobbles. The black of the riot police melds with the black of the anarchists through a yellow mist of tear-gas. Iron bars vie with nasty-looking truncheons. Definitely time to go; but not before I have a photo of the moment. The Black Bloc, much to their chagrin, are very photogenic.

If I'd thought about it, I would have realised that it was a stupid thing to do. As I raise my camera, a masked figure crashes in from the left and shoves me violently in the back. I stagger a few feet down the kerb. He rams an iron bar up about three inches from my nose.

'No photos!' he says. 'Fuck off!'

I fuck off.

Eventually, we catch up with the pink-and-silvers. They reach the fence around the Red Zone at the same time as a group of Italian pacifists arrives. The fence is high and huge, jammed across the tiny medieval street like a counter-revolutionary barricade. A line of very tooled-up riot cops faces us on both sides of the fence, twitching in anticipation. Robin and I exchange looks. Then everybody sits down.

For almost an hour, they remain sitting; a mass of bodies, singing songs, performing the odd bit of radical theatre and occasionally approaching the fence, where they are driven back by the humourless police. It's overwhelmingly good-natured; from the activist side at least. But I can't see us getting over the fence. Eventually, Robin approaches me with a guilty look on his face.

'I don't know about you,' he says, 'but I'm a bit . . . well, bored. I want to see some action. Look at that fence. We could easily get over that.'

'Go on then. I dare you!'

'I just don't really want to sing songs all day. I don't even know the words.'

I have to agree. It's time to see what is happening in the rest of the city. Later on, we will wish we'd stayed where we were.

Down the hill, at the Brignole train station, the White Overalls are arriving from the giant, open-air athletics stadium where many activists have been sleeping. The White Overalls – *Tute Bianche*, in Italian – are a world away from both the Black Bloc and the pink-and-silvers. Vehemently 'anti-ideological', the White Overalls, an Italian movement which emerged from a network of squatted 'social centres' in the 1990s, oppose neoliberalism as they oppose the dogmatic alternatives to it proposed by the traditional left. Some of them are members of a network of similarly dressed activists known as Ya Basta!, which comprises a number of Zapatista support groups dedicated to solidarity with the EZLN and their message both inside and outside Chiapas. Their presence here is just the most obvious sign of the influence of the ski masks of Mexico on the hundreds of thousands on the streets of Italy.

The White Overalls have evolved a tactic for events like this known as 'violent non-violence'. Rejecting both the Black Bloc approach (smash the place up, attack the police) and the pacifist opposite (refuse to participate in any physical confrontation), the White Overalls are dressed in defensive body suits made of old life-jackets, plastic bottles and foam rubber bed rolls. They carry plastic shields and wear old bike helmets on their heads. They are about to engage in their favourite tactic – bouncing through the police lines, truncheon blows bouncing back off them. They refuse to return the blows, but they are determined to push back, or break through, the police lines. Watching them confront the police gives a very clear picture of where the real violence comes from – and that's the idea.

But today it's not working. The White Overalls have been infil-trated from both sides; the police are attacking them, viciously, and some violent protesters are using their ranks as cover. Cobble-stones and tear-gas canisters are flying; the air is thick, heavy and acrid. A running battle is raging, and it's getting uglier by the minute. Meanwhile, around the corner from the Brignole station, extreme elements of the Black Bloc have set fire to litter bins and cars, filling the air with filthy black smoke. Shops and garages are being trashed and looted, off-licences are being raided. Whoever is under those masks, they're not here for the politics. A whole street is burning and the police are doing nothing about it; they're here, at the station, laying into the White Overalls.

Robin pulls a scarf he's been wearing round his neck up on to his face, to form a mask. From his pocket he pulls a pair of swim-ming goggles.

'Right,' he says.

'Where did you get those?' I ask, jealously.

'It was really hard to find them,' he says. 'Sorry, man, I would have got you some, but it was the last pair they had. All the fancy dress shops are closed. I reckon it's Berlusconi's orders. Got to be.' He pulls the goggles on. They have pink plastic mermaids on them.

'They're kids' size,' he explains. 'It was all they had. I look fucking stupid, I know.' Not as stupid as me, though. I don't even have a bandana, let alone a gas mask.

'Come on then,' says Robin. We advance into the mêlée. Within ten seconds a cloud of gas thicker than mud envelops us. I can't see a thing, my eyes are on fire and my face is ballooning. I stagger down a side street and collapse on a wall with my head in my hands. Robin doesn't last much longer.

'These goggles are shit!' he exclaims, emerging from the yellow cloud. 'I look stupid *and* they're shit. I want my money back!' I'm too busy trying to find my eyes to respond. Robin takes charge.

'Don't rub your eyes,' he says, 'it makes it worse. Here, put your head back.' There's a sound like the unscrewing of a bottle, then liquid cascades down my face.

'*Fuck!*'

'Keep your eyes open, man.'

'What the hell is it? It's as bad as the gas.'

'Vinegar and water, and lemon. Wait a bit. It works.'

And it does. It takes a good thirty seconds, but I can see again. Robin's bottle contains a variant of 'Seattle solution', the liquid pepper-spray medicine that was wheeled around the streets of that city in giant dustbins during the anti-WTO protests of 1999. Only this one's for tear-gas. It's a different recipe.

'What do we do now?'

'We can't get anywhere that way. We'll never get past the police lines. Wait till the gas clears and we'll go and see what's happening.'

A few minutes later we venture out into the streets again. Thirty yards away I see three cops carrying an unconscious *carabiniero* back towards their vans, blood on his face, his eyes closed. Injured protesters are slumped on pavements, bruised and sometimes bloodied. Plumes of smoke and muffled explosions are rising from scattered parts of the city; we can see them beginning to disperse above the rooftops all around us. Wherever we go, running battles are being fought. I see police chasing photographers with truncheons; battering peaceful protesters. And then I begin to see, on the faces of the activists streaming past me, away from the station, towards the sea, a look that doesn't seem to fit. Not defiance, anger, determination, frustration: something else. Something I don't like at all.

Half an hour later, Robin and I have managed to wend our way, somehow, away from the carnage and up to a requisitioned school on a hill overlooking the sea, where non-violent activists have been meeting, training and planning for the past week, and where independent media operations are based. The faces there wear that same look, and when I look at the pictures and reports streaming on to the computer screens in the media centre I know why.

Down near the station, a few streets away from where Robin and I have come from, an Italian protester, Carlo Giuliani, has been shot through the head by armed *carabinieri*, then run over by a reversing jeep. Photos are already on the wires, being sent all over the world; a body lifeless on asphalt, gas clouds and blue-helmeted cops on all sides, his blood a river in gutters that were meant for rain. The whole room is deathly quiet. Something, somewhere, has gone horribly wrong.

It doesn't get better; it gets worse. The next night, the *carabinieri* raid the media centre itself, and a gym across the road where activists have been sleeping. They attack people with truncheons while they sleep; they beat journalists unconscious in the street outside; they punch, kick, grope and batter defenceless people who offer no resistance, painting the walls and floors with sheets of their blood. People are carried out in body bags, still alive. Others are arrested, taken to the police station and tortured. Some are stripped naked, others forced to sing fascist songs from the days of Mussolini. The next day the police present the media with a cache of 'weapons' they claim to have gathered in the raid – petrol bombs, hammers, axes, knives – to justify what they have done.

Investigating magistrates will later accuse the police of planting the weapons to justify their brutality. In the coming months, questions will be asked in the Italian parliament about what the police did in Genoa. MPs will call for the resignation of the interior minister. Prime Minister Berlusconi will be forced to initiate a parliamentary inquiry, and the head of the Italian police will admit that his officers employed 'an excess in the use of force'. Three senior policemen will be sacked. The morning after the raid, though, none of this has yet happened, and none of it matters. We have just taken part in the biggest 'anti-globalisation' demonstration in history. We have *made* history. And not one of us feels good about it. Not one of us knows what to think, where to turn or what to do next. Not one of us is intact.

Later that day, from their chandelier-strung palace deep inside the Red Zone, the G8 leaders issue a statement. 'The most effective poverty reduction strategy,' it says, 'is to maintain a strong, dynamic, open and growing global economy. We pledge to do just that.'

This, for most people, is the 'anti-capitalist' or 'anti-globalisation' movement. In just a few years, those terms have become as common as front-page pictures of 'anarchists' (a catch-all media term for dissidents of any stripe) in stand-offs with lines of police dressed like something out of *Robocop*. On the streets of London, Genoa, Prague, Seattle, Melbourne, Barcelona, Durban, Seoul, Washington DC . . . every time there is an international economic summit, there are rings of protesters sworn to close it down.

Such stand-offs, as this book aims to show, are actually the tip of a much bigger and more significant iceberg. They are not the whole story of this movement; they are not even its most important chapter. Yet they have thrust it very effectively into the limelight all over the world. They have helped swell its numbers. They have forced the issues that it holds dear on to the agendas of politicians, journalists, business leaders and ordinary citizens the world over. And whatever you think of them, they are remarkable, historic, unavoidable and increasingly regular events. They help define our age.

To really understand confrontations like Genoa, though, you need to take a step back, to the first, and still the most magnificent, of the now commonplace global summit shutdowns. For if this movement was born in Chiapas on that January day in 1994, it was baptised, with tear-gas and pepper spray, on the streets of the American city of Seattle on 30 November 1999.

That day, as the newly christened World Trade Organization met to set out its first trade round, 50,000 people came out to meet it. Unions, farmers opposed to genetically modified crops, anarchists, environmentalists dressed as sea turtles, priests, militant taxi drivers, a coalition of radical greens and steelworkers, longshoremen, Zapatista solidarity groups, Colombian tribespeople fighting the destruction of their forests, Ecuadorian anti-dam protesters, Chinese democracy campaigners and thousands more took to the streets. There they clashed with thousands of police dressed like Darth Vader with painfully ironic Nike swooshes on their specially made gloves, who pepper-sprayed pensioners and attacked peaceful protesters *en masse*. The mayor declared a civil emergency and the WTO's much-trumpeted trade round collapsed in chaos as tens of thousands of people besieged its compound. 'This,' they roared, in a slogan that has since followed their movement to every continent on Earth, 'is what democracy looks like!'

The world woke up. Something was happening, and it was something different. This wasn't just another showing of the disgruntled old left – the slogans, the tactics, the organisational principles showed that. The demands of this new and untested coalition were many and diverse, and sometimes contradictory, but were couched, like those of the Zapatistas, in a new language. The

Seattle protests were organised by no single group, had no leaders, no one ideology. They were impolite, they were novel, they were radical, they were determined. And they were spectacularly successful.

If it hadn't been for the 'Battle of Seattle', none of us would be talking about globalisation in quite the same way; it is not an exaggeration to say that the world would not be quite the same place. If the Zapatista uprising was the first post-modern revolution, Seattle was the first post-modern street protest.

Seattle crystallised something that hadn't been in evidence before; something newly, and self-consciously, global. On the day that the protests there began, hundreds of thousands took to the streets in dozens of other countries around the world, in solidarity. Activists rallied around the Australian stock exchange in Brisbane and the presidential palace in Manila, in the Philippines. In Delhi, near the spot where Gandhi was cremated, 500 slum-dwellers, farmers and students set fire to a statue representing the WTO. Thousands marched through Cardiff, Limerick, Prague, Berlin, Rome, London, Halifax, Bangalore, Washington and Tel Aviv. Dockworkers went on strike in California, protesters chained themselves to the railings outside the chamber of commerce in Dijon, and over 1,000 people from sixty villages rallied their bullock carts in India's Narmada Valley, site of a vast dam-building project. No one, anywhere, was alone.[3]

From the launchpad of Seattle, there was no stopping this new surge of rebellion – whatever it was. In January 2000, the World Economic Forum in Davos, which had been meeting quietly among idyllic Swiss Alps since 1971, was besieged by more than 1,000 protesters, forcing its delegates to undergo horrific deprivations: 'One Asian minister complained that he was stranded without his chauffeur, and quite unable to move,' explained an outraged *Daily Telegraph*.[4] The next year they came back in greater numbers, and did it all again.

In February, activists in Thailand picketed the UN Conference on Trade and Development in Bangkok, burning chillies in frying pans and filling the air with stinging smoke in a traditional Thai 'cursing ceremony' aimed at the promoters of globalisation. In April, thousands of Bolivians took to the streets of the city of Cochabamba in a week-long 'water war' against privatisation, while Washington DC was brought to a standstill by 30,000 people converging on the World Bank and IMF's annual meeting.

On May Day 2000, a day of action against the global economic order rippled across the world. Later in the month, 80,000 people took to the streets of Argentina to reject the International Monetary Fund's grip on their economy. In Prague, in September 2000, 20,000 members of the same coalition that had frozen Seattle trapped delegates to the World Bank and IMF's annual meeting inside their conference centre for twelve hours, then rounded off their victory by besieging the city's opera house and ruining their evening's entertainment. At the same time, another 20,000 converged on the meeting of the World Economic Forum in Melbourne, Australia, and solidarity rallies burst on to the streets of 110 cities around the world.

It went on. Over the next two years it went on in Thailand, India, Indonesia, Australia, New Zealand, South Korea, Brazil, Mexico, Argentina, the USA, Bangladesh, the Philippines, France, Canada, Papua New Guinea, Pakistan, Ireland, Belgium, Poland . . . the list is too long to print in full. It went on in Genoa, and despite what happened there, it went on afterwards, elsewhere. It went on, bigger than before, after 11 September 2001, when the pundits said it was, or should be, dead. It mutated like a virus and it continued to spread. It is still spreading.

Who could give a name to this new movement, pin it down, hem it in, control it? If you talked to ten people who considered themselves a part of it you got ten different ideas about what it was. Some called it 'anti-globalisation'. Some called it 'anti-capitalist'. Some called it a 'pro-democracy' movement, others a 'social justice' movement. Tony Blair called it 'an anarchists' travelling circus'. *The Economist* said it was 'winning the battle of ideas'. The influential American journalist Thomas Friedman said it was 'a Noah's ark of flat-earth advocates, protectionist trade unions and yuppies looking for their 1960s fix'. What Clare Short dismissed as 'misguided, white middle-class activists' Noam Chomsky called 'the first real promise of a genuine International'. Everybody had an opinion. Few of them tallied.

While the analysts and pundits discuss it, debate it, dissect it or dismiss it, it keeps growing. It is a global network of millions; one that has fused together in a remarkably short time and which has regularly outfoxed the forces of the Establishment. It is the biggest story of the age, the biggest political and social movement for generations; perhaps the biggest ever. And it wants to change the world.

Where has this come from, and why? The last question is probably the place to start. For it is impossible to understand this movement without appreciating the historical moment it emerged from; a moment we are still living in.

The world, as most of us have probably noticed, is currently undergoing rapid and all-consuming change – economic, social, political, technological – which is sweeping away traditional political structures, old economic models, social certainties, national divides. Nothing is the same. The great clash of ideologies that defined the twentieth century died with the collapse of the communist bloc. Capitalism won the Cold War, and now it is ramming home its victory by triumphantly raising its flag on the political battlements of every nation on Earth.

Everything is up for grabs. On a newly interconnected planet, in which corporations, investors and bankers in distant cities can pull the economic rug out from under entire nations, wrecking whole economies in hours if their interests are threatened, 'politics' has taken on a whole new meaning. From Brazil to Britain, South Africa to Germany, Russia to Mexico, New Zealand to Japan, politicians from left and right are morphing into a managerial class of hemmed-in technocrats who see no choice but to make their peace with the market. There is nowhere else to go. There is no alternative. We have reached, so many of them say, with either a triumphant smile or a resigned sigh, the end of history.

There is a fashionable word for this: 'globalisation'. It is a term that is as widely used as it is loosely defined. The word tends to conjure up vague mental images in people's heads – pregnant Thai women working twelve hours a day in sweatshops with no toilet breaks; grinning Masai warriors e-mailing each other on laptops in the middle of the Serengeti – which help determine whether you are for it or against it without ever having to explain what it actually is.

The one thing that people do seem to agree on, though, is that globalisation is something new: an economic and technological revolution that will lead, depending on your view, to either the Elysian Fields or to Hades. Either way, things will change beyond recognition, as humanity enters a new and unique phase in its development.

One commentator on this new process has well described the social and economic upheaval that globalisation has brought into being: 'All fixed, fast frozen relations, with their train of ancient and removable prejudices and opinions, are swept away, all new-formed ones become antiquated before they can ossify. All that is solid melts into air, all that is holy is profaned, and man is at last compelled to face with sober senses his real conditions of life and his relations with his kind.'

This is as poetic a description of the social effects of globalisation as has yet been produced. The same writer's observations of its economic effects are similarly sharp: 'All old-established national industries have been destroyed, or are daily being destroyed. They are dislodged . . . by industries that no longer work up indigenous raw material, but raw material drawn from the remotest zones; industries whose products are consumed, not only at home, but in every quarter of the globe. In place of the old wants, satisfied by the productions of the country, we find new wants, requiring for their satisfaction the products of distant lands . . .'

The writer of this dissection of the revolutionary power of globalisation was Karl Marx, in *The Communist Manifesto* in 1848. It demonstrates nicely that while the technology, the circumstance and the speed of what we are undergoing may be new, what underlies 'globalisation' is something very much older. What it is, despite all the cant and waffle that has been issued on its behalf, is the latest phase of an economic system known as 'capitalism', which has been with us for at least half a millennium.

Capitalism has gone through many phases since the Industrial Revolution in Britain in the late eighteenth century first made it a force to be reckoned with. When Marx was writing, in the mid-nineteenth century, its very existence seemed threatened by a wave of revolutions that were toppling, or threatening to topple, regimes across Europe. Later, towards the end of the nineteenth century, fed by the markets, mines and sweated labour of Empire, capitalism became as global, rampant and unfettered as it had ever been. This phase was known as liberal capitalism, or simply 'liberalism', from whence we get the clunky term 'neoliberalism' – a new version of a very old story. Then, as now, it fed the rich by punishing the poor, and raised the industrial nations of the West to dominance by marginalising the lives, cultures, economies and aspirations of the rest of the planet. Then, as now, it led to a worldwide popular uprising which found its most forceful expression in Russia in 1917. The historical comparisons can be uncanny.

For a while, after the revolutions of the early twentieth century, after the Wall Street Crash of 1929 and the Second World War, it looked like rampant capitalism was a thing of the past. Hemmed in by regulations, welfare states and strong labour unions, limited in its ambitions by the end of Empire and a determination not to repeat the mistakes of the past, it seemed almost as if humanity had bucked the trend and learned from history. Then, in the 1970s, came Milton Friedman, the radical 'new right' economist who believed that unregulated markets, left to themselves, could solve every problem worth solving. General Pinochet in Chile, followed swiftly elsewhere by Margaret Thatcher and Ronald Reagan, had a go at proving him right, and the economic winds they unleashed became hurricanes with the decisive collapse of the Eastern Bloc in 1990.

The rigid, utopian ideology of international communism was dead. In its place came another ideology: one equally utopian, equally rigid and equally immune to human suffering – the dream of a global free market.

The pursuit of this dream, we have been assured for years, is the best – the only – way to meet every challenge facing humanity, from abolishing poverty to preventing environmental catastrophe. Sit back, let the market work its magic, watch the cake grow, eat until you're full. Yummy. And yet almost three decades of chasing this dream have shown it to be a nightmare for much of the world.

Compare, for instance, the world today with the world as it was before the neoliberal experiment began in the 1970s. Measured in conventional economic terms, we are certainly richer. Gross world product in 1960 was $10 trillion; today it is $43.2 trillion – over four times as high.[5] Where that wealth has gone though, is another matter entirely.

In 1960, the 20 per cent of the world's population that lived in the rich industrialised countries of the West had thirty times the income of the poorest 20 per cent of humanity. Today, we have seventy-four times as much.[6] A stunning 2.8 billion people – almost half the world's population – live on less than $2 a day, and this figure is 10 per cent higher than it was in the late 1980s.[7] The richest 1 per cent of the world's population receives as much income as the poorest 57 per cent. The richest 10 per cent of the population of just one country – the USA – have a combined income greater than the poorest 2 billion people on Earth.[8] The assets of the three richest people on the planet are more than the combined GNP of all the least developed countries put together.[9]

At the same time, inequality has increased within countries as well as between them. Even in those rich nations, inequality has been increasing sharply since the market really began to bite in the

1980s.[10] In Britain, for example, Margaret Thatcher's neoliberal experiment succeeded in increasing the percentage of the population living below the poverty line from one in ten to one in four.[11]

Rising global inequality is not a new trend; it can be traced back to at least the early nineteenth century. But globalisation has accelerated it massively, to the point where, today, the world is more unequal – more un*fair* – than at any point in human history. This, in a nutshell, is globalisation's story – the rich getting richer, and the poor getting poorer. This fact alone undermines the empty promises of wealth-for-all held up by its promoters. And this fact alone is probably the single biggest reason – though by no means the only one – for the accelerating international uprising that is the subject of this book.

Private corporations, as any activist will tell you, are among the most obvious beneficiaries of this process. Over the past decade, they have become politically and economically dominant in a way that is unprecedented in human history. Together, the world's ten biggest corporations control 85 per cent of all pesticides, 60 per cent of all veterinary medicine, 35 per cent of all pharmaceuticals and 32 per cent of all commercial seed.[12] Of the world's 100 biggest economies today, 51 are corporations; only 49 are nation states. General Motors is bigger than Thailand. Mitsubishi is bigger than South Africa. Wal-Mart is bigger than Venezuela.[13] It is a stunning accretion of private political and economic power.

And yet the free-market project continues. At the international level, treaties like NAFTA and a host of other less well-known agreements, formal or unofficial, cement the hold that private interests are gaining over every aspect of economies, societies and cultures. Meanwhile, a triumvirate of global institutions – the World Bank, the International Monetary Fund and the World Trade Organization – are loathed by activists and praised by neoliberals for driving that project onwards.

The World Bank and IMF, set up in 1944 to rebuild a shattered post-war world, morphed in the 1970s and '80s into the attack dogs of advanced capitalism. They loan money to 'developing' countries to build infrastructure projects, stabilise their economies or, more recently, promote social programmes. In return, they demand that countries 'restructure' their economies according to models drawn up by their in-house economists. Typically, in return for Bank or IMF help, a country will be expected to slash its public spending, begin a process of privatisation, open its borders to trade and investment, focus its economy on export-led production and encourage foreign corporate investment.

This makes more sense when it is understood that it is the world's most powerful countries which run the Bank and the Fund, both of which apportion votes to government representatives according to how much money they receive from them. Both institutions are thus effectively run by rich countries, but operate only in poor ones. The Washington-based technocrats who devise their policies used to proudly call them 'shock therapy'. In the name of trade, they have shocked millions across the 'third world' into penury, and continue to do so.

Over at the World Trade Organization, meanwhile, the powers of national governments are quietly being given away in the name of trade. The WTO was set up in 1995 to oversee the final creation of the neoliberals' market utopia. Its vast dossier of international laws is designed to knock away all and any 'barriers to trade' by banning countries from subsidising their industries, protecting vulnerable economic sectors, passing laws that inhibit trade flows and corporate freedoms or generally preventing competition from doing its work.

Unfortunately, a corporation's 'barrier to trade' is often a citizen's environmental protection law, social programme, public health regulation or community support scheme. What NAFTA is doing to the Zapatistas of Chiapas the WTO is doing to the rest of us. Its rules have already been used to force the USA to rewrite its Clean Air Act to allow dirtier imported gasoline and drop import bans on shrimp caught without turtle-friendly nets. The WTO has instructed the European Union to stop favouring banana imports from small Caribbean producers over those of the US-based Chiquita corporation, which operates vast, chemical banana farms in Latin America. It has declared the EU's ban on potentially cancer-causing hormone-injected beef from the USA illegal. It has instructed Japan to raise the legal level of pesticide residues in its imported foods.[14] Every time that the WTO has been faced with a choice between upholding the interests of corporations and upholding environmental or social protection laws, it has ruled in favour of corporations.

As with the Bank and the IMF, it tends to be the rich countries which set the agenda at the WTO. In theory, every country has one vote in its meetings; in practice, many key decisions are made in secret meetings attended by only the world's most powerful governments. Many poor countries cannot even afford to send representatives to some of its meetings, while rich nations will send along a bevy of ministers backed up with armies of corporate lobbyists to shape the world trading framework, as ever, in their own interests.

This is 'globalisation'. Not grinning Eskimos downloading screensavers; not cheap flights to eco-tourist lodges in the Amazon; not more cultural understanding or world peace. Instead, a political project, pushed by the powerful and sold to the rest of us as an unavoidable, evolutionary development: as inevitable as the tides and just as difficult to turn back. It is as much about power and control as it is about trade or economic growth: control of resources, control of politics, control of the arguments that shape the values of societies.

If you are 'anti-globalisation', this is what you are against. And what you are part of is a worldwide people's movement that is being built from the ground upwards. At present, it has no name. It has no name because it is diverse, it has no leaders, it has no manifesto and it has no marketing budget. Its two most common epithets are the 'anti-capitalist' and 'anti-globalisation' movement, neither of them all-encompassing and both of them negative. Activists prefer more positive names, like the 'social justice' or 'global democracy' movement, both of which sound like they have been drawn up by committee. Most people, including me, simply call it 'the movement', but its name doesn't matter.

What matters is what it stands for. What matters is that, if you are part of this, you are part of an uprising against a world in which power is marginalising more people than at any time in history. A world in which the hard-fought-for democratic project is under threat from an inhuman economic experiment. A world in which people are redesigned to fit the economy, rather than the other way round. What you are part of is a gathering force of dissidents who have had enough, and will have no more.

What you are part of is a revolution.

The Bolivian city of Cochabamba sprawls unglamorously across the high Andes, the thin mountain light lending it a curious aura of unreality. Its airport is one of the world's highest, but has little else to be said for it. This is fortunate, because I don't get much time to see it. I'm here to attend a global activist conference, which I'm hoping will give me more of an idea of how the movement organises itself. Also here is my girlfriend and fellow-traveller Katharine, who has promised to meet me from my plane.

Meet me she does. As I wander into the arrivals hall she leaps at me and grabs my arm before I can even say hello.

'Come on, let's go!' she says.

'What? Can I get my luggage first?'

'No. Yes. OK, but hurry up. And don't mention the conference.'

'I wasn't going to. Why not?'

'Just don't. Don't look suspicious! Quick! I've got a taxi.'

'What *are* you talking about?'

In the taxi, pulling away from the glass buildings of the airport and heading across the bleak *Altiplano* to the edge of the city, I find out. Dozens of people arriving in Bolivia for the conference have been detained at the airport and threatened with deportation. Katharine only escaped because she got altitude sickness when she arrived and had to run straight for the toilets. When she got out, most of the people she had been travelling with had been detained, and she spent an hour frantically phoning around people she knew in the country, and the conference organisers, trying to do something about it.

'I didn't know what to do,' she says, relaxing slightly as the taxi takes us away. 'I hung around in this tourist shop at the airport for ages until the police had left. I was pretending to browse, but the staff were getting suspicious. I almost bought one of those stupid hats just to show I was a tourist, but I thought I'd rather be deported.'

The local government, it turns out, is trying to prevent this conference of troublemakers from getting together in its territory. It has done so by branding the activists 'terrorists' and trying to have them all thrown out of the country – most of the attendees, including me, have tourist visas. It wouldn't normally matter, but when the authorities want an excuse to clamp down on perfectly legal dissent, they can use it. And they have a perfect excuse. The date is 15 September 2001, America's 'war on terror' is four days old, and already, peaceful protesters are in the firing line.

The 'terrorists' in question are an international activist network known as People's Global Action (PGA). PGA was one of the driving forces behind the rise of the global movement that I found myself a part of in Prague and Genoa, and I am hoping that I can learn more from them about how that movement has come to be where it is.

On the lip of a dusty hill in Cochabamba, in an innocuous complex of school buildings, PGA is holding its third international conference. The gardens are planted with jacaranda trees, in full and beautiful bloom and a hot sun is beating down from a thin Andean sky. PGA has been given use of some of the school buildings for a week, even as classes go on. Dark-skinned children mill about buying Coke from snack stands and slouching from class to class as, under trees and in unused classrooms, uprisings are planned.

Katharine and I, having escaped being sent home, arrive the afternoon before the conference begins, sign in and wander around the banner-strung buildings. Agendas are being set, conversations held, workshops planned. Multi-ethnic, multi-national gangs of people are wandering around under the trees or sitting on the blossom-coated lawns smoking and talking, haltingly, in each other's languages. School bells ring, bees buzz and, in a purple jacaranda between the school hall and the garden, a tiny hummingbird flits between the blossoms. It's a world away from Genoa, and yet invisible ties bind the two cities together. For the story of PGA mirrors the story of the global movement itself.

The birth of PGA was inspired by the Zapatistas. At the end of the Encuentro in Chiapas in 1996, the Zapatistas issued a call to create an 'intercontinental network of resistance, recognising differences and acknowledging similarities' which 'will strive to find itself in other resistances around the world'. It would be a 'network of communication among all our struggles and resistances, against neoliberalism, and for humanity'. PGA is that network. Conceived at the Encuentro, PGA was officially born at a meeting in Geneva in 1998, created by 300 people from 71 countries. It is, as its 'members' are keen to stress, not really an organisation at all – it is rather a method: a means by which grass-roots groups around the world can link their struggles together, and hopefully strengthen themselves and each other as they do so.

Then, as now, the hallmarks of PGA were simple – and the marks left on them by *Zapatismo* are clear. Only grass-roots movements are involved – no established NGOs, no political parties, just the chosen representatives of community groups and activist 'cells'. All oppose globalisation and all the hallmarks of neoliberalism, and all are prepared to use non-violent civil disobedience to challenge it. All are committed, too, to building new systems in a new way – devolving power rather than replacing it, looking for a political order based on 'decentralisation and autonomy'.

PGA took the new political forms, the new ideas about power and the new methods of making things happen that had come out of Chiapas, and ran with them on a global scale. The result was events like Seattle, Prague, Genoa – and the global movement we have today. For it was PGA – not PGA alone, by any means, but certainly PGA in the role of inspiration and key player – which helped create the kind of 'take on a big summit' action that came to define the first stage of the anti-globalisation movement. Its first success was in 1998. As the G8 met in Birmingham, over sixty-five demonstrations against it sprang up in twenty-nine countries. It was an unexpected international co-ordination of dissent and, at the time, nobody knew quite where it had come from. It had come from PGA, and its next destination was to be Seattle.

Like the rest of the movement it helped spawn, PGA has an almost fanatical devotion to the concept of 'horizontal organising' – working in networks, not hierarchies, with no appointed leaders. The whole conference, the whole network, is run along these lines – no one representing anyone else, or PGA as a whole. Decisions are taken by consensus, with majority votes, and no person or organisation is obliged to do, or agree to, anything they don't like. It was the same set of principles I saw in Genoa, and in Chiapas, and understanding them is crucial to understanding the global movement as a whole.

What characterises PGA, I am to discover, is what characterises the global movement: diversity. Diversity of aims, of tactics, of race, of language, of nationality, of ideas. There is no manifesto, no line to follow, no leader to rally behind. This diversity is what leads critics outside the movement to assume that it doesn't have any ideas. After all, if it did, surely it would write them down, publish them, form a party, get a charismatic leader and march forward to take power? That's how politics is supposed to work. This, on the other hand, is gloriously anarchic, in the best sense of the word. This is a politics in which means matters as much as ends.

Sometimes it's hard to come to terms with this, even for activists. You might be standing in the middle of some mass action or conference or spontaneous uprising, thinking, Who started this? Who organised it? *Who's in charge here?* Police officers and politicians, imbued instinctively with a 'take me to your leader' mentality, have never believed the movement when it answers, 'Nobody and everybody.' How can events as stunning as Seattle or Genoa have no centralised organisation, no leader who decides and declaims, whom people follow, and who we can arrest to neuter everybody else?

But they don't, and this in itself is a revolutionary idea – not a new one, but one that's rarely been put into practice. So much so, that even as part of it, it's a leap to give that question – 'Who's in charge here?' – the answer it deserves: Everyone. No one. Oh yeah: Me!

This approach is part of what has made this movement so effective. Broad-based, local and national networks, run by communities and linked internationally, more often than not, by the Internet, have proved themselves capable of bringing together very large groups of people in very short spaces of time. This way of organising has been called 'swarming', and has been the subject of many excitable pseudo-academic treatises over the last few years. Like the Zapatista rebellion, networks like PGA have been defined in many ways by the Internet. That was how Genoa was organised (mobile phones help too), that was how the Zapatistas came to the world's attention, and that is how, to a large extent, PGA runs its shop. The success of Seattle has even been put down by some to one over-riding factor: the police hadn't discovered the activists' e-mail lists.

Internet activism, unlike more traditional forms of mobilising, cannot easily be crushed. It is democratic, non-hierarchical and entirely in keeping with the global nature and principles of the movement. It also gives birth to new forms of protest – 'cyber-squatting', for example, when hundreds of people log on to a corporate website and crash it in protest at company activities. Or the so-called 'Dracula strategy' – using the Internet and e-mail to expose something to the light which its creators would rather keep hidden.

This was used to its best effect so far in 1998, when the text of a global treaty being quietly drawn up by the Organization for Economic Co-operation and Development – the Multilateral Agreement on Investment (MAI) – was leaked to a group of Canadian activists. The agreement, which would have given multinational investors the power to sue national governments and gut democratic control over foreign investment, was sent around the world to websites and e-mail lists in a matter of minutes. A rapid mobilisation began, and before even many government ministers knew what was in the treaty, a worldwide campaign was in progress against it. Exposed to the light, the MAI shrivelled and died, when politicians who would previously have waved it through pulled out of negotiations in the light of public glare. The victory was justly celebrated by the *Financial Times*, which grumbled, accurately, that the MAI had been 'ambushed by a horde of vigilantes whose motives and methods are only dimly understood in most national capitals'.[15]

The 'swarm' had its first scalp. Within twelve months, at Seattle, it would have another. Ironically, the Internet, engine of financial and corporate globalisation, had become the engine, too, of the globalisation of resistance; a vital tool for the creation of a global network of dissent that could probably not have been created without it.

PGA could not have been created without it either. Now, here in Cochabamba, on the first full day of the conference, hundreds of people are sitting around in the unused school hall on red plastic chairs discussing where it will go next.

Exactly how many people are here isn't clear, but 151 groups from 43 countries applied to attend the conference. Not all of them came, but of those that did, PGA applied its usual policy of ensuring that 70 per cent of them were from the 'developing' world. The result is that it is their concerns which largely set the agenda: an eye-opener for those who have read so many times in the press that this is a movement of spoilt middle-class white kids with nothing better to do.

During our week here we will be listening to talks from community groups, swapping tactics and strategies, rewriting PGA's manifesto, planning forthcoming days of action (the WTO meeting in November is the next biggie) and deciding on what issues the network will focus on for the next few years. We will also be chewing a lot of coca leaves. Bolivia's union of coca farmers – the *Cocaleros* – are one of the local organisers of this conference, and are keen to explain how the USA's 'war on drugs' (about as effective as its 'war on terror' so far; the drugs are winning) is, *de facto*, a war on them. They are small mountain farmers who have been growing coca plants for generations – the locals chew the leaves or make tea from them, as a mild stimulant. The plants are also the basis of cocaine, so the USA has decided that the way to prevent American kids taking drugs is to aerially fumigate vast swathes of Latin America with powerful pesticides. This, with any luck, will kill a lot of coca plants and opium poppies. It will also kill a lot of livelihoods, traditions and industries, such as those of the coca farmers, and probably a few people into the bargain.

This policy has already had the effect of radicalising people like the coca farmers. It also has the indirect effect of ensuring that everyone at the PGA conference has to chew a lot of coca leaves in a gesture of defiance to the *Yanqui* imperialist aggressor. This is unfortunate because, with the best political intentions in the world, coca leaves are revolting. As we sit digesting our lunch, women farmers approach us one by one in their bowler hats and rainbow shawls, vast sacks of coca leaves around their neck. People take handfuls and slip them into their pockets, or chew them until they think no one is looking and then slip the resulting gobby mess under a bush. But it's the thought that counts.

Despite the coca, I am inspired by PGA. For the first time, I am beginning to see with my own eyes how truly global this movement is. It's one in the afternoon on the first day of the conference, and I'm sitting in the hall, eating lunch on one of a row of trestle tables that fill the room. On my table sits an *adivasi* tribal woman from Bangladesh, an ecologist from Russia, a union representative from Canada, a stocky member of Ya Basta! who I last saw through a haze of tear-gas in Genoa, a Chilean human rights activist who was tortured under Pinochet, a Maori from New Zealand, a local student volunteer and two female *cocaleros* whose mobile phones keep going off in the middle of their meals. In other hands, such a convergence of worlds could lead to conflict or incomprehension. But here, with common forces affecting all, they have been brought together, and the results are fascinatingly fertile.

The topic of conversation around the table at lunch is the topic that will recur throughout the gathering: September 11th, and how it will change the world. Already, the US is using the terrorist attacks as an excuse to push its free-trade agenda even faster than it had been doing on September 10th – using a sickening 'idea' that their trade representative, Robert Zoellick, has called 'countering terror with trade'. It is also clear that the crackdown on 'terrorism' is likely to include conveniently sweeping attacks on dissidents of all stripes, whether peaceful or otherwise. Already we have heard American senators comparing anti-globalisation protesters to al-Qaeda. Everyone is nervous, but no one is being put off.

'I think we could be seeing a new McCarthyism,' says a blond, bearded union organiser from Canada. 'For "communism" read "terrorism". The governor of Cochabamba seems to have got the message already. Open season on us. It could be bad.'

'What we must do,' says a very serious old woman from Ecuador, 'is issue a statement against terrorism. But against state terrorism as well. The sort of terrorism that America has been sponsoring in Latin America for so many years.' There is general agreement on this point, and murmurs of consent break out around the table, in stages according to the speed at which people are translating the conversation for those who don't speak English.

'What we have,' says a short, stocky, Afro-Colombian man in a frightening rainbow shirt, who has travelled here from the former freed slave colonies of Colombia, 'is a system where we are the horses and they are the riders! And they have whips!' More nods, this time slightly vaguer. A few people light cigarettes, despite the polite signs pasted up above all the doors, and the talk goes on. A grizzled old farmer from Lake Titicaca says that the world is divided into a 'culture of life and a culture of death' – with capitalism and terrorism on the same side. No one is quite sure what to do, or what the world will now become. In this, at least, they have something in common with the rulers of the world.

Lunch can't go on for ever, though; we have an appointment with the history of the city to keep. There is a reason that PGA is meeting in Cochabamba, and we're about to have the details of it explained to us. What happened here just a year before we arrived has already gone down in the annals of this movement as one of its most famous victories; one that has made Cochabamba as symbolic a place to activists as Chiapas or Seattle.

In the school gym, we gather to listen to a talk by a local man who has already become a legend within the movement. Oscar Olivera, a short, unassuming former shoemaker and union leader, has come to tell us how he, and others who are here with him, led what he calls 'the first victory against the neoliberal economic model' in Cochabamba two years ago.

The story started, Olivera explains, in 1999, when the city's water system was leased to a consortium of multinational companies which, it later turned out, was a subsidiary of the US engineering mammoth Bechtel Enterprises. The World Bank ('Our dream is a world free of poverty') told the Bolivian government that if they wanted international debt relief they had better privatise Cochabamba's water system – and they had better not subsidise prices to help the poor pay their bills.

None of this was new in Bolivia, which, in exchange for accepting help from the IMF in 1985, was forced to restructure its economy along US-designed neoliberal lines. Bolivia followed globalisation's recipe for prosperity to the letter: it opened its markets to foreign corporations, slashed government spending, and privatised everything that wasn't nailed down. The result, after eighteen years of this, is that Bolivia is the poorest country in

Latin America. Sixty-five per cent of its people live below the poverty line (in the countryside, it's greater than 90 per cent), nearly 12 per cent of urban Bolivians are out of work, and for the country's rural indigenous people – who make up more than 70 per cent of the population – unemployment rates are even higher. The gap between the rich and the poor has widened and an increasing number of Bolivians are beginning to feel very cheated indeed.[16]

The Bechtel consortium was given a long-term lease on Cochabamba's water system for an undisclosed sum. For its money, Bechtel got control not only of the city's water delivery infrastructure, built by the government, but also of the ancient irrigation systems of local farmers, and of community wells, none of which were the government's to sell. And they were allowed to start charging for it.

And charge they did. In January 2000, the first private water bills arrived in the homes of the Cochabambans. 'Within a month of Bechtel taking over the water,' says Oscar, 'all the bills had gone up. Some by as much as 300 per cent.' People living on the minimum wage of $60 a month were expected to spend $15 of it just to keep their taps running. Bechtel were asking the poor of Cochabamba to pay more for their water than some World Bank economists paid in Washington. 'They are a very stupid company,' says Oscar, simply. It was to cost them dear.

In January 2000, Cochabamba ground to a halt as a new community body known as the *Coordinadora*, led by Olivera and the others who are with him today in the gym, led a four-day general strike in protest. The government sent in 1,000 troops. Street children, women, peasant farmers and thousands of local families were tear-gassed by police as they tried to march to the centre of their city. A shaken government promised a review of the water rates and of Bechtel's performance, but the deadline for that came and went with nothing to show for it but promises.

By now, the *Coordinadora* and its tens of thousands of followers were demanding the cancellation of the contract with Bechtel.

No chance, said the government. Bechtel had signed a binding contract: the water was theirs for forty years. And Bolivia's reputation for international stability was riding on this: if the government allowed popular pressure to topple this privatisation, it could all end in tears.

For Bechtel, it did. In April, the *Coordinadora* led a 'final battle' against the unbending government and the dismissive consortium which closed the city down for four days. A running battle between thousands of its people surged through the streets. The *Coordinadora* leaders were arrested then released, martial law was declared, protesters shut off the city with blockades and soldiers fired on crowds, killing a seventeen-year-old boy. Protests began in other parts of Bolivia, as people took to their own streets in solidarity.

After a week, the government caved in. They warned Bechtel that the safety of its staff couldn't be guaranteed, and the water men – all of whom had been shipped in from abroad – took to their heels, stopping only to grab the computers and the company's cash as they fled the city. The government announced the cancellation of the contract with Bechtel, and a stunned citizenry realised that it had won.[17]

The reverberations of the Cochabamba 'Water War' rang around the world, inspiring activists and making investors jittery. Bechtel decided the only fair response was to sue the government of Latin America's poorest country for $25 million in 'damages' for loss of potential earnings. Cochabamba's water was placed in the hands of a new public company, whose board included members of the *Coordinadora*. The Cochabambans had turned something very big on its head: not just a water company, not even just a major privatisation, but an assumption of inevitability; a myth that there is no alternative, that private will always beat public and that people are no longer active citizens but passive consumers. 'It can be done,' says Olivera, simply. 'We know, because we did it.'

It's a warm afternoon, a few days into the conference, and in the school hall, small groups of people are sitting in corners charged with rewriting key parts of the PGA manifesto, which is to be given a spring-clean.

'So,' says a pencil-sucking man sitting on a wall, 'should it be "northern concept of the nation state" or "northern corporate nation state"?'

'What if we take out "concept"?' suggests his partner.

'Mmmm . . . maybe. OK, how about "an emancipatory anti-capitalist perspective struggles" . . . er . . . "struggles for the idea of self-determination and opposes the concept of the capitalist nation state"?'

'I like it!'

Eventually, the groups break up and come together again as a whole, for there is serious business to discuss. We form a circle of chairs in the hall, which is marked by all the signs of a gathering of curious rebels: indigenous flags, posters, badly painted renderings of Che Guevara, EZLN videos, tables of books in Spanish about the inevitable collapse of capitalism. Banners are strung across the windows, bearing slogans that are found all over the activist diaspora – slogans like 'our resistance is as transnational as capital', and, my favourite, the direct translation from the original Zapatista threat/promise: '*Estamos en todas partes*' – 'We are everywhere.'

The subject under discussion is direct action, a topic which no one in PGA seems able to keep off for very long. The *cocaleros* would like us to take a trip with them to a nearby army base at Chapare and stage a demonstration against Plan Colombia. Others are worried that, what with the 'terrorist' crackdown and all, this might not be a good idea. A heated but polite debate ensues.

It had always seemed unlikely that this conference could break up and go home without some form of civil disobedience taking place. For all this week's talk of 'sustained local campaigns' being the way forward, PGA is still an organisation that was born out of non-violent direct action – 'NVDA'. This was one 'hallmark' of PGA's manifesto that wasn't going to be touched by the rewriting session: 'A confrontational attitude, since we do not think that lobbying can have a major impact in such biased and undemocratic organisations, in which transnational capital is the only real policy-maker.'

It doesn't get much clearer than that. Direct action, civil disobedience, is in PGA's lifeblood. It forms part of a belief that I will come across wherever I find this movement: the belief that direct action – taking politics into your own hands – is not simply a lobbying tool, an outlet for frustrations or a means of pursuing a goal, but is an end in itself.

If big summit protests now follow a familiar pattern, so does the furious debate that takes place after every one about what they achieved, where they go now and whether they are justified. But what's often lost in the media scrum is the importance of protest on a personal level. Those who would debate the purpose, point and future of direct action without ever having been a part of it will never know the personal power that being one of so many people moving in the same direction can give you. They will miss a great deal of the point – that getting people up and moving, personally inspiring them to take things into their own hands rather than vote or petition or ask someone else for it – allowing people to *live* again – is at least half the achievement. It may not bring capitalism to its knees, but what it does do is to give many thousands of people a taste of the power they have by joining together and taking things into their own hands. That power is unequalled, and once you have tasted it, you are never the same again.

Evening is here on the last day of the conference, and the scent of jacaranda blossoms is flooding the schoolyard. Tomorrow morning, horribly early, those going to protest at Chapare will set off by bus. This evening, though, it's party time.

In the hall, we're having a multi-national entertainment session. Bolivian kids are demonstrating ancient dances which mock the *conquistadores*. A Mexican man is providing a rendition of a deeply worthy play about capitalism which, fortunately, is in Spanish. A guy from Bristol gets a huge round of cheers for his fire-breathing. Tiano, a Maori who has no interest in half measures, wants to perform a Maori drinking song with his friend but can't persuade anyone to lend them a guitar and, in any case, is 'not pissed enough to make it work properly'.

Later, the evening descends into mass dancing in and around and outside of the hall. I am being swept off my feet by Virginia, a woman of utterly boundless energy from South Africa, who has been telling me that, if I want to see what people are really doing to fight privatisation of their services, I should come to Johannesburg. I have promised to take her up on her offer. In the meantime, she is trying to teach me to *toyi-toyi* – the hip-wiggling South African tribal dance that became a symbol of resistance to apartheid, and is now becoming a symbol of resistance to globalisation. 'Move your hips, Englishman! Your *hips*! *Do* they move?' she keeps screaming, before joining Katharine in a round of mocking female laughter.

As the dancing goes on, and the night draws in, and everyone gets progressively more drunk, including me, I look around me and I realise something. It's when everyone is up and moving, ripping and running around in mad circles to the Che Guevara song, under a waving, multicoloured, chequered flag; the symbol of the *campesino* farmers of Latin America. I'm being swung from South African to Colombian to ecologist to anarchist, from Brazilian to Bangladeshi, from *cocalero* to tribesman, all of them grinning madly, most of them dancing badly and me worst of all.

It's when I look around and see that everyone who surrounds me – all colours, from all corners, all together even as they are so far apart – all of them, all of these people, are determined and somehow together. I realise that they have between them something too powerful to wash away. You'd have to kill all these people, and the hundreds of thousands more they represent, to stop this movement. And as the pipes and drums roll on and the circle turns faster, throwing people half off their feet, I can't see anything that will shut them up, shut them down, make them go home quietly and stop causing so much trouble. Apart from winning.

3 **apartheid: the sequel**

'South Africa is in the hands of global capital. That's why it can't meet the legitimate aspirations of its people.'

GEORGE SOROS, FINANCIAL SPECULATOR, 2001

'He says that when the poor rise, they will rise against all of us.'

MOJANKU GUMBI, THABO MBEKI'S LEGAL ADVISER, REVEALS HIS BOSS'S FEARS, 1996

A young black man in a red T-shirt bearing the legend 'Soweto Electricity Crisis Committee' is hauling himself up a telegraph pole in a Soweto suburb. When he gets to the top, he reaches into a leather bag slung around his shoulder and pulls out a pair of pliers and a knife. He spends a couple of minutes doing something technical to the wires, then lowers himself down.

He makes his way over to an electricity meter mounted on the side of a nearby house, and swings a pickaxe at it. It splinters and tears away from the wall. He makes some adjustments to a jumble of wires sticking out of the wall with a knife, using a bin bag for insulation. Then he stands up, dusts himself down and approaches the house owner, an old woman who has been watching anxiously from her doorway.

'You now have electricity,' he says, grandly. He flicks the woman's light switch, and her tiny front room floods with light for the first time in weeks. She begins to sniff, gratefully.

'Now I'll be able to drink tea in the morning, instead of water!' she sniffs. 'Oh thank you!'

The man is one of dozens of illegal 'reconnectors' who roam Soweto restoring the electricity of people who have been cut off for non-payment of their bills. He is part of 'Operation Khanyisa' – operation light-up – a campaign of resistance to the steadily rising cost of basic utilities – water, gas, electricity, rent – that is hitting the poor in this, and other, townships. Collectively, Soweto owes the state electricity company, Eskom, almost one billion Rand – about $80 million – in unpaid bills.[1] But Soweto has 70 per cent unemployment, and most people simply cannot afford to pay. Eskom's response is to cut them off by the thousand. Their response is to reconnect themselves.

The man in the red T-shirt says that the government promised free electricity to the poor before the last election, and hasn't delivered. He is not alone in feeling angry; across Soweto, people say that their bills are rising and rising, and that their government is to blame. Reconnection is dangerous, difficult and illegal, but the people say that they have no choice but to take the law into their own hands; they say they are desperate.

The Sowetans are right: their electricity bills are rising. They are rising because Eskom is being prepared for privatisation, and the South African government, on the advice of the World Bank, will not subsidise prices for the poor blacks in places like this. The poor blacks whom the ANC was supposed to liberate; the poor blacks who thought that, in 1994, when Nelson Mandela came to power and apartheid finally dissolved, their country was finally in their hands.

Something is happening in the new South Africa; something that was never supposed to be part of the landscape in this liberated, post-apartheid nation. Electricity cut-offs, water cut-offs, evictions, rent hikes – all have been increasing since the ANC came to power. The gap between the rich and the poor has been growing, and the poor have been getting poorer. And in South Africa, 95 per cent of the poor, unsurprisingly, are black.[2]

Across the country, discontent is spreading. People are beginning to talk of a 'war on the poor' – a war led by the ANC government. Some are saying that they are actually worse off now than they were under apartheid. It seems almost impossible to believe. Yet the claims continue to be made; and they are growing louder. What on earth is happening to the Rainbow Nation, and why?

There is no poverty inside Johannesburg airport. There are a lot of South African flags – the green, gold and black model that replaced the old apartheid flag, and which symbolise this still-young nation – and, in the bookshops, there are whole shelves of books about or by Nelson Mandela. Many have pictures on their covers of the moment he walked free from prison, his fist clenched, into the world's glare. I can still remember that moment myself. It seems difficult to believe that it could have gone sour so quickly.

If it has, there is one man who can begin to explain why. Patrick Bond is a Johannesburg academic and veteran anti-apartheid campaigner. Before Mandela's ANC government came to power in 1994, Bond helped them to draft their new economic policies. He used to be an insider; now he is a bitter critic of what he claims the government has become. He has kindly agreed to show me around and put me up for the duration of my stay, despite having never met me before. 'Phone me when you get into Jo'burg,' he told me. So I do.

'Welcome to South Africa!' he says, answering the phone instantly. 'How about I come and pick you up from your hotel tomorrow? There are some things you might want to do. In the morning, I can take you to a meeting, if you'd like, where the South African left are trying to formulate a response to what's happening in Zimbabwe. Interesting stuff about land reform. Then there's lunch with a local union man, he's quite high up and he wants to meet you; he's keen to talk about the situation here with privatisation. Then at 4:30 there's a meeting about the forthcoming WTO summit in Doha. And after that . . .'

Patrick talks like a Kalashnikov, and on the bad phone line I can hardly get a word in. Perhaps I don't need to; I seem to have found an ideal guide.

When he picks me up the next day he's as full of energy in person as he was on the phone. Slim, academically dressed, with square glasses and neat brown hair, he is, it turns out, a human dynamo with more than enough enthusiasm for both of us. Which is handy, because I'm still jet-lagged.

Patrick lives in a Johannesburg suburb called Kensington which, like most other overwhelmingly white suburbs in South Africa, is defined by big gates, loud dogs and armed-response signs. His house has big gates, a loud dog, and an armed-response sign, and on the evening of my first full day in the country I am sitting in his kitchen, which looks out over Johannesburg. Patrick has poured us both large gin and tonics, and is telling me his version of South Africa's story since apartheid ended.

In 1990, South Africa's president, F. W. de Klerk, revoked the ban on the ANC, released Nelson Mandela from jail and announced a process of bringing democracy to South Africa. Mandela's ANC rallied itself for the inevitable – an election victory and, at last, government. While this was a prospect that excited the vast majority of the nation's people who didn't have white skins, it worried others: not just the rump of racist whites who had little say in the matter and knew it, but the stock markets and much of the business community.

'The ANC was allied with the South African Communist Party and COSATU, the trades union congress,' Patrick explains. 'They still are. And the ANC had traditionally a very progressive platform. The markets didn't like it. The stock exchange took a dive in 1990 just because Mandela said publicly that nationalisation was still ANC policy.'

In 1994, the first democratic election in South Africa's history swept the ANC to power. They inherited a shattered country: economic growth stalled at just over 1 per cent, unemployment between 20 and 30 per cent, depending on which figures you used, inflation at 10 per cent.[3] More significantly, society was polarised in an almost unique way.

'Ninety-five per cent of the poor were black,' says Patrick, sipping his drink, 'and another four per cent were "coloured" – mixed race. Only one per cent of the poor were white or Indian. The wealthiest five per cent of the population – all white, of course – were consuming more than the bottom eighty-five per cent put together.'

South Africa in 1994 was one of the most unequal countries in the world. More than half the country lived in dire poverty, less than a third of black South Africans had access to basic services such as electricity or tap water, and land distribution was among the most skewed on Earth.[4] In short, the poor were black, the rich were white, and it was the rich whites who controlled the economy, the capital, the land and the political process. The 1994 election changed the last of these; now, the ANC decided, was the time to change the rest.

Before the election, the ANC had rolled out, to great fanfare, its proposed means of changing it: the 'Reconstruction and Development Programme' (RDP). The RDP, which Patrick helped to write, was to be an ambitious programme of economic reconstruction and social improvement. 'The first priority,' it stated, 'is to begin to meet the basic needs of people – jobs, land, housing, water, electricity, telecommunications, transport, a clean and healthy environment, nutrition, health care and social welfare.' This was to be achieved through 'programmes to redistribute a substantial amount of land to landless people, build over one million houses, provide clean water and sanitation to all, electrify 2.5 million new homes and provide access for all to affordable health care and telecommunications. The success of these programmes is essential if we are to achieve peace and security for all.'[5]

This was unequivocal stuff. It was also short-lived. By 1996, the RDP was dead, its most ambitious plans shelved, many of its targets (though not all) unmet, the ministry created to oversee its progress quietly closed. The ANC's experiment in nation-building had lasted just two years. In its place came something altogether more unexpected – and very much more painful.

In 1996, the government unveiled a new economic programme – the 'Growth Employment and Redistribution' programme, or GEAR. For many of the party's erstwhile supporters, GEAR was a nasty shock.

Unlike the RDP, which had been drawn up after long consultations with communities, NGOs, unions and others, GEAR had been drawn up by a cabal of fifteen economists and launched on to the party, and the country, with no consultation. 'Two of the economists were from the World Bank,' explains Patrick, thinly, 'and a lot of the rest were from big South African banks and conservative economic thinktanks.' It showed.

In one fell swoop, GEAR publicly realigned the ANC's entire economic approach. It moved the party from being a government of social democrats to being a government offering up the most unashamedly neoliberal policy platform in Africa. GEAR accepted that growth was more important than redistribution, and that widespread privatisation and foreign investment was necessary for that growth. It tacitly accepted the impossibility, in a market-led world, of carrying out many of the government's proposed social programmes, including widespread land reform, public works schemes, state housebuilding projects and free utilities for the poor.

Rather than the language of national reconstruction, GEAR talked the language of the markets – the language of 'greater labour market flexibility', 'economic stability', 'sound fiscal policy', 'foreign direct investment' and 'strong export performance'. Behind it all lay a familiar mantra: private capital would create the wealth, and a free market would distribute it.

'GEAR is a capitulation to the markets,' says Patrick now, draining the last of his gin and tonic, 'but also to established power within the country. Essentially, democracy arrived, and the ANC got into power and there was kind of a deal – the white businessmen said to the ANC, "OK, you chaps can have the state, but you let us get our money out of here." In the meantime, you've got the World Bank sniffing around even before the ANC got into power – housing and infrastructure and land reform policies were influenced by them in the mid-1990s, which is why they failed. The ANC has bought into a very one-sided Faustian pact.'

That, at least, is Patrick Bond's take. South Africa's ANC president Thabo Mbeki has his own. He explained it at the press conference at which GEAR was launched in 1996, when a journalist asked him if this economic about-turn made him a neo-Thatcherite. 'Just call me a Thatcherite!' he grinned.[6]

Whatever the ANC's precise motivation, the results of this national realignment are now becoming clear. According to its opponents, almost a million jobs have been lost to GEAR. South Africa's unemployment rate is now estimated, conservatively, at 25 per cent, and may be as high as 40 per cent. Twenty-two million

South Africans, in a population of 42 million, still live in absolute poverty,[7] and the proportion of black South Africans living below the poverty line has increased dramatically since the ANC came to power – from 50 per cent to 62 per cent.[8]

GEAR's World Bank-approved policy of 'cost recovery' has only exacerbated this. Most notably, it has been estimated that close to 10 million South Africans have had their water cut off, 10 million have had their electricity cut off, and 2 million have been evicted from their homes, as a direct result of this policy – all for non-payment of bills which, in a country in which half the population gets by on around $2 a day, most have no ability to pay.[9]

In the townships and homelands today, a feeling is beginning to grow that few, if any, had ever expected. A feeling that the ANC, the great liberators, are selling out their own people. If this is true, two questions present themselves. Why? And what are the people going to do about it?

Downtown Johannesburg is one of those places you're supposed to be terrified of (high crime, boarded-up shops, dodgy characters walking the streets) and which the guidebooks say you should avoid. White businesses rapidly moved out of the city centre when black people were finally allowed to move in, in the early 1990s, taking their money with them, and large swathes of the city centre are now a commercial desert. But it's not nearly as bad as everyone says, which is handy, because I'm lost in it.

It takes me a good half-hour of wandering litter-blown streets and getting lost under flyovers before I find the undistinguished brown office block that I'm looking for. It is surrounded by graffiti, which says things like 'Bush is a racist pig' and 'Down with GEAR – forward to a socialist future'. I duck inside.

I'm here to talk to George Dor, who runs the Johannesburg branch of the Alternative Information and Development Centre, one of the groups that is mobilising against the government's economic plans. I want to see what groups like the AIDC are up to, and what popular support they have. Their office is high up in the building, next to that of the local branch of the ANC. I have to walk past giant 'Vote Mbeki' posters to get there. Inside, in a small complex of rooms shoehorned into the end of a corridor, I wait while George gets off the phone.

The room is covered with posters. One is from the Prague solidarity march they had here in 2000. 'Don't borrow from the World Bank,' it says, 'scrap the apartheid debt.' There's an antiprivatisation forum poster that says 'Boycott electricity payment – boycott privatisation – boycott racism'. In the corner is a giant orange puppet wearing badges that say 'let the market decide' and 'flexible work rules OK'. I feel strangely at home.

A minute or so later, a tall, angular white man with a long chaos of lank brown hair, khaki shirt, cords, greying stubble and thick, square glasses approaches me. He looks both friendly and harried. George Dor shows me into his office, piled high with papers, old posters, reports and the like and sits down. The AIDC is the hub of the activist wheel in Johannesburg. It runs workshops, writes reports and liaises with community groups. The AIDC was also responsible for the birth, in 1996, of the first visible manifestation of South Africa's new resistance to globalisation.

CANSA – the 'Campaign Against Neoliberalism in South Africa' – was a small, tentative coalition of defiance which came together to oppose a visit to the country by the IMF's managing director, Michel Camdessus, who was coming to discuss a new loan with the government. The small but loud rabble that was CANSA met Camdessus at the airport and harassed him into his limousine, and since then, though CANSA itself, in name, has more or less stalled, the cause it promoted has taken off, carried forward by groups like the AIDC which were involved in its creation.

Since CANSA pounced on Camdessus in 1996, resistance to neoliberalism in South Africa has coalesced around GEAR, which has been, much to the ANC's chagrin, an excellent tool to educate South Africans about the effects of globalisation on their lives.

This resistance can be broken down into three groups. First there are NGOs like the AIDC, and their umbrella group, SAN-GOCO – the South African National NGO Coalition – which is increasingly critical of the ANC and fundamentally opposed to GEAR. Secondly, there are the ANC's allies in the so-called 'tri-partite alliance' – the South African Communist Party and COSATU, the trade union congress. The Alliance was the key to breaking apartheid, but GEAR, and the ANC's love-in with the market, are now straining it as never before.

Since 2000, COSATU has organised regular marches, rallies and strikes against privatisation and the effects of GEAR. In October 2002 it called its 2 million members out on a nationwide general strike in protest at continued privatisations. 'We did not fight for liberation,' runs one of their most popular and ubiquitous slogans, 'so that we could sell everything we won to the highest bidder.' The communists, meanwhile, are growing so hostile to the ANC that a split between the two parties is looking increasingly likely.

Finally, there is the growing grass-roots resistance – the kind of community defiance exemplified by the Soweto Electricity Crisis Committee and their roving gangs of red-shirted reconnectors. In townships all over the country, anger is turning into action; electricity and water reconnectors, anti-privatisation forums, anti-eviction groups, 'concerned residents' committees and more nebulous, unofficial stirrings of opposition to the on-the-ground results of the ANC's market-led policies.

It is this last strand of opposition that is going global. Virginia Setshedi, who tried so hard to teach me to dance back at the PGA meeting in Cochabamba, is deputy chair of the Soweto Electricity Crisis Committee. I will bump into her, and others from the townships, a few months later in Brazil, when activists from all over the planet gather for the World Social Forum (see Chapter 6). A group of South African activists attended the second Zapatista Encuentro. They are part of an international anti-debt network, and are making connections with other communities in other countries, in Africa and elsewhere, which are resisting water and electricity privatisations. Their finest hour so far was probably in August 2002, when, together with activists from all over the world, up to 40,000 people took to the streets of Johannesburg during the UN's 'Earth Summit' to protest at the hijacking of the international and national political agenda by corporations.

It is this growing current of broad-based community opposition that probably worries the ANC most. If it is able to link up successfully with the disgruntled trades unions, and continue to forge links with the wider global resistance movement, its impact could be huge.

George Dor is one of only a handful of people on the Johannesburg NGO scene trying to deal with a rapid growth of interest in this kind of opposition. He's been working to drum it up for years, but it can get overwhelming.

'Mun, it's hard,' he says, exhaling slowly. George is the complete opposite of Patrick; chaotic rather than manic, slow-burning rather than octane-fuelled. 'I don't know how I get the time to eat, sometimes. But it's exciting, too. Things are snowballing. Organised political resistance to neoliberalism here is still formative, but it's growing very fast. Work around globalisation is starting to take root in other organisations, and starting to take hold in the wider communities. People are starting to get interested in why the ANC is going down the neoliberal route, what this means for them, why things aren't improving on the ground – why things are getting a lot worse.'

The ANC itself, of course, is not happy about the work that people like George are doing. Not happy at all.

'The ANC's attitude to what we do is interesting,' says George. 'It's basically "Who are you? Civil society? What are you for? Why don't you just close down? We led the struggle, we *are* the mass movement and now we're in government." Government has bred arrogance in them very quickly. They will always accuse everyone who even questions them of being "counter-revolutionary". Resentment is starting to build against that. It is slow, and still small, but at the same time, much bigger than even a few years ago. Things are starting to develop, people are starting to understand the issues and feel strongly about the issues – and the global issues, as they relate to what is happening on the ground here in South Africa. Last year, for the World Bank meeting in Prague, we had a lot of people and organisations getting active, held workshops, had public forums. We had a very colourful march. That's what those puppets outside were for.'

'Nice puppets.'

'Yeah, they're not bad, are they? They were very last-minute. In any case, if you want to see what we do on these occasions, you're here at the right time.' And I am. It's November 2001, and next week the World Trade Organization will be holding its first ministerial meeting since the débâcle of Seattle. It's a biggie: the WTO needs to nail down the new round of trade agreements that it was prevented from achieving in 1999. If it fails again, the entire organisation will be in jeopardy. So it has no intention of failing. To make sure that no protesters get near this time, it has decided to hold its meeting in a desert in Qatar, a conveniently repressive and inaccessible nation. It's a step on even from Genoa; this time, the whole nation will be its Red Zone.

In Johannesburg, as in hundreds of other cities around the world, anti-WTO actions will be taking place on 9 November. George is the man charged with making this one happen. 'Over the next week, we're organising a series of workshops and discussion groups about the WTO, which will culminate in a street protest on the 9th,' he says. 'Most people here have no idea what the WTO even is, let alone what effect it has on their lives. I hope that if we can start to change that, we'll see more mobilisations. If you want to come along, I'm doing a workshop in Soweto in a couple of days. You might find it interesting.' He grins. 'I think it's going to be a good one.'

Durban, unlike Johannesburg, is a city worth visiting, and plenty of tourists, from both inside and outside the country, do.

Lounging on the edge of the Indian ocean, the city was once a key Afrikaner holiday destination for those who wanted a whites-only Victorian seaside fantasy. Today, though, it is less of a fantasy. I have come here to see what the sort of struggles that Patrick and George talk about actually mean to people's lives.

As in Johannesburg, a rebellion is happening in this city. In June 2001, as the UN's World Conference on Racism began, the Durban Social Forum, organised by NGOs and community groups, staged a huge march. Their declared aim was to march 'against the South African government and its conservative economic policy, GEAR, that is making the poor poorer'.[10] Twenty thousand people took this message to the streets of Durban, shouting 'ANC – agent of global apartheid!' and 'Mbeki – don't sell our future!' It was Africa's Seattle.

Meanwhile, around the edges of the city, in the old townships where the blacks, the Indians and the 'coloureds' were herded by apartheid, a more constant, more local and more difficult battle is taking place day after day. The city government is busy evicting people, cutting off their water and electricity, and sending them to jail when they resist. And the more this happens, the more they resist.

I am sitting in the back seat of a car, belting down a motorway towards a place that, once I have seen it, I will never be able to forget: Chatsworth. An old Indian township on the edge of Durban, Chatsworth is the scene of an increasingly vicious clash between the ANC and the people. In the front seats of the car are a pair of frighteningly effective and uncompromising activists with fire in their bellies and frustration in their hearts.

Ashwin Desai, a South African Indian, went to school in Chatsworth; he's now a doctor, a writer, an activist, a community hero and an ANC hate-figure. Heinrich Bohmke is a lawyer, an activist, and an ex-ANC member, who is now as disillusioned with the party as anyone gets. Both were imprisoned by the apartheid regime, and both are seeking a new approach to political change in the country. They have been working for the past few

years to help the people of Chatsworth, and other Durban townships like it, resist eviction, cut-offs and destitution. Heinrich and
Ashwin are street-fighters – literally and metaphorically. Both have
strong opinions on, well, everything, which they are currently
laying out for me at 70 miles an hour.

'I'm sick of the fucking left!' Heinrich is saying, as he drives. He
wears a sensible, tucked-in shirt and trousers, and little rectangu-
lar glasses. He looks like a lawyer, and talks like a revolutionary.

'There are two lefts in South Africa,' he goes on. 'One is old and
bureaucratic and ossified, and the other is new and creative and
still unformed. There's all this intellectual Marxist shit, and then
there's people in communities doing things they need to do. But
they don't connect it to some great neoliberal project, they just do
it. I've stopped even referring to myself as "left". It's so patronising
and disempowering, calling yourself "left" or "progressive". We
need a new vocabulary.'

'Right!' says Ashwin. 'And we need to connect up these struggles. Connect them up nationally, and internationally, with all
those other movements that are out there. It's starting to happen,
but it's slow. Instead of always asking the state to give us what we
deserve, we need some way of taking it. These people in Chatsworth are angry, man. Guys are turning up with guns and
throwing them out of homes they can't afford to pay for.'

'But it's so hard, Paul, in this country,' cuts in Heinrich. 'People
are so sick of struggling. And there's still this great legacy of liberation to deal with.'

'There's a lot of *energy*, you know,' says Ashwin, 'but how do
we harness it? How do we make sure that COSATU or the ANC
don't harness it? Or some little bunch of fascists? You know
organised labour won't work with us – they just won't. They've
got their little power base, and they're going to defend it, whatever the consequences. They're so fucking shortsighted. You
know, during the racism conference, we held a community
march of the poor. We had 20,000 people on the streets. Next
day, COSATU holds its own march, and gets about 9,000 people

out. Next day, the ANC holds *another* one, and they get about 2,000 people!'

Heinrich changes gear determinedly. 'But at least people are starting to break through the barrier of illegality,' he says. 'They've given up expecting the government to do right by them. But then, you know, we have these leftie intellectuals in Jo'burg who are just waiting for Pretoria to have a change of heart and invite them in to sort out the economic programme. Whenever we mobilise for any sort of confrontation here it's always, "Well, comrade, we support your struggle, but we're worried about your analytical fucking framework, and your tactics." Your *tactics*, man! People are dying, literally, and they're worried about tactics.' I'm suddenly glad that Patrick isn't here.

'You've come at an interesting time, Paul,' says Ashwin. 'We're entering a new phase of political activism in this country. Hein and I, we both feel it's time for new approaches. As a movement we need to start proposing things, getting out there, doing things ourselves. You know, Zapatista-style. Taking it back; communities doing it themselves, instead of always reacting to whatever shit the government gives them. A lot of activists here are stuck in old ways of reacting to injustice. We need some new ones, man, and fast.'

'Sounds like a good idea,' I say.

Off the motorway, through the suburbs and out on the very edges of the city, strung along an abandoned railway line, Chatsworth sprawls, ugly and unashamed. We stutter down a dirt road, past gangs of grinning, shoeless black and Indian girls. At the end of the track, we park the car.

'This is it,' says Ashwin.

A creation of the notorious Group Areas Act of 1950, the act which, more than any other, created apartheid by requiring that non-whites move to designated areas – 'townships' on the edge of cities, and, later, 'homelands' in the countryside – the Chatsworth township was, and largely still is, for Indians. Forty years old, and home to 300,000 people, it is, today, a place that would make the worst British inner-city estate look desirable. I step out of the car and look around me.

Yellow and maroon tenements with corrugated roofs cling to a long ridge. Many have smashed windows and all have barred doors – crime is rife here. Communal taps outside the houses are capped with devices designed to make them unusable, and are padlocked down. The poor have not been paying their way. What was once grass is now scrub and dust, the roads are pitted with holes and the children's playground looks lethal. Gangs of teenage boys mooch around, bored, and kids play on piles of old tyres and low-hanging tree branches. There is little else for them to do; many have no schools to go to; many, too, have unemployed parents. There are no jobs for people like this.

The state – the very existence – of Chatsworth cannot be blamed on the ANC; it is a product of forty years of apartheid, under which those with non-white skin were treated like the animals the government believed them to be. Neither is it the fault of the new government that, nine years after apartheid finally fell, people still live in places like this. The point, say people like Ashwin, Heinrich, and the residents of Chatsworth, is not that the government is being slow to deliver, but that it is not delivering at all.

'Everyone knew that after apartheid, there'd be a huge backlog in social services, and it would be unrealistic to expect nirvana, or even just a decent standard of living, immediately,' says Heinrich. 'What is generating these struggles is not a failure to deliver, but a veritable *attack* on the poor. Government is not just leaving poor communities in misery, it's actually *cutting off* the little social support that they have in order to keep the national budget within a figure demanded by the Washington consensus. The ANC sees itself as being able to position the country as one of the best options among "emerging markets" by making these gestures to international capital. For people here, those fucking gestures lose them their homes.'

Chatsworth's people have lived in misery for decades. Eviction notices were served on them in such quantities during the 1970s and 1980s – often on unemployed families, for being in arrears by the equivalent of a few pounds – that mass protests ensued against the apartheid government. When the ANC government was elected in 1994, with the promise of mass housing provision for the poorest, hopes were as high in Chatsworth as elsewhere.

What followed, though, was an increase in evictions, and cut-offs of electricity and water. Durban's city council, now under ANC control, was employing the 'cost recovery' ethic that the World Bank was so proud of the ANC for adopting. 'Normal business practice demands that if tenants can't pay rent, they must be evicted,' said the council's acting director of housing.[11] Unemployment in Chatsworth was, and is, around 70 per cent, and many of its residents had the same problem as the Sowetans: they simply couldn't pay. Like the Sowetans, they believed the government's promise of free services for the poor, but what this promise turned into was a patchily enforced guarantee of mini-mum amounts of water and electricity for all.

The promised amounts were tiny – 6 kl of free water a month per household in Chatsworth, and a promise of 50 kw of free electricity that has not been delivered – and both were hedged in with small print. The free water, for instance, is only available to those who owe no money to the water company, which cuts out most of the poor of Chatsworth. The free electricity, meanwhile, is available only to those able to pay for installation of a pre-paid meter, which is conveniently impossible to reconnect if it is cut off. Then there are the evictions, for non-payment of rent: evictions which began to run into the hundreds after the ANC took control of the council. Evictions of old men and women, families with babies; whole legions of the poor.

By 1996, Durban city council was dusting down its apartheid-era combat gear, and moving into Chatsworth with police dogs and tear-gas, to forcibly evict, or disconnect water and electricity from, hundreds of its residents.[12] Chatsworth's people began forming community groups and linking up with those in other townships. Protests were held when local councillors came to town. Gangs of armed bailiffs stormed daily into the township to find themselves confronted with rings of residents determined to resist them. Battles ensued, bottles, stones and sticks were thrown. Sometimes the council men would turn tail, sometimes they would hit back, with tear-gas, rubber bullets and side-handled batons. Hard, vicious, physical confrontations went on for hours, days, weeks. The people of Chatsworth had had enough.

Today, because of this resistance, there are fewer evictions. But there are still regular disconnections, and poverty is still intense. Yet I can feel, all around me, a sense of dignity, and a sense of community that seems to defy the pressure from above. As we arrive, the residents are staging an event to try to keep that community spirit alive. It is Diwali, the Hindu festival of light, and the people of Chatsworth are holding a 'festival of no lights' to celebrate both Diwali itself and the community's resistance to the sort of cut-offs that leave them without working bulbs.

A red, white and blue marquee has been set up on an area of common ground, inside which singing, dancing and performances are taking place on a small stage in front of lines of chairs. Groups of young girls, faces painted, are dancing shyly, women are singing, and a wide-boy compère is making the audience laugh. Outside, groups of men are stirring curry, rice and dahl in huge, ancient iron pots. They insist on feeding me first. In return, I have been designated official photographer for the event, on the grounds that I am the only one with a camera.

I wander around snapping, and talking to mothers and grand-mothers, who tell me that they are fighting the government because, in the words of one, 'What else do we do?' A group of young men hanging around by the broken swings tell me that the ANC is worse than the National Party that preceded it; at least you knew where you stood with apartheid, they say. 'A lot of families who've been evicted in Durban,' one boy told me, 'have just got nowhere to go. There are whole families living out in the bush. They've got nothing left.'

Inside the houses, the situation is even worse than it appears from the outside, as I discover when a shy, middle-aged woman lets me use her toilet. The rooms are tiny, filthy, crumbling; plaster is falling from the walls, floorboards are rotting, plastic bags are stuffed into holes in the broken windows. It is a tiny, three-room tenement with primus stoves, broken chairs and decades of accumulated filth that can never be scrubbed away. I ask her how many people live there. 'Six,' she says. She looks embarrassed and I don't know what to say.

Outside, Ashwin is wandering around high-fiving and back-slapping, chatting and plotting. Everybody here knows him. We end up sitting on a low stone wall together with Heinrich, watching the festivities and eating more curry. I am trying to digest both my food and my experience. I can't remember ever having seen such human misery in my life – nor such dignity and determination in the midst of it. It makes me feel small, depressed and angry. I don't know what to say, and I tell Ashwin how shocked I am.

'Yeah,' he nods, through a mouthful of dahl. 'You can't come to this place and not be shocked. I'm *still* shocked, man. *Look* at all this' – he sweeps his arm across the grim vista before us. There is a look in his eyes that must have been there many times before.

'These people are *fighting* to be allowed to stay in houses that fucking *animals* shouldn't have to live in,' he says, fiercely. '*That's* why we have to fight. And we have to move this fight on from just being reactive. We need to start setting the agenda ourselves, or all we're doing is fighting a rearguard action to stop the worst things that the government is throwing at us.'

'It is a *war* on the poor,' interjects Heinrich. 'Look at what the government is doing – all the unnecessary pain they're causing people like this. The government has volunteered to dismantle its tariff barriers faster than it's required to by the WTO, even though it will cause unnecessary unemployment. These people are being evicted, cut off . . . and it doesn't stop there. You used to get a childcare grant of 450 Rand a month if your kid was under eighteen. Now it's been slashed to 100 Rand if your kid is under seven. You're suddenly expected to pay school fees – you never used to . . .' Ashwin is nodding again.

'What you're seeing here,' Heinrich goes on, 'and I really hesitate to say this, even now, but it's true – is a dismantling of even what *apartheid* gave these people – puny as that was. If there was a rent boycott under apartheid, the National Party didn't dare send in the troops, because there would have been mayhem. The ANC can do it, and they can do it in the name of development.'

'Yeah,' nods Ashwin. 'It's true. And you know, to oppose this is *totally* legitimate – to oppose both the process and the government that pushes it. It's damn hard, man, to oppose the ANC in this country – damn hard. They're still the liberators to so many people, but what we have to do is build a culture where opposing the ANC is progressive.'

'We all lived under a Nazi-like regime,' says Heinrich, 'and we defeated it – and that defeat took heroic things. People still have those memories. Now, the party that has hijacked that victory – that has come to stand for that victory – is out doing all this to its people . . .' – he shakes his head – 'even I have trouble sometimes, having to make that call, having to stand up and say "Down with the ANC!" But it needs to be done.'

'The world looks to South Africa now for inspiration,' says Ashwin. 'We need to spark a new form of opposition that has an international resonance. The question is, how do our struggles in places like this link with the Seattles and the Genoas? We need to, because to fight disconnection and to ignore the World Bank or the IMF or whatever, is fighting the symptoms not the cause. On the other hand, I wish the people in Genoa would come down here and see that trying to smash international institutions without winning support from communities like this is never going to work. Neither work on their own. If we can link them, we get a truly international movement.'

'Ah, but it's so fucking hard, man,' says Heinrich.

'It's hard,' agrees Ashwin, 'but we have to make the break.'

It's a warm November morning, and about forty people are gathered in Pimville Library in Soweto to learn about the World Trade Organization. I am back in Johannesburg, this time in its biggest and best-known township. The lime-green room heaves with the red T-shirts of the Soweto Electricity Crisis Committee and the yellow T-shirts of the Johannesburg Anti-Privatisation Forum. The AIDC is running a teach-in before the WTO meets next week. George, who is running the workshop, is exhausted – he's already done three this week in other townships. He stands in front of the whiteboard at the front of the room, brushing his hair out of his face. All eyes are on him; eyes belonging to rotund middle-aged women in headscarves and African dresses; angry young bucks in 'No to privatisation' T-shirts, interested young mothers, curious teenagers. It goes without saying that everyone in the room, apart from George and me, is black.

'We're gathered here today,' begins George, after an APF man has introduced him to everyone, 'to discuss this thing called the World Trade Organization.' He writes 'World Trade Organization' on the board with a blue marker pen. 'People around the world are going to be protesting about this WTO next week, because they're very unhappy about what's happening there. So let's have a look at it. Who knows anything about it?'

There is a sea of blank faces. One man raises his hand.

'It is an economic muscle,' he says, 'organising the world into one global economy – but for the rich, not for people like us.'

'No,' says another man, 'I think it is about job creation, so that countries can organise themselves for economic development together.'

'I think the WTO has organised the G8.'

'Governments of the north want the WTO,' says another man, 'because they want our wealth! That's why the APF says no to the

WTO and no to privatisation!' He seems to be reading from a sheet.

'I don't think the WTO will create jobs,' says a young woman. 'I think they exist to make a profit for companies. How will this give us jobs?'

'The WTO is like the World Bank and IMF,' chips in the sheet-reading man again. 'They want to generate more profits for the capitalist class. That is why the APF says no . . .'

'OK,' says George, 'right. Anyone else?' An old man, who's obviously been thinking about this, raises his hand.

'The problem,' he says, 'is that the WTO doesn't take into account different ideologies. They impose sanctions on countries that don't fit into their economic model. They give countries no choice about how to develop themselves.'

'OK,' says George, 'there are a lot of ideas here. Let's talk about them. First, I'll tell you about the history of the WTO. It's a very new organisation. It's only five years old . . .'

An hour or so later George is explaining the WTO's agreement on Trade-Related Intellectual Property Rights – or TRIPS – to his engaged audience. TRIPS, according to the WTO, globalises patent protection, copyright, trademarks and the like, to prevent unfair theft of ideas or designs, and 'protect innovation'. It means that something patented in one WTO member country is patented in all of them, and that undermining that patent is illegal.

South Africa, meanwhile, has a law allowing the government to make use of 'compulsory licensing' of drugs in times of national emergency – taking away patent rights from a company and mass-producing cheaper versions of the drug. South Africa, in which 4.7 million people – one in nine of the population – is HIV-positive, has a national emergency on its hands by any standards, and virtually everyone agrees that providing free or cheap AIDS drugs to the poor is a moral necessity. Everyone, that is, except thirty-nine of the world's biggest drugs companies who, in 2001, brought a legal case against the South African government, saying its cheap drugs policy was illegal, and quoting TRIPS to back them up.

AIDS activists in South Africa initiated an international campaign against the drugs companies, which forced them to drop their case amid a wave of international revulsion. Under pressure, the WTO eventually issued a statement insisting that TRIPS did not prevent governments like South Africa's breaking patents in times of widespread health emergencies.

'That's what the WTO says,' George explains. 'And yet the American government has taken Brazil to the WTO for doing exactly the same thing – producing cheap drugs and breaking patent laws. Thailand is doing it too. So let's look at laws. In South Africa, we have a law – you're not allowed to murder your neighbour. If you do, what happens to you?'

'Arrested,' murmurs the room.

'Right. The police come and take you away, and then you go to court. So if, say, Thailand keeps producing cheap AIDS drugs, breaking the TRIPS law, what do you think will happen?'

A pause.

'Thailand will be arrested?' volunteers a man.

'Er . . .' says George, 'well, yes, in a manner of speaking, I suppose. Thailand will be taken to a closed WTO tribunal, and if it loses its case, sanctions will be imposed on it.'

'But that's not fair!' shouts someone from the back.

By the end of the meeting, everybody seems to agree: it's not fair. George is talking about government support for industry, and why WTO rules require South Africa to phase it out.

'A lot of Western Cape canning companies have closed recently,' he says, 'because the government is no longer allowed to subsidise them under the WTO. And yet, in Europe, governments subsidise their farmers by billions every year—'

A woman puts her hand up. 'But that's economic oppression!' she says, simply.

'Yes,' says George, 'it is economic oppression.' A ripple spreads around the room.

'Are our trade ministers stupid?' asks a large, colourful woman, who has been growing increasingly agitated since the meeting began. 'Don't they understand what they're reading before they sign it?'

'Yes, they understand,' says George. 'Now, do you understand why South Africa has lost a million jobs under the WTO?'

'Yes!' roars the room.

'These people in our government at top level,' says a man over to one side, 'they should be doing what we want them to do! That is their job!'

'Yes!' shouts everyone again.

'So what can we do about this?' says another woman. 'Our first enemy is ignorance. I didn't know anything about the WTO at all until today. How can we fight this?'

'We must fight it!' shouts an old man. 'We are being sold! We are *always* being sold! We *must* fight it!'

As the workshop winds up, everyone is busily discussing how to organise transport to central Johannesburg for the march next week. All of them, to a person, want to stand up and be counted. In the corner of the room, meanwhile, writing busily on a very full-looking notepad, sits Dudu Mphenyeke, one of the leading lights in the Soweto Electricity Crisis Committee.

Dudu has lived in Pimville for decades, and helped to set up the SECC in July 2000, after her electricity had been cut off. She's now the SECC's public relations officer, and has seen the organisation that she helped to create soar from 17 initial members to over 5,000 today. She wears a giant square badge on her red T-shirt that says 'Third World Within'. I ask her what motivates the SECC to keep going.

'We regard electricity as a right,' she says, simply, 'and we feel it is better to break the law than to break the poor – to break the community. That's what the government is doing. The free water and electricity that they promised before the election – it's not been implemented.' I ask if she agrees with Ashwin and Heinrich, that the government is conducting a 'war on the poor'.

'Oh, life in Soweto has got worse,' she says, matter-of-factly. 'It was better under the apartheid government. We didn't have any cut-offs, we didn't have water leakage, we didn't have a situation in which even a person with a diploma from university was short of a job. It's really alarming. People are being retrenched, unemployment is going up, companies are being privatised . . .' She sighs, and looks me full in the eye.

'We feel,' she says simply, 'that this government has brought more misery and more poverty than before. They are making things easier for business people – reducing their taxes to make it easier to make profits – and making it more difficult for workers; more difficult for ordinary people like us.' She sighs again, and shakes her head.

'We don't have freedom yet in South Africa,' she says, 'and we feel deceived.'

Two days later. Tomorrow is 9 November, when the AIDC's anti-WTO march will be held, and George is zipping around the city trying to drum up what he needs to make it work. I have promised to help with the props, and so it is that I find myself in a giant disused factory-turned-arts-space, which smells inexplicably of peanuts, painting everything and anything that could potentially be used by the people who will be turning up tomorrow. Four or five members of a local arts collective have promised George that they will make him some props at short notice, and I am helping them out.

We spend all day brainstorming and crawling around the floor with pens, pots and paintbrushes, and by sundown we have an interesting collection of items to show for our efforts. It includes a giant cardboard puppet of the WTO-loving Trade and Industry Minister Alec Erwin; he wields an enormous hammer, stamped with the letters 'WTO', over a giant yellow representation of Africa, upon which are printed the words FOR SALE. It also includes twenty cardboard water glasses ('WTO water – 1 Rand 50'), four giant top hats painted with dollar signs and stripes, with accompanying cardboard fat-cat cigars, a collection of cut-out medicine bottles with 'Stop AIDS, stop TRIPS, affordable medicine now!' printed on the side, and three giant cloth anti-WTO banners of which we are all quietly proud.

The morning of the 9th dawns bright and clear, and in the small car park outside the AIDC offices, a vanguard of demonstrators is gathering. George has given me the job of explaining and distributing the props, which we have transported from the peanut factory in his ancient, rattling car. A keen crowd gathers around me as I open the boot.

'OK,' I say, picking up Alec Erwin, gingerly, 'this is Alec Erwin. He's got a WTO hammer, see . . .' Someone grabs Erwin and parades him around the car park in a circle, to enthusiastic cheers.

'Hang on – wait a minute. This is Africa, obviously. It's, er, for sale. He's supposed to be hitting it with the WTO, you see, so you have to carry the two next to each other.' Now that I explain it like that, it seems, well, a bit silly. But nobody cares, and Africa is swiftly and keenly claimed.

'Right, who wants to be an American capitalist?' The dollars-and-stripes top hats are being tried out for size before I've finished the sentence.

'Don't forget the cigars,' I bring a handful of crudely painted rolled-up cardboard things out from the boot. 'Capitalists need cigars.'

'Dagga!' shouts someone, grabbing one of them. There is a ripple of laughter. Dagga is the South African word for marijuana.

'It's not dagga, it's a capitalist cigar.'

'Capitalist dagga!' The cigars are in people's mouths in two seconds, and imaginary dagga smoke is being blown to the heavens. Within a minute, all the other props and banners are eagerly seized, so it looks like our day wasn't wasted.

Half an hour later, in the city centre, the march is about to begin. The Sowetans have arrived, joining people from other townships and the city itself. The prop-carrying crew are dancing around wildly in the middle of a square, and the place is a mass of

T-shirts; the red and yellow of the Sowetans, and others, worn by those who have turned up independently, with slogans like 'Corporate globalisation is global apartheid', 'Landlessness = racism', and – my personal favourite – a Nike swoosh, emblazoned with the words 'Just vom it'.

A few minutes after my arrival, a car pulls into the square with a pair of speakers attached to the roof. It's being driven by Trevor Ngwane, a man who is rapidly becoming a new South African folk hero ('Trevor is our Marcos' claims Patrick, enthusiastically). A former ANC councillor for Soweto, thrown out of the party for opposing privatisation plans for the city, Trevor is now a leading light in the Johannesburg Anti-Privatisation Forum, works for the AIDC, chairs the Soweto Electricity Crisis Committee and roams both South Africa and the world giving talks in his booming gravelly voice which rarely fail to grab the attention. This is a man who has given billionaire financier George Soros a tongue-lashing via video link at the World Economic Forum. This is a man who can unashamedly mount a stage in front of thousands of people in Washington DC and *toyi-toyi* while singing 'The World Bank – *haai!* – is the devil – *haai! haai!*'. The ANC must be rueing the day it drove him away.

Naturally, I have been wanting to talk to Trevor since I got to the country. When I get a chance to grab him I ask him what he thinks community groups like the ones he is involved in can actually achieve. What has the Anti-Privatisation Forum done, for instance?

'The APF tries to link unions with community organisations,' he explains. 'It is a coalition open to anyone who opposes privatisation and is willing to go public about it. But it also gives a new political dynamic and perspective.' The key issue at the moment, he says, is to break people out of their refusal to criticise the ANC.

'We need to get over that. Take myself: when you part with an organisation you've been building and working hard for over the years, you don't enjoy it!' He laughs – a deep, long, attractive sound. I ask him if the ANC is worried about what people like him are currently up to.

'Ooh yes!' he grins. 'There is *no* doubt in my mind. They are *definitely* worried about us. What I have noticed now is that they are no longer coming to the people as the ANC – but as "the state". They're the state now – they're no longer a social movement. That's how they relate to us. We are "counter-revolutionary", they say! But more and more people are no longer listening.'

The march is starting. Trevor jumps into his car and grabs the microphone, leading us slowly through the streets of the city, yelling slogans as he goes.

'Mbeki – away!'

'GEAR – away! Away!'

'WTO – away!'

'Capitalism – away! Away!'

'Viva South Africa! Viva!'

It doesn't take much to get a South African dancing, and as soon as the march moves off, everyone is at it; *toyi-toyi*ng through the streets. I bump into Virginia, who can't stop laughing at our apparent inability to meet without being surrounded by dancers. The crowd keeps moving, carrying giant puppets, shouting along with Trevor and waving at the police, who have gathered around us in those horrible, huge, square armoured cars that you used to see on TV in the 1980s hosing people down in the townships. Now, the drivers are black. There are maybe 300 people here, but they have enough energy, and make enough noise, for 3,000.

A few streets into the march, Patrick arrives, breathless. As usual, he is overworked. He's also depressed, though Patrick depressed is still a bundle of energy. He's just been at a meeting with some ANC policy-makers, where he and a colleague were trying to persuade them that their privatisation policies were damaging the very people they claimed to have been struggling to liberate. What did they say to that, I ask.

'Ha! They said we were counter-revolutionaries, of course. So we showed them a video – people in Soweto rising up against the cut-offs. They went very quiet after that. It was unanswerable. Then we pointed out that they promised free electricity at the '99 elections.'

'So are they going to do something about it?'

'No. They see their role now as selling privatisation to the poor. That's their version of liberation.' We turn a corner, still marching and shouting, followed by baton-swinging police. Patrick is introducing me to everyone he knows, which seems to be everyone.

'Paul, here's someone you should meet. Lucien, this is Paul. Lucien's one of our leading anarchists.'

'There's no such thing as a leading anarchist, Patrick,' says Lucien.

'Wolfram,' Patrick says to a frail old man with kind eyes walking three paces behind us, 'this is Paul. Paul's writing a book about the movement. Wolfram's one of our leading liberation theologists. You two should exchange numbers.'

In a couple of long strides, Patrick has latched on to someone else.

'Nhiania, this is Paul. Paul, Nhiania is a leading activist from Swaziland. You'll find this very interesting . . .' I wonder whether I should offer Patrick a commission.

'Privatisation – away! Away!' Trevor is bellowing, through his speakers.

'AMANDLA!' yells the crowd. *Amandla* is a word I have been hearing a lot since I got here. It is the Xhosa word for power. South Africa's people have been liberated from apartheid; real power, though, is proving much more elusive.

I have two days left in the country, and there is one thing left for me to do. I have to talk to someone from the party that is supposedly responsible for all this, and ask them what is going on; get their side of the story.

Thus it is that I find myself on the fifth floor of the ANC's imposing Johannesburg HQ, sitting in the office of Michael Sachs, the party's head of policy and research. Sachs is an influential figure in the party, and has promised to give me the government's side of the story. I sit down, say that, yes, I would love a cup of tea, thanks, switch on my tape recorder and ask him why so many people feel deceived by his government.

'Well,' he says, slowly, 'I think firstly one has to put it in the context that we have won an overwhelming majority in four elections now. Every month there are about ten by-elections in this country and the ANC continues to enjoy popular support in those elections. I'm not saying nobody feels deceived by the ANC, or there is no dissatisfaction in the country – clearly there is, but just put it in perspective.'

There's a lot of unhappiness, though, I say, with what you're up to. For example, it's difficult to find anyone with a good word to say about GEAR – even your partners in the Alliance seem to hate it.

'There is a lot of unhappiness,' says Sachs, frankly. 'Yes, there's a lot of criticism of GEAR. The economic policy we adopted in 1996 was conservative. It has many parallels with what one could call structural adjustment programmes. It's about fiscal discipline, it's about macro-economic stability, it's about overcoming debt. There has been the introduction of market mechanisms into what were previously wholly publicly owned and managed institutions. There's been a very lively and open debate about this.'

That debate seems to be loudest outside the ANC, I say. And the party's keenness on pleasing the markets at the expense of its own people is what is angering so many people. GEAR—

'Well, look, we're kind of post-GEAR now anyway,' he says, interrupting. 'There's been a relaxation of that tight fiscal discipline, but look, yes, there's a lot of . . .' He pauses, thinking, for a very long time. 'If you place what we are doing in the context of a national democratic revolution, which is what we see ourselves as being in government to deliver . . . it's a situation that is really very difficult – basically no other revolutionary movement has had to contend with a unipolar world. Certainly not since the creation of the Soviet Union has any revolutionary movement taken power in such unfavourable global conditions – such an unbridled victory for finance capitalism – finance capital being ascendant ideologically, and having a hegemony that is unparalleled in history.' He pauses, looking tired, then resumes his litany of downgraded expectations.

'We achieved democracy in 1994,' he goes on, 'and immediately had to confront the issue of globalisation. We embarked on a very steep learning curve. In that kind of context you have the adoption of conservative macro-economic policies. Maybe they could have been less conservative than they were. Maybe there could have been more social spending. But I have no doubt that if we had embarked on some kind of Keynesian socialist project in 1994, we would have been defeated by now, as the ANC. Macro-economic stability, in a globalised world, is the condition for us to continue our objectives, which are about provision of social services, which are about transforming this country from a racially skewed economy into one which is more egalitarian.'

But what, I say, if the pursuit of that stability compromises what you say are your goals? What if the pursuit of that stability becomes your goal? People have told me that their lives have got worse since the end of apartheid, and they blame you.

There is a long pause, again, while he chooses his words.

'Look,' he says, finally, 'you're operating in a world in which you're forced to make compromises . . . and I think that if you believe that the state is not attempting to discipline capital and ensure that social services are available to the people, then you would have a wrong impression. The standards of living of people in the urban areas may have declined since 1994. It's been a very austere macro-economic plan, but we're dealing with a crisis that was not of our own making. Given that our democracy came about in the year that the WTO was created – given those pressures, I think we should be given credit for what we are achieving. It's not as if we never make mistakes, or I'm trying to paint a picture that everything is rosy and there's no room for improvement.'

But you're not just reluctantly putting up with globalisation, are you, I say, you're pushing it on further and faster. This very minute, your trade minister is at the WTO pushing for a new trade round – the only African trade minister to do so. You've upset a lot of your close neighbours by doing it. You're removing your tariffs faster than you're required to by the WTO . . .

'Well, we don't oppose the WTO,' he says, deftly side-stepping the point. 'We'd never join a call to abolish it, or to abolish the World Bank or the IMF. We think you have to engage with these institutions. But – look . . . there's not a sell-out. I don't believe there's been a sell-out. Certainly there are elements within our own ranks that believe in capitalism. But that's always been the case in the ANC; we've never been a socialist party. The approach we take is saying, how do we engage with globalisation? And if we engage with it in a way which is unrealistic, that is dictated to by what are probably good principles, but which don't recognise the reality of a unipolar world with the strength of finance capital which exists out there . . . you've got to take these things into consideration, and say, how do you advocate the most productive agenda in that context?'

This is turning into one of the starkest admissions of governmental powerlessness in the face of globalisation that I've ever heard. I'm beginning to admire Sachs for his frankness.

'You know,' he says, gesturing at nothing in particular, 'you can't just go and redistribute things, in this era. Maybe if we had a Soviet Union to defend us we could do that but, frankly, you've got to play the game – you've got to ensure that you don't go on some adventure – you know, you *will* be defeated. They were defeated in Chile, they were defeated in Nicaragua . . . you can't do it now . . .'

In the meantime, he says, it's not true that services are getting worse everywhere.

'Services *are* improving,' he insists, his tone decisive. 'There's no doubt about that. In terms of rural development in this country, people are getting water, they are getting electricity. Maybe the cost of living's gone up, and for the urban working classes, things haven't been easy in the last five years. Globalisation blows horrible, stinging winds across your economy. But there's still no doubt that the state is popular and democratic, and there's no doubt that it is extending services to the poor. There is popular discontent, there is no doubt about that, but I don't think people are about to abandon the ANC.' South Africa's NGOs, he says, do not have a mass base anything like the size of the ANC's. And as for the 'anti-globalisation' movement that they are hooking up with – it 'has a problem'.

'I mean, it's not like communism or socialism, which, for all their faults, at least had a vision of what they wanted to replace international capitalism with. This movement does not have this, yet. You can go round to the mayor's house and cut off his electricity, but what do you propose that the state, or whatever, puts in place of the system which causes these problems? I don't think this is necessarily inherent in this movement, I think it's probably just a stage in its development, that it has not yet got to the point where it can say, "This is what we would like to see." I mean, people like me – I'm against capitalism, we're all against capitalism, we all think that exploitation of men by men is wrong, but that's not enough. In the South African context, what is the political alternative to the ANC? Should we adopt, say, similar policies to Castro, who is one of the ANC's closest friends? Should we be out there condemning imperialism? If you do those things, how long will you last? There is no organisational alternative, and no real policy alternative to what we're doing.'

He sits back in his chair, and exhales. My tape recorder continues to whirr. The sound of typing comes through the wall. South Africa's ANC government must be one of the most admired on the international stage. It had a vast network of hopes resting on it. It already seems to have abandoned most of them; including its own. Globalisation has pulled the rug out from under the feet of the Rainbow Nation's liberators more effectively than apartheid ever did. To Michael Sachs' credit, at least he's honest about it.

'It's tough,' he says. 'I'm not going to pretend that there isn't dissent within our own ranks about all this. I'm not saying we're doing everything right – but we're trying, you know?'

On my last day back in Durban, Ashwin and Heinrich had given me a lift to the airport, and we were all hanging around waiting for my plane back to Johannesburg. We were sitting in a typically soulless airport café, drinking coffee to the sound of tinned muzak, and discussing everything and nothing, when Ashwin said something very interesting. He was talking about the South African struggle, and what, according to him, was at the heart of it.

'What was the whole struggle about, from the beginning?' he demanded, rhetorically. 'It was about saying, we won't work in your mines – we want our land, we want control. We don't want the fucking vote – the vote is *meaningless* unless we can run our own economy. That's what we want. People assume our struggle ended when Mandela gave us the vote – that that was what it was all about. It wasn't – it was about economic rights as much as political ones. We have a right to control our own economy, to use our own resources, to buy and sell our own things. And it's a *gripping* question for people, you know – how come we have all this land, all this gold, and yet the IMF and the World Bank and the stock markets tell us what to do? How come we have the vote and yet we are not free? And people are starting to see this now. Our struggle is not over. The struggle of the twenty-first century is the struggle for the right to run our own economy.'

What Ashwin had hit on was precisely what Michael Sachs, in a more roundabout way, was nudging at in his office that day. Something which reflected, independently, similar words I had heard in Genoa, in Chiapas and in Cochabamba, and which I would hear elsewhere, as I spoke to activists in very different countries, in very different circumstances. It was a simple idea, but one which runs like a seam through the global movement: political freedom without economic freedom is meaningless.

South Africa provided me with only the starkest example of this fact, but it can be seen all over the world. The activities of governments are severely constrained by the free flow of capital and investment which characterise the process of globalisation. Put crudely, but accurately, if any government tries anything radical and dangerous, like land reform, nationalising industries, reining in corporations, redistributing wealth – anything, in other words, which threatens that country's status as a safe place to make profits – business, and investment, will up sticks and move elsewhere.

American journalist Thomas Friedman, one of globalisation's loudest and most ferocious defenders, has famously called this the 'golden straitjacket'. He speaks in glowing terms of the process that has been one of the movement's biggest complaints: 'As your country puts on the Golden Straitjacket,' he explains, 'two things tend to happen: your economy grows and your politics shrinks . . . [The] Golden Straitjacket narrows the political and economic policy choices of those in power to relatively tight parameters. That is why it is increasingly difficult these days to find any real differences between ruling and opposition parties in those countries that have put on the Golden Straitjacket. Once your country puts on the Golden Straitjacket, its political choices get reduced to Pepsi or Coke – to slight nuances of taste, slight nuances of policy . . .'[13] This, Friedman thinks, is a good thing. Good or bad, it makes a mockery of the often-heard claim that free markets and free societies go hand-in-hand. The reality, as South Africa shows so well, is that globalisation eats democracy for breakfast.

South Africa has strapped itself firmly into the golden straitjacket and the result has been a timid government, restrained by the dead hand of global capital from even attempting to achieve its more radical ambitions. The result, seen starkly, is a revolution betrayed. The ANC government has made its decision: to surrender to the power of the global market, and hand their people what crumbs they can gather from its table. Maybe this is understandable. Maybe it is cowardly. Whatever it is, they are not alone.

But their people are not alone either. Not alone in their outrage or their resistance. Not alone in the growing realisation that economic, not just political, independence is something to be fought for. That fight has begun, and it doesn't look like stopping any time soon. South Africa's long walk to freedom is not over yet.

4 **the church of stop shopping**

'All of us in the Coca-Cola family wake up each morning knowing that every single one of the world's 5.6 billion people will get thirsty that day . . . If we make it impossible for these 5.6 billion people to escape Coca-Cola . . . then we assure our future success for many years to come. Doing anything else is not an option.'

COCA-COLA ANNUAL REPORT, 1993

'I asked the president, "What can we do to show support for America?" He said, "Mom, if you really want to help, buy, buy, buy."'

BARBARA BUSH, MOTHER OF GEORGE W. BUSH, 2001

It's the hair that does it. The hair is visible three blocks away, a vast golden skyscraper of a bouffant glinting in Manhattan's winter sunshine. The hair and the teeth. The teeth are like sarsen stones, and the grin which they collectively form is wide, friendly, deeply cheesy and pointing in my direction. This could be no one else. He rides a bicycle, its chain lock slung around his neck.

'Paul?' says the Reverend Billy, grasping my hand very firmly indeed. 'Bill. So sorry I'm late.' He looks down at the paper cup in my hand, in the bottom of which are the cold dregs of a Starbucks latte.

'Now, you didn't pay for that, did you?' he says.

The Reverend is displeased, and decides that what we both need is some 'real coffee'. I dispose of my paper cup and we make our way across Astor Place, away from the biggest Starbucks in Manhattan and towards a battered green coffee truck, owned by a friend of Billy's, which is blasting out jazz from a couple of rickety speakers and serving what is, indeed, much better coffee than Starbucks have ever dreamed of.

'My man,' says the coffee truck owner to Billy, 'how goes it?'

'Well,' says Billy, 'very well. One of your finest cappuccinos, I think. No, wait – make that two.'

The Reverend Billy is the founder and spiritual leader of the Church of Stop Shopping, and he is on a mission from God. His mission is to save New York, to save America, to save the world from the scourge of consumerism. A scourge visited upon the unbelievers like the plagues of Egypt; sent down from on high to homogenise their neighbourhoods, destroy their small shops and cafés, substitute independence for dependence and hand control of their streets to a buccaneering gang of multinational corporations who will decide what they buy and take their money for doing so. The Reverend Billy has come to save them – to save us – from all this, and I have come, today, to Astor Place, to have my sins absolved (specifically, the purchase of that latte) and to listen to the Reverend explain to me how he intends to do it.

We wander a few blocks downtown, the Reverend pushing his bicycle and pointing out, every few yards, this or that local landmark which stood proudly independent for years and which is now a McDonald's, a Disney Store, a Borders, another Starbucks. We seek refuge in one of the few places in midtown Manhattan that is not yet owned by a multinational chain – Jones Diner, a sixty-year-old American classic, all chrome, steel, neon, plastic, hamburgers and grits (whatever they are). It exudes James Dean, Humphrey Bogart, Steve McQueen. I've seen this kind of thing in films, so I know.

'This is one of the last human-scale places in the neighbourhood,' says Billy. 'They want to knock it down. They want to build an "executive development".'

'Hey, you!' says the diner's owner, popping up from behind the stainless steel counter. He wears a striped apron and a little white hat. He is pure diner, pure New York, pure America. This is my first time in this country, and everything already looks terribly familiar.

'Hey you!' repeats the owner, waving at Billy. 'We don't like your sort in here. You look like trouble.' Both of them are grinning. This is obviously a well practised ritual.

'Fine,' says Billy. 'We'll go and eat in Starbucks instead. They have little shrink-wrapped biscuits. We don't need character in our neighbourhood anyway, we'd rather have corporate cool.'

'Turkey's the special,' says the diner man.

'Then bring us turkey, please, my good friend,' says the Reverend. The diner man disappears into the kitchen, and Billy turns back to me, teeth flashing like homing beacons.

'Let's talk,' he says.

Since he first took his vows, the Reverend Billy has been waging a one-man crusade against consumerism, in a style that is all his own. Others who object to the rash of Starbucks, and other such corporate chains, from bookshops to burger bars, spreading across their town, destroying local competition and bleaching the character out of their neighbourhoods, might perhaps choose to boycott the chains. Might write a letter to someone, may even go so far as to stand outside the store holding placards and shouting 'no more Starbucks', or something similar. Billy doesn't think any of this works, and he's probably right. Billy thinks that in a new world – a world of wall-to-wall consumerism, mass advertising, information overload – in a world like this, protest must be as new, as shiny, as reinvented, as the economy itself.

Billy wants people to understand that when they buy a Starbucks coffee they are buying a lot more than a drink, and he wants to get the message across in a way that people cannot possibly ignore; in a way, indeed, that they might even find amusing. And so, on a chosen day, at a chosen time, Billy will enter Starbucks, his hair towering and magnificent, his teeth gleaming, his body encased in a dog collar and white tuxedo, and he will begin to preach.

In his stentorian wail, his well-enunciated words, his talent for self-publicity, he will treat the assembled customers to a sermon on the evils of 'Frankenbucks'. He will tell them about the genetically modified, Monsanto-brand bovine growth hormones in Starbucks' milk. He will tell them about the battles the company has engaged in to prevent its workers joining trades unions. He will tell them about Starbucks' corporate policy of 'clustering' many outlets at once in parts of town where there are local cafés, and expanding the clusters until only Starbucks is left. He will tell them about the company's use of prison labour to package its products.

Most of all, he will preach the gospel of anti-consumerism; will tell tales of devastated neighbourhoods, cannibalised by chain-stores and left out in the sun to die. He will amuse and infuriate, the Starbucks employees will shuffle their feet, the branch will begin to empty and, if he's lucky, Billy will be thrown out, still preaching. He loves being thrown out.

This is just one – the most basic – of the tools in the Reverend's armoury. He will also, on occasion, initiate 'cellphone operas', in which members of his congregation will wander the store shouting loudly into cellphones about anything from slave labour on coffee plantations to low-paid employees, their conversations rising to a co-ordinated crescendo. Billy has also written a number of scripts for suggested 'spat theatre', which anyone, anywhere, can perform – loudly, of course – in their local Starbucks with a friend. One features a couple loudly discussing their imminent sex in the Starbucks toilet. In another, an ex-prisoner pops in for a coffee and discovers that the packaging he's just bought was glued by him while he was inside. Another, entitled 'Where My Latte Gets Its Bovine Growth Hormones', features two lovers whose relationship has been sponsored by Monsanto.

All this explains quite adequately why Starbucks hates and fears the Reverend – so much so that they distributed a memo to all their New York employees entitled 'What should I do if Reverend Billy is in my store?' Hide, perhaps.

The Reverend Billy, in his more sober moments, is plain old Bill Talen, an actor and writer who, after many years treading the boards, decided that he needed a new direction. Bill had always wanted his art to change the society it reflected, but it took the birth of the Reverend to really begin to have the effect he wanted. His alter ego was inspired by a number of factors – an old friend who was himself a priest, his own Calvinist childhood, America's television-evangelist tradition, and what was happening to New York's Times Square.

This was in the mid-1990s, when mayor Rudolph Giuliani was at the height of his campaign to clean up New York – part of which involved a scheme to transform Times Square from a haunt of 'low lifes' to a playground for tourists and consumers.

'Anyone who looked like they had character was out,' says Bill, plunging into his freshly delivered plate of turkey, 'because they were creating a mall in Times Square. It had been full of preachers, ranters – a place where all sorts of people would come and shout at each other about their beliefs, and nobody asked why. The end of that was the start of a very deliberate process, and we see the results today. Places like Times Square and SoHo are now very commodified, and the streets are not really public spaces any more.'

Bill believed that the community, and the city, he valued was being sold – sold to some of the biggest retail corporations on the planet. From this belief, the Reverend was conceived; and at the Disney Store in Times Square, he was born.

'I decided to don my uniform,' he says. 'Dinner jacket like a tel-evangelist, and the collar. I created a theology based on standing up outside the Disney Store.' He morphs into the Reverend mid-sermon: 'MICKEY MOUSE IS THE *ANTI*-CHRIST, CHILD! DON'T *GO* INTO THAT STORE! DON'T GIVE YOUR MONEY TO THE PEOPLE WHO PAY THEIR SWEATSHOP WORKERS A DOLLAR FOR AN EIGHTEEN-HOUR DAY! SAVE YOUR SOUL!' A middle-aged man eating his lunch quietly in the stall behind us looks round to check he's not in any danger from this shouting lunatic.

Before long, the Reverend was inside the store, co-ordinating cellphone operas about anorexia and Barbie dolls and being regu-larly evicted by large, unamused security guards. He press-released all the theatre critics in New York – 'A new play is opening at the Church of Stop Shopping, starring the Reverend Billy and friends, opening in the Disney Store, Times Square.' Hundreds of people came to watch. It was part of the play that Billy and friends would jump up on to the counter and stop the cash registers; bodyguards shouting at him from both sides – 'they were my proscenium arch' – would be incorporated into the performance.

Bill, it is clear, loves every minute of this. He is loving just telling me about it. But it should go without saying that this is not mere entertainment. This is politics.

'The corporations are pushing into public space so thoroughly that it's not public space any more,' he repeats. 'It's an amazing pri-vatisation process going on in New York at the moment – the streets, the very fundamental of public space, are no longer ours. I moved from the Disney Store to Starbucks for a reason. Starbucks believe they're selling a lifestyle, they're selling meaning, they're selling community, they're involving us in a consensus about what it means to be a neighbourhood – it's completely delusional. The opposite is happening; we have fluorescent, hushed, centrally planned chainstores all over New York now, and gradually, the sassy verbosity that you love about this place, the ability of regular people to tell amazing stories – all that is considered a market, and that "market" is having so many brands pushed on to it that it is being murdered.'

In the wrath of the Reverend Billy, global interests are assailed by a very local sensibility. It is, says Bill, the neighbourhood striking back.

'I take my cue from what is happening in my neighbourhood,' he says. 'Is it a healthy neighbourhood? Are people looking each other in the eye, telling stories, circling each other with playful insults? Do they feel they belong there, will they rise up and defend each other? That's a healthy neighbourhood. The transnationals *need* us not to have neighbourhoods. They want to mall-ise us. They want our relationship with each other to basically happen through a credit card. The transnationals are a totalising presence – their major market is to persuade the individual that they will not enjoy direct access to their own lives – their dreams, their desires, will be mediated through their presence, their image, through what they sell.' He soaks up the last of his gravy with a slice of flimsy white bread.

'That's where I get my politics,' he says. 'I am defending my neighbourhood's right to not be mediated.'

If consumerism really does mediate our desires, then the USA, the original consumer society, must be the most mediated place on Earth. Consumerism – every man and woman's right to be able to buy anything they want, and now – has been a driving force behind the American Dream for decades. The United States, of course, is by no means the only country whose national purpose has become entwined with rampant material consumption: every country in the 'developed' world, to different degrees, is engaged in the same consumer crusade. Poorer nations, sheepishly following the Western development model, are beginning to catch up – their new, and usually tiny, middle classes proudly sinking their teeth into KFC bargain buckets while most of their population have to walk miles to find water. But the USA, as ever, is the nation which does it biggest and best.

The United States of America, with just 5 per cent of the world's population, consumes 30 per cent of the world's resources, including 25 per cent of the world's fossil fuels – the cause of global climate change. By the time a baby born in the US in the 1990s reaches the age of seventy-five, he or she will have produced 52 tons of rubbish, consumed 43 million gallons of water and used 3,375 barrels of oil. The waste generated each year in the US would fill a convoy of ten-ton rubbish trucks, which would stretch over halfway to the moon. The amount of energy used by 1 American is equivalent to that used by 6 Mexicans, 38 Indians or 531 Ethiopians. Almost 60 million adult Americans – over a third of the population – are overweight, and there has been a 42 per cent increase in childhood obesity in just twenty years – a pandemic which has been blamed on overconsumption of both fast food and television.[1]

To ensure that this profitable spiral continues, corporations shovel an estimated 12 billion display adverts, 3 million radio commercials and over 200,000 TV commercials into the American consciousness every single day.[2] American teenagers are typically exposed to 360,000 adverts by the time they graduate from high school, which seems to have the desired effect: 93 per cent of American teenage girls say that their favourite hobby is shopping.[3]

Few aspects of life in the Land of the Free (Market) are exempt from this assault on the mind. Children, for example – a growth market – are ruthlessly targeted. Coca-Cola and Pepsi have branded entire schools, paying them up to $20 per pupil in exchange for selling a set number of drinks on campus, and banning the products of their competitors. Channel One, a commercial TV company, beams daily 'educational' programmes into 12,000 American schools on free, donated equipment – on condition that the pupils watch adverts aimed at their target demographic. Procter & Gamble sponsors school lessons on oral hygiene. Campbell's Soup created a science 'lesson' where pupils compared the viscosity of one of their sauces to that of a rival. Kellogg's created an art project where sculptures were made out of Rice Krispies.[4]

None of this is particularly exceptional, and all of it makes good business sense. Children in the US directly spend $24.4 billion a year, and adults spend a further $300 billion a year on their behalf.[5] 'If you own this child at an early age,' said the former president of the clothing chain Kids R Us, apparently with no sense of rising horror, 'you can own this child for years to come. Companies are saying, "Hey, I want to own the kid younger and younger."' The head of the Prism Communications company said much the same: 'They aren't children so much as what I like to call "evolving consumers",' he explained delicately.[6]

Adults, meanwhile, have their own challenges. There is barely a foot of space in the USA that has not been bought up by corporations trying to flog their goods to the increasingly overspent American. Toilet walls, petrol pump nozzles, cash machines, mobile phone messages, spam e-mails, stickers on oranges, the backs of bus tickets, not to mention millions of billboards, newspaper, magazine and TV ads – few places are exempt from corporate attempts to create new needs to be met. And with straight adverts increasingly old-fashioned, twenty-first-century corporations have turned their attention to buying up public space, in what one critic has called an 'enclosure of the cultural commons'.[7] Go to see a sports event, in a land obsessed by baseball, basketball and American football, and you may find yourself in the Continental Airlines Arena (formerly Meadowlands), the FedEx Field (Washington), the Staples Center (Los Angeles), or the presumably soon-to-be-swiftly-renamed Enron Field (Houston). You may find yourself staring up at a historic public landmark which has been given a corporate facelift – the Empire State Building, for example, lit up, as it was in August 2002, in 'Snapple Yellow' to celebrate the drinks company's thirtieth anniversary. You may find yourself at a branded festival, in a logo-swathed public park or on the campus of a sponsored university.

If this is too down-to-earth for you, there may soon be more celestial opportunities to extend your consumer choice. Pizza Hut recently succeeded in getting its logo pasted on to the side of a Russian space rocket, and then topped even this achievement by delivering 'the world's first space-consumable pizza' to cosmonauts on the International Space Station. 'Wherever there is life, there will be Pizza Hut pizza!' declared the company's chief marketing officer, who had perhaps been watching a little too much *Star Trek*. Pizza Hut is not alone; Radio Shack, Lego and Popular Mechanics all paid to have astronauts promote their products on the space station.[8] If this all sounds amusing but harmless, it may be only the first step in the commercialisation of space; for years, corporations have been exploring the feasibility of putting giant billboards in orbit, which would promote their products in the night sky from the Caspian to the Kalahari.

With such a bombardment of exhortations to spend, it is not surprising that the American people have been obeying. Per capita consumption in the USA increased by 45 per cent between the 1970s and the 1990s.[9] Unfortunately, and perhaps not coincidentally, so did rates of obesity, depression, eating disorders, family breakdown, crime and income inequality. The proportion of the population describing themselves as 'very happy', meanwhile, failed to increase at all – in fact, it fell by 4 per cent.[10]

So whatever happened to the American dream?

The Reverend Billy thinks he knows: he says that consumerism killed it. This is not exactly a new message, of course. But Billy is not alone in believing that if it is to be implanted in the minds of his fellow Americans as firmly as exhortations to Just Do It, Think Different and Come to Marlboro Country, the medium of communication will need to be as sophisticated, arresting and unexpected as the most successful advertising campaigns. There is a term for this: it's called culture jamming, and, like consumerism itself, it is spreading like a rash from the shores of America to the wider world.

Kalle Lasn is a man who enjoys explaining it. Lasn, a determined, middle-aged troublemaker, is the founder of *Adbusters* magazine, a Canadian vehicle for challenging the consumer culture. Set up by a group of ex-advertising executives, *Adbusters*, which calls itself a 'journal of the mental environment', has a language, and an approach, all of its own. It popularised the concept of the 'subvert' – producing spoof ads which so closely mirror the original that the subversive message they contain drops into your subconscious just as easily. It talks of 'meme warfare' (the battle for control of the mind), 'Manchurian consumers' and 'uncommercials'. Like the advertising industry it sets out to undermine, *Adbusters* can get a little, well, pretentious, but Lasn is an expert at finding the words to explain what culture jamming is, and why America needs it.

He explains it best in his book, *Culture Jam.*[11] 'America,' he writes, 'is no longer a country. It's a multi-trillion-dollar brand . . . American culture is no longer created by the people . . . we ourselves have been branded . . . American cool is a global pandemic.' Lasn says that the point and purpose of culture jamming is to 'strike by smashing the post-modern hall of mirrors and redefining what it means to be alive'. Like the Reverend Billy, Kalle Lasn and his crew at *Adbusters* are waging war for the right to live their lives unmediated by what global corporations say is vital, necessary, entertaining. Substance, say the culture jammers, not style. Reality, not image. Self-definition, not brand recognition. 'The only battle still worth fighting and winning,' says Lasn, 'the only one that can set us free, is The People versus the Corporate Cool Machine.'

'Consumerism' might seem a nebulous target for political resistance: the sort of thing you can only complain about when you live in a country rich enough to afford it. But people like Kalle Lasn and the Reverend Billy are concerned that consumerism has attained what the Italian revolutionary Antonio Gramsci called 'cultural hegemony' – it is such a dominant and ingrained value within our culture that it goes virtually unquestioned. If this is true, and if the result is that manufactured culture is replacing real culture, then the means of questioning those values, say the culture jammers, need to be clear, clever and subtle. They need to be able to get under the skin of a population so used to being bombarded with messages plugging consumer materialism that having a Nike swoosh shaved into the back of your head can win you plaudits in the playground. This, say the jammers, is nothing short of cultural warfare – warfare in which culture is both something to be defended, to be re-created – and to be used as a weapon.

What really gets activists exercised is the extension of American consumption patterns – and all the values and the assumptions they are based on – to the rest of the world. Nobody can have failed to notice this happening, apparently inexorably, over the past few decades, as markets expand, borders are opened and barriers to trade removed. Western consumerism has broken through its geographical boundaries and is spreading itself all over the map.

The result of this, say critics, is the homogenising of cultures. A global market requires global tastes, and global tastes require global values. If, for example, as they have made clear many times, the corporate mission of both Coca-Cola and Pepsi is to have everyone on Earth drinking something made by them every day, then everyone on Earth must want to drink carbonated, sweetened, canned drinks. To want to drink them every day, they must first have offloaded the drinks of their own culture, and with them the myriad strands of tradition and history that make their culture different from the one which created Pepsi and Coca-Cola.

More even than that, though, they must have adjusted to the kind of environment in which refrigerated carbonated sugary drinks are on sale from vending machines in every town, in which drinks are bought not made, in which global corporations out-compete local producers and in which a fast-paced, urban consumer lifestyle necessitates regular 'refreshment'. The same goes for hamburgers, jeans, jeeps, trainers, hair gel and shoulder bags. This is not, in other words, about fizzy drinks at all: it is about culture. All over the world, the extension of the consumer machine that the culture jammers say is eating America is steamrollering the world's many cultures, leaving a rootless, cosmopolitan global mono-culture in their place.

The result is the bleaching of the human rainbow. It is the same massive cultural airstrike that leads to women buying acidic skin-lightening cream in India and Africa, to look more like the cool white people on satellite TV, and Chinese children under-going tongue operations to make their English more acceptable to the ears of their global masters. It is the polar opposite of that 'world made of many worlds': it is a global mall, in which corporations expand by eating up the small, the local, the unique and the different – colonising and commodifying everything we could ever need, and then selling it back to us.

There is, as any economist will tell you, a sound economic reason for this. Capitalism has long been subject to what has been called a 'crisis of overproduction'. An increase in the availability of resources and the efficiency of the technologies needed to trans-form them into goods has, for over a century, been accompanied by fairly static demand for those goods in the West. It was to increase demand for consumer goods, to create new needs and to transform luxuries into necessities, that everything from the adver-tising industry to the fashion industry came into being. But markets can only expand so much within any population; to give yourself a serious chance of offloading that surplus production, increasing your profits and market share and outbidding your rivals, you need to expand your markets elsewhere.

In the late nineteenth century, when Western market expansion was tied up with imperial dominance, arch-Empire builder Cecil

Rhodes was at least able to be frank about this process. 'We must find new lands,' he said, 'from which we can easily obtain raw materials and at the same time exploit the cheap slave labour that is available from the natives of the colonies. The colonies would also provide a dumping ground for the surplus goods produced in our factories.'[12] Today, say activists, the words are couched but the motivation is the same: new markets for Western goods, and hang the consequences.

All this, say supporters of globalisation, is apocalyptic nonsense. Yes, markets expand; yes, corporations have increasing access to many countries they wouldn't have done before. Yes, McDonald's, Coca-Cola, Levi's, Starbucks, Disney and all the rest are springing up in remote corners of every country. Yes, the world is homogenising, but that's because people want it that way. 'McDonald's does not march people into its outlets at the point of a gun,' protests *The Economist*. 'Nike does not require people to wear its trainers on pain of imprisonment. If people buy those things, it is because they choose to, not because globalisation is forcing them to.'[13]

There are many answers to this. Answers that point out the stranglehold that Western multinationals have on the global economy. Answers that explain how international trade rules prevent countries from building up and supporting their own cultural industries against those from outside. Answers that point to the virtually unchallengeable dominance of Hollywood (which makes 85 per cent of the films watched in the world),[14] MTV and all the rest over the world's cultural landscape. Answers that question just how 'free' a choice is when it is made on the back of a multi-million-dollar advertising onslaught in countries where people are barely educated enough to read.

This battle will go on, because the global movement has its own answers; answers that come not just from America, the belly of the consumer beast, but increasingly from people elsewhere, who resent the dominance of Western culture and the dissolving of their own. Against the endgame of a bleached, smoothed-out, branded planet, the same in essence from Brisbane to Bombay, the movement offers up an alternative of diversity. Only real people, in real places, say activists, can create real culture. It doesn't come from branding consultants huddled in halogen-lit dens halfway up office blocks that look the same from Singapore to Cincinnati. It comes from the ground up, not the top down, and however hard the corporations try, it can't be bought.

What Kalle Lasn calls 'the second American revolution' – a struggle to decommodify The People – appears to have begun.

If you conduct a search on the Internet for the California Department of Corrections, you will come across two websites. The first, an official site of the state government, will tell you everything you could want to know about the state's 'correctional facilities', list the ten most wanted escaped fugitives and show you some charming photos from Death Row. If this is the sort of thing that cranks your chain, you can even apply for a job with them online.

If it isn't, the other site might interest you more. The other California Department of Corrections is an underground coalition of culture jammers dedicated to 'correcting' advertising billboards. This they do with spraycans, paper, Letraset, creativity and the cover of the night. Like the almost venerable Billboard Liberation Front (which recently celebrated its twenty-fifth anniversary), also based in San Francisco, they are engaged in what is probably the longest-running form of culture jamming there is.

'Reworking' billboards so that their message is 'subvertised' is becoming common in the cities of the West. The Billboard Liberation Front, who, like the California Department of Corrections, stubbornly refuse to reveal themselves to the outside world, say they do what they do because 'old-fashioned notions about art, science and spirituality being the peak achievements and the noblest goals of the spirit of man have been dashed on the crystalline shores of acquisition'.[15] They, too, say they are engaged in 'cultural warfare'. They, too, are not alone.

Residents from San Francisco to New York to Bristol to Toronto to Cape Town to Bangkok to my home town of Oxford regularly wake up of a morning to discover that what was a billboard ad for Marlboro is now a plug for Marlbore, that Gap Athletic has become ap Ath etic, that Charles Manson is the new face of Levi's, that L'Oréal is now essential not 'because you're worth it', but 'because you're stupid'. Such 'fauxvertising' can range from the strikingly funny to the embarrassingly humourless, but it always works best when it is so professionally done that the result is indistinguishable in style and execution from the original. British versions of the BLF and the CDC include the Bristol-based ABBA (Anti-Billboard Brainwashing Action) and the Londoners NASA (New Advertising Standards Authority), but much billboard liberation is done by small groups of cultural guerrillas with no names or pack drill, just a spontaneous desire to make mischief and reclaim public space.[16]

While billboard liberation spreads with consumerism itself, the cultural guerrillas of the global movement are adopting more and varied ways of jamming the medium to insert their own message. *Adbusters*, as well as producing its own 'subverts' and TV spots, which corporate-owned US TV channels regularly refuse to air, has instituted an annual celebration of anti-consumerism, 'Buy Nothing Day', which is celebrated in over thirty countries every November. In Sweden, anti-consumerist Santa Clauses visit shopping malls and shout about the joys of not shopping. In Ireland, a 'conga against capitalism' occupies a Dublin shopping centre. Sheep take to the streets of San Francisco, bleating 'buy mooooooore stuff', and 'sweeeeeaaaatshops'. Zombies shuffle through Cairns, Australia, with barcodes on their torsos, wielding shopping bags. Culture jammers outside a mall in Seattle offer shoppers a 'credit card cut-up service'.[17]

Meanwhile, a global network calling itself the Fanclubbers is doing its best to annoy the chainstore retailers of the world. Their favourite tactic is buying something – often, if there are enough people involved, buying a lot of things – and then immediately returning them, with a message attached. In London, a group of Fanclubbers went *en masse* to NikeTown, bought a batch of sweat-shirts, and then immediately returned them on the grounds that they all had 'dirty marks' on them – the marks being the Nike logo.[18]

Elsewhere, 'Whirl-Mart' are wandering into Wal-Mart stores wearing white jump-suits, and processing up and down the aisles for an hour pushing empty trolleys and informing curious cus-tomers and riled staff that they are participating in a 'consumption awareness ritual'. In New York, the Surveillance Camera Players are performing pointed, silent street theatre into some of the 3,000 CCTV cameras that dot Manhattan, in a show of protest against the watched society and the enclosure of public space. SCP branches from Sweden to Lithuania do the same. In London, activists hand out spoof newspapers – the *Evading Standards*, the *Hate Mail*, the *Financial Crimes* – to commuters. American activists did the same during the IMF/World Bank meetings in Washington in 2000, with the *Washington Lost*, which contains such headlines as 'In Moving Ceremony, New US Consumers Are Sworn In', and 'Fat America Starves Africa to Keep Humanity's Total Body Weight Unchanged'.[19] In Thailand, photo-activists re-stage Vietnam war photos in shopping centres to make a piquant point about a new American invasion – commercial this time, not military.

Then there is RTMark, a kind of web-based clearing centre for subversive ideas. RTMark, which has set itself up as a limited lia-bility corporation, is a centre for people to come together on projects designed to upset the corporate and political world. People post ideas on their website for culture-jamming projects they want to carry out, and list how much, if any, money they need to do it. Others can then join in or fund them, anonymously if necessary.

Their first success came in 1993, when a military veterans' organisation donated $8,000, via RTMark, to the 'Barbie Libera-tion Front', who used the money to switch the voice boxes of 300 Barbie dolls with 300 GI Joe dolls in the shops. Another corker came during the 2000 presidential elections, when RTMark set up a fake George Bush supporters' website which the president's men scrambled to close down. The battle became a major news story in the US, especially when Bush, asked what he thought about the fake site, opined that 'there ought to be limits to freedom' – a quote he has yet to live down.

At the time of writing, ideas looking for support and/or funding on RTMark's site include a project to 'build or use an existing pirate radio transmitter and use it to broadcast home-made and seemingly sincere advertisements for the major corporation of your choice on to existing radio signals'. Another, noting that Wal-Mart had started allowing people with motor homes to camp in its car parks overnight, seeks to 'recruit thousands of hippies and homeless to camp in Wal-Mart parking lots nationwide on the same night . . . Design special cardboard boxes to sleep in highlighting the destruction corporations are doing to our communities. Get nationwide media coverage.' There are plenty more ideas.[20]

The corporate response to the growth of such activities has been, in many cases, to try to grab them for themselves. In recent years, a number of examples of the consumer culture trying to co-opt the very act of dissent against it have appeared. Thus we have seen the Gap, a favourite target of activists for its use of sweatshops, running a window display which includes red banners and fake graffiti sprayed across the outside of its windows. Nike has spoofed anti-sweatshop protesters in its own adverts for football boots ('The most offensive boots we've ever made') and set up a fake grass-roots protest group, supposedly to complain that their boots were so well made that they put non-wearers at a disadvantage (hold your sides in!). Diesel has used staged protest photos to sell jeans. Black Bloc-inspired catwalk costumes, complete with ski masks, have appeared in the Sunday supplements. What all of this tells us is that in a consumer society, everything is for sale: even resistance to consumer society. It can play havoc with your head. Is even culture jamming being jammed?

Sometimes, it seems. But the point about culture jamming is that however hard the corporations try, it keeps coming back, evolving, being reborn in ways which no one expected. It keeps competing for that cultural hegemony.

The hard question is how effective any of it is. Culture jamming is certainly fun, but can it really succeed in doing more than pricking the skin of an increasingly global consumer culture? Is it not, on occasion, a bit, well, sanctimonious? And is playing what are, at root, basically old-fashioned pranks really the best way to challenge the hegemony of consumer capitalism?

I am sitting in a hot spring somewhere in the Arizona desert. The February sun is high and determined, the smell of sulphur is in the air and the bare trees are stark against the thin blue sky. On the horizon, across brown miles of scrub and dust, are snow-capped mountains. This natural spring is one of a complex in a remote and dilapidated ranch that used to be owned by the Rolling Stones. It sits in the centre of Apache territory, where one of the world's most effective guerrilla wars was fought by one of the last free tribes of North America against the European invaders. Anyone from Geronimo to Mick Jagger could have been in this pool before. Right now, though, there is just me and, six feet away, buck naked, with only a green rubber ring to cover his modesty, Special Agent Apple of the Biotic Baking Brigade. He is lying on his back and smiling vaguely into the sky.

'Isn't this great?' he says.

I have to agree. It is great. I've been here two days, sleeping in the back of a car I hired and stupidly drove all the way from San Francisco to get here. This is the annual gathering of the radical American environmental group Earth First!, which turns out, upon closer inspection, not to be a million miles away from the British version – a lot of workshops, dreadlocks, wind chimes, skunk and the exchanging of tips on the best ways to disable road-building machinery and chain yourself to digger axles. Earth First! (the exclamation mark is obligatory), almost two decades ago now, provided today's movement with one of its prototypes for unyielding radicalism and determined direct action. Since then it has lost some of its own momentum, but it still seems to be good at holding get-togethers in wild and beautiful places. Agent Apple is someone in both Earth First! and the Biotic Baking Brigade. He is a culture jammer *par excellence*, and before he gets out of the pool, I'm hoping he's going to tell me more about it.

The Biotic Baking Brigade has become a legend in its own lunchtime. Its pioneering combination of slapstick, politics, wordplay and gastronomy has inspired imitators around the world, and a veritable mass of cells across the US. The BBB began life in California, where Apple then lived, in 1998. Inspired by the visit of Milton Friedman, the godfather of neoliberal economics, to a conference in San Francisco, Apple and a few friends baked an organic coconut cream pie in celebration. Apple then put on a suit, slid the pie into a briefcase, wangled his way into the conference and gently pressed the pie into Friedman's face. 'These neoliberal economists offer us pie in the sky,' he told the press afterwards. 'I brought that pie and gave it back to him.'

Thus was the BBB born, its avowed purpose: 'Speaking pie to power.' In the months and years to come, the original California cell perfected its tactics: locally made pies, organic if possible, to be thrown full in the face of the intended victim, the pieing to be followed by a press release stating, in the unique language of the BBB, a combination of politics and brilliantly awful pastry-based puns, the reason for the attack. And it worked. The BBB's tactics were aimed at getting political messages across in a way that the press would pick up on and people would empathise with, and even enjoy.

In the months and years that followed, Apple and the BBB hit Robert Shapiro, then head of the biotech company Monsanto; Charles Hurwitz of the Pacific Lumber company, which was busily deforesting ancient woods near the BBB's California home; and even Carl Pope, head of the US environmental group the Sierra Club, who the BBB accused of co-operating with loggers. Then, in

1999, the BBB's reputation went global when three of them pied San Francisco mayor Willie Brown in a protest against his policies on homelessness in the city. Brown took them all the way to court, a process which ended in the 'Cherry Pie Three' being sentenced to six months in prison.

Since then, what Agent Apple calls the 'global pastry uprising' has spread from Burma to South Africa, from Britain to Germany and from Canada to Chile. It has landed flans in the face of Bill Gates, Bernard-Henri Lévy, Clare Short, Ann Widdecombe, Sylvester Stallone, Keith Campbell ('inventor' of Dolly, the cloned sheep), the former heads of both the IMF and the WTO, Helmut Kohl, Jacques Delors . . . The list is still growing.

According to 'Subcomandante Tofutti' of the BBB, the Global Pastry Uprising – described by Apple as 'an underground network of militant bakers who deliver just desserts to those in power' – is inspired by the Zapatistas. They pie people who use power without responsibility, and they like their victims to be pompous, powerful, often obscure and devoid of a sense of humour. They are a grass-roots gastronomic retort to a faceless economic process and they have, says Apple, with an almost straight face, the 'moral pie ground'.

'Pieing is definitely a critical element in culture jamming,' Apple tells me, lazily pushing himself off the side of the pool with his big toe. 'It's a form of direct action that is not violent and yet delivers a powerful message. It's a form of visual Esperanto, a universal language. Everyone can understand it. To see politicians dripping with cream – who could resist it?' Moreover, he says, splashing his hands duckily at his sides, in a world in which the traditional left, and traditional forms of opposition have become 'boring, bureaucratic and unproductive', the *entartistes*, as they are known in the French-speaking world, have something new to offer.

'In today's world, when everything is about image and image-management, it's a way of breaking through that control, and sending our own message, creating our own image. I wouldn't be surprised if at this stage PR firms are training their clients in what to do if you're pied.' I wouldn't be surprised either. But there must, I say, be a point at which pieing passes its sell-by date. And what about culture jamming as a whole? Can it really make a difference?

'Sure,' he says, splashing again. 'Pieing is just one weapon in a whole toolbox of resistance, but the pie is a very effective vehicle to communicate issues that otherwise wouldn't get a hearing. We have got the issues of homelessness, logging, the global market, corporate control, consumerism – we've got it all into the media and into people's consciousness in a way that wouldn't have been possible if we'd just held some rally or something. Also, though, you have to think tactically, and this applies to all the culture jamming-type stuff that goes on in America. In American society, the forces arrayed against dissenters are massive. We have the biggest military force in the world, the biggest budget for the security services in the world, the highest prison population, etc. The climate of paranoia among dissidents here is extremely high. It's been that way for a very long time, and Bush's "war on terror" has just made it a lot worse. Culture jamming, in that context, is a tactic. It's a guerrilla approach. It's not about violent confrontation with the state or the system, but it is a really positive way of getting your message across.'

There's more, too, says the Special Agent, who has now abandoned his rubber ring to float lazily in the middle of the pool flicking dead leaves around with his hands.

'I mean,' he says, 'the traditional way of opposing policies or systems you don't agree with – you know, lines of Socialist Workers selling their papers on the streets . . . it's just a joke. Your average person will look at it and think it's a complete waste of paper. Whereas, for instance, a well done billboard – your average person is going to have much more chance to look at it, really get involved in it, understand – and get a kick out of it, and begin to think about it. The value of questioning authority should not be overstated, and culture jamming is one of the best ways to get those questions across in a way that people can appreciate.'

'I think that to a large degree the battle for the future is for people's hearts and minds,' continues Apple. 'It's not about armed struggle or even traditional types of mass resistance right now – there's none of that kind of thing in the Western world at the moment. It brings on such a wave of repression from the state and often a wave of revulsion from the populace – culture jamming has the opposite effect; of inspiring people. And because of the guerrilla tactics, you can't really stop it in the way you can stop more traditional forms of resistance. It's a lot more decentralised.' He bobs to the side of the pool.

'I guess I should think about getting out. Are you going on this hike? They're going to climb a mountain. I can't decide whether to go.' He looks like he should get out, but really has no inclination to at all. It's a damn fine morning.

'You know,' he says, philosophically, 'there's just something incredibly powerful about *laughing*. I think Beaumarchais wrote that sometimes a man must laugh, lest he cry. If you can't use humour, then you're bound to fail. And you probably deserve to.'

I am in a motel room in Colorado, and I am exhausted. It is late evening, and America is bigger than I thought it would be. For some reason, I imagined that a jaunt from California to Arizona to Colorado would be in the same league as a trip from London to Bristol. I was very wrong, and now I am knackered, lying on my bed with a grim takeaway pizza trying to find something on one of the sixty channels of my TV set that I can watch without being overcome by a faint feeling of nausea. Eventually, I strike gold: *The Simpsons*! This is just what I need. It will ease my tired brain, take my mind off how greasy my pizza is and prevent me from taking anything too seriously. I settle down to watch. This is what I get:

The Simpsons title sequence.
Immediate ad break: skin cream, doughnuts, parcel service, mobile phones.
Start of cartoon: 6 minutes.

More ads: mobile phones ('free up your wireless life'), Taco Bell, triple mascara, chewing gum, local radio, medical insurance.

Cartoon continues: biting satirical critique of American gun culture (7 minutes).

More ads: evening news ('Is Bin Laden dead? A special report!'), cheeseburgers, steakhouse, grillhouse, Jeep Liberty, Coca-Cola, baseball game, new hit series.

Cartoon continues and ends: 7 minutes.

More ads: blockbuster movie with Kiefer Sutherland, local phone company.

The Simpsons closing credits.

This is my first time in the USA. I am evidently a bit naïve. I have never seen anything like this. I am depressed. I give up on my pizza and go to bed.

The next morning I wake up under a beautiful midwestern sky and open my quilted curtains to see the warm, brown foothills of the Rocky Mountains rising above me in welcome. Still dazed from my journey (a train from San Francisco this time), and my first experience of US television, I go for an hour-long walk to the top of the nearest hill before breakfast and come back feeling a lot more human. I am in Boulder, Colorado and, aptly, I have come, among other things, to talk to a man who is keen to explain that advertising and branding are far from the only means by which consumer society instils its ideology into the consciousness of its citizens.

In fact, say many activists, in the US and elsewhere, advertising culture is not even the most insidious means of communicating the consumer message. At least you know where you are with advertising; know it's paid for, know it's trying to condition you, to persuade you, trying to prise open your wallet. On the other side of the fence, though, sits the news media that is such a proudly trumpeted feature of democracies the world over; a feature, say many, that is part of the problem, not the solution.

In the US, the mainstream media is accused by activists of reflecting and promoting the self-obsessed, throwaway society – mediating the world in the image of free market globalisation. They have an unavoidable point. The American media – particularly the airwaves – are among the most nakedly commercial in the world, with a panoply of commercial TV channels, radio stations and publications whose reason for existence is to 'deliver audiences' to their advertisers. Virtually all of the country's TV and radio stations, newspapers and magazines are reliant on the ad-space buying power of corporations. This leads, inevitably, to those corporations having both direct and indirect influence over what is published or broadcast.

At the most obvious level, corporations are always keen to ensure that their adverts are not featured within or next to 'inappropriate' features. 'The Coca-Cola Company,' wrote Coke's advertising agency in a memo to magazines, 'requires that all insertions are placed adjacent to editorial that is consistent with each brand's marketing strategy . . . We consider the following subjects to be inappropriate: hard news, sex, diet, political issues, environmental issues . . .'[21] Such corporate *diktats* are far from exceptional. *Adbusters* provided another striking example a few years ago when it revealed some of the responses it got from US TV networks to attempts to buy space for its 'uncommercial' for Buy Nothing Day. Despite the high production values of the commercial, and the fact that the money was on the table, not one channel would air it. Given reasons ranged from NBC's 'we don't want to take any advertising that's inimical to our legitimate business interests' to CBS's starkly Stalinist 'this commercial . . . is in opposition to the current economic policy in the United States'.[22]

Then there is ownership. The vast majority of TV and radio stations, magazines, book publishers, film producers, record producers and even theme parks are owned by just ten multinational 'entertainment' corporations – AOL Time Warner, AT&T, General Electric, News Corporation, Viacom (which owns the publisher of this book), Bertelsmann, Disney, Vivendi, Liberty and Sony. Lest any non-Americans start to feel smug, six of the above companies control vast chunks of the media in the rest of the world, too, and the chunks are shifting in size and shape so fast that if I were to quote a figure now, it would be out of date by the time you read it.

The outcome of allowing key sources of a nation's information, news and cultural expression to be controlled by an ever-narrowing cabal of giant profit-making entertainment corporations can be seen anytime a television set is switched on in America. The attitude of Disney's Chief Executive, Michael Eisner, sums up the issue as well as any activist could when he explains his company's mission: 'We have no obligation to make history, we have no obligation to make art, we have no obligation to make a statement. To make money is our only objective.'[23]

This situation has arisen as a direct result of a progressive demolition of regulations designed to protect public service media from the cultural fires of the market. Since the 1980s, regulations which prevent cross-media ownership, stop particular companies dominating the market and ensure the continued existence of local and community-based media have been progressively rolled back, partly as a response to aggressive lobbying from the media giants. Since George W. Bush's Republican elite took power in 2000 and consolidated it in 2002, the pace has been accelerated.

The Federal Communications Commission, the body charged with overseeing media regulation, has been placed in the hands of the free market ideologue Michael Powell (son of Secretary of State Colin) – a man who, when asked the definition of 'public interest' replied, 'I have no idea.'[24] Powell has placed a swathe of regulations 'under review', including laws designed to prevent single corporations owning large numbers of radio stations, controlling TV and newspapers in the same area of the country and guaranteeing 'independent voices' in local TV. In February 2002, the FCC overturned two significant regulations: a sixty-year-old rule that prevented any TV company reaching more than 35 per cent of the national audience, and a rule preventing a company from owning a cable channel and a broadcast station in the same city. There are more such 'market openings' on the books.

This phenomenon is looking likely to be repeated worldwide as globalisation provides new 'market opportunities' in the unfortunate, benighted nations of what one media consultant has called the 'underscreened, undermalled, still-waiting-for-cable world'.[25] AOL Time Warner's former head Gerry Levin publicly declared his ambition to 'have corporations redefined as instruments of public service'[26] in a forthcoming WTO agreement – the General Agreement on Trade in Services (GATS), which media companies are working hard to influence. GATS, they hope, will outlaw or weaken national and regional regulations protecting public service media and limiting corporate ownership. But whether they get it through the WTO or some other means, there is no doubt what the global media empire-builders want: the kind of control over information and entertainment that they have in the USA, writ global.

The chances of the media being 'free' under such circumstances seem pretty slim. This is precisely why a growing number of people within the movement see the mainstream media as a threat, rather than a potential ally. David Barsamian is one of them, and as I sit talking to him in a noisy coffee shop in Boulder, I see what links the arguments of the culture jammers to the work of people like him. I see that this is about a battle for information: a battle for the right to tell the stories that shape your society.

Barsamian is founder and director of Alternative Radio, a station he set up, with virtually no experience, as an experiment in 1986, and which now has its programmes featured on 125 stations internationally, reaching millions of people. Increasingly one of America's most respected, and most uncompromising, media critics, Barsamian is intense, smart and fast-talking, with a sharp-shooting grin, wide glasses and a mop of greying hair.

I have already been down to Alternative Radio's less than palatial (and all the nicer for it) office which, as Barsamian puts it, is 'situated to correspond with its position in the mainstream mass media: down an alley, behind a house, on top of a garage', and have been loaded up with *gratis* tapes of recent programmes. They include 'Michael Parenti: The Manufacture of History', 'Robert McChesney: Corporate Media and the Threat to Democracy', 'Eqbal Ahmad: Terrorism – Theirs and Ours', and 'Arundhati Roy: A Writer's Place in Politics'. Alternative Radio would not describe itself as easy listening.

'Look at the big picture,' Barsamian instructs me. 'Look at what has happened to American journalism. Ben Bagdikian's classic book *The Media Monopoly* has always been the primer for what is happening to our media. It came out in 1983, and in it he identified fifty corporations that controlled most of the media in the United States. Second edition came out – twenty-eight. Third edition – twenty-three. Fourth edition – fourteen. Fifth edition – ten. The latest edition, which came out in 2000, identified six corporations. And these corporations are now subsumed in even bigger corporations. CNN and ABC are controlled by Disney. NBC is controlled by General Electric. These are no longer news-gathering organisations in control of their own destiny. They're controlled by entertainment companies interested in maximising profits.' He sighs, but quickly. Barsamian does everything quickly. He has to be in seventeen other places today, most of them at once; he's that sort of person.

'This concentration of monopoly control of information poses a *serious* threat to democracy,' he goes on. 'It's not just people who would call themselves left-wing or progressive who should be concerned about this. People like Thomas Jefferson and James Madison – conservative theorists – said that the citizenry need a broad range of opinions in order to make their own decisions on the important issues of the day. Opinion should range from A to Z. Today, the range of opinions in the United States is from A to B. American democracy has significantly suffered because we don't have a lively media.'

Barsamian, like others, says that the media, as a result of corporate ownership, profit-seeking and deregulation, is more interested in producing entertainment than information, education – or news. This, he says, is no surprise – it's the inevitable result of turning your information-producing power over to a handful of competitive, profit-making private companies.

'Corporate control drives the media here not to generate coverage but to generate profits,' he says. 'Investigative reporting is virtually eliminated – there's still a bit left in print journalism, but in electronic journalism it's been virtually eliminated. In-depth stories take money and they take time. The corporate concentration of the media really constricts the scope for news reporting, news gathering and the kind of background that is required to understand something. So instead of explanation on, say, Afghanistan, we get good versus evil, liberty versus hate, black versus white. Which side are you on? Are you with us or with the terrorists? Good news reporting is about explaining the grey areas. Corporate control of information is structurally unable to get into those grey areas – it's too expensive, it takes too much time, it doesn't deliver the profits in the same way.' He stirs his tall latte, frantically.

'People aren't *stupid*,' he says insistently, as if someone had suddenly appeared from under the table and challenged him to prove otherwise. 'Stupidity is *constructed*. There's a lot of propaganda about the American people being apathetic – they just want to watch football and drink beer. That's not because there's some genetic basis for it, it's constructed. It's constructed by a media and educational system that says: your role as a citizen finds its ultimate fulfilment as a consumer. Not as someone who is involved in important decisions about where money is spent, how US foreign policy decisions are made – any of those things. You're supposed to focus on why the Denver Broncos may not have a good team this year because the coach has made bad decisions about the running backs. On issues like that, you can debate, you can be very vitriolic . . . but on important areas of foreign policy, life-and-death national decisions, whether we should bomb Afghanistan – you're supposed to roll out the flag, wrap yourself in it, say, "I am a loyal American, I will follow my leader."'

If this is the case, I say, what can be done to tackle the media's control of information, and the values it promotes?

'Well,' he says, without pausing to think, 'the problem is that the media in general, especially the electronic media, won't give the necessary explication needed to deconstruct events for the listener. It's all soundbites, eyebites, you know. What tends to happen in those circumstances is the mouthing of slogans, things that every-one believes in – that the United States defends freedom, that the US is the beacon of democracy, as George Bush puts it – you don't need to produce any evidence because you're supporting conventional wisdom. Whereas if you say, rightly, that the United States has been, for a long time, a major supporter of international terrorism, then the reaction is – "what?" You need time to explain that, to expand on it, you can't just produce the usual media soundbites. People demand answers, you have to explain the CIA training terrorist gangs in Central America, the financing of the *Mujahideen* . . . You need to provide facts when you're challenging conventional wisdom in a way that you don't if you're shoring it up. It means that real journalism – challenging journalism – needs more time, and needs to be allowed to explore the issues in a way which modern news simply does not allow. What does that mean should be done? It means breaking up the corporate concentration of media ownership for a start, rather than encouraging it. It means getting the Federal Communications Commission, which is supposed to defend the public interest, to stop defending the busi-ness interests of Wall Street and Madison Avenue. But it also means that those of us who like to complain about it should get going on our own media. The potential to do that, and the ease of doing it, exists as never before.' He's finished his coffee now. He fiddles with the spoon anyway.

'The corporate concentration of media ownership is a dagger at the throat of democracy,' he says. 'That's what this is. A dagger.'

Barsamian probably feels like a lone voice on this subject some-times. He isn't, though; questioning the ideology and the work of

the mass media, and attempting, sometimes successfully, sometimes not so, to provide alternatives to it is a preoccupation of
activists worldwide. A movement that wants to get across ideas
that few have even considered – ideas that challenge authority not
just physically or politically but philosophically, ideas about
values – is unlikely to get a fair hearing in the mainstream media,
and rarely does.

One obvious but telling example. When I looked through the
newspapers and watched the TV news reports after the Genoa
protests, I heard and saw virtually nothing about the debates that
had gone on for a week before the protests. For a week we had
gathered in a complex of tents on the seashore and discussed the
problems with, and solutions to, everything from currency speculation to corporate regulation, changes in agricultural policy to
land reform. Organisations from all over the world had met and
made links and engaged in intelligent debate about the state of the
world. And all we saw in the press was bricks, tear-gas, bullets and
broken windows.

This picture is repeated wherever protesters gather; as a rule –
one which is occasionally but rarely broken – the mainstream
media either report violence or, if there is no violence, they report
nothing. In Genoa, 300,000 people marched and demonstrated;
the street battle became the news and the issues were forgotten.
The next year, in March 2002, 500,000 showed up in Barcelona to
discuss and object to the European Union Summit. There was no
violence and, consequently, virtually no coverage. This, to activists,
is only the most obvious and widespread example of a media that
regularly refuses, or seems unable, to represent their concerns
properly. Their solution to this is straightforward: they create their
own media.

This, in itself, is nothing new – political movements have
always done it, from little magazines, newsletters and free papers
through to party propaganda sheets. The differences today are
two-fold. First, in a movement obsessed with diversity and decentralisation, alternative media tend to reflect these principles – there

are no newspapers, radio stations, websites or anything else which can claim, or would claim, to represent 'the movement' as a whole. Like the movement's political organisation, its media are not centralised.

Secondly, though, the new technology that has developed symbiotically with the globalisation process has enabled alternative media to flourish in a way that it has never been able to before. In a world in which digital cameras and camcorders cost only a few hundred pounds, desktop publishing programmes can produce professional-looking magazines in a few hours and a homemade website can give a handful of committed people the ability to communicate with millions of others, worldwide, in a matter of minutes, alternative forms of information distribution at last have a chance of becoming genuinely influential, and genuinely popular. How long this will last – how long the Internet, for example, will remain a largely free and democratic medium – remains a hot topic for debate. But while it does, the potential to, in David Barsamian's words, 'get going on our own media' exists, in spades.

The best and most systematic attempt to do this so far has been the rise of Indymedia, an increasingly global network of locally controlled websites (and in some cases, radio stations and video projects) which aims to offer 'grass-roots, non-corporate coverage' of events. Indymedia (favoured slogan – 'Don't hate the media, become the media') began life during the Seattle protests in 1999, when a group of writers, web designers, activists, filmmakers and others put together a website to provide the news from the WTO meeting and the attendant protests that the mainstream media weren't providing. The site received 1.5 million hits during the summit, and in the four years since then, Indymedia has gone global.

At the time of writing, there are ninety-one Indymedia sites in thirty-one countries, ranging from Israel to Finland, Nigeria to Spain, Indonesia to Colombia, India to Russia. Indymedia provided up-to-the-minute coverage in Genoa and were viciously attacked by the police for their pains. Indymedia Chiapas provides the latest on the Zapatistas, and while I was in South Africa, I attended one of the first meetings of the country's Indymedia centre, which was in the process of being born.

And yet Indymedia, as such, doesn't exist. There is no central office, there are no paid staff, there are no rules, not even any one agreed mission statement. Funding comes from donations, no advertising is sold and no political party, creed or corporate line is toed. Some people involved are trained journalists, but most are not, there are no official hierarchies. Its journalists do their meeting, planning and co-ordinating by e-mail and in chatrooms. Anyone can publish anything on an Indymedia site, and the various Indymedia centres are linked with each other only in loose, unofficial ways. What really links them together is a desire to tell the news that the mainstream media is not telling, or to provide unnoticed or ignored angles that you won't read elsewhere.

Thus Indymedia will run the stories behind events like Genoa, Prague, Seattle or Durban which don't get into the papers or on to the TV bulletins. It will tell the story of the siege of the Church of the Nativity in Jerusalem from the point of view of those inside. It will run features on the street-level popular assemblies springing up in Argentina as a result of that country's IMF-inspired economic collapse. It will showcase resistance to water privatisations in India and anti-Zionist demonstrations in Israel that you would otherwise be very unlikely to hear about.

Indymedia is built around a virtual obsession with two things – horizontal organising and open publishing. The first is self-explanatory – it is that old loathing of hierarchies that Indymedia activists share with the movement as a whole. The second is a direct response to the increasing control of information by profit-making corporations, and their use of that information to promote consumerism, globalisation and the values that come with it.

Indymedia journalist Matthew Arnison describes open publishing as a 'revolutionary response to the privatisation of information by multinational companies'.[27] The principle, as demonstrated on Indymedia sites, is simple: anyone can publish anything. There are no professional journalists or editors who decide what is or isn't news, no corporate filters and no one line – though a dissenting, anti-globalising tone is shared by all Indymedia outlets. What this means, as anyone who has used Indymedia will tell you, is that there can be an awful lot of crud among the better quality material: lies, mistakes, conspiracy theories, the odd bit of hate-mongering.

In this sense, Indymedia is like the journalistic version of a group conversation rather than a monologue; it is the reader creating the news. Not all of it will be worth reading, but Indymedia assumes that most people are intelligent enough to tell good journalism from nonsense. 'Media corporations assume the viewers are stupid,' writes Arnison. 'In their eyes, the total creative potential of the audience is *Funniest Home Videos*. Creative people do not buy more stuff, they make their own. This is a problem for media multinationals. They do not trust their audience to be creative. It might be bad for profits . . . but it's OK. The audience doesn't trust the corporate media either.'

Indymedia is hardly set to replace mainstream news reporting. It has neither the reach, the resources, the expertise, the audience or the desire. But it is a phenomenon, and an important one. In Indymedia – which is replicated in kind if not in scale by other open publishing outlets on the Internet – the movement has found at least the beginning of an answer to the fears that the Reverend Billy, Kalle Lasn, the Billboard Liberation Front, Agent Apple and David Barsamian all articulate. Fears which, with everything I've seen, I can't help sharing. Fears which can be wrapped up in two words: cultural enclosure.

We are in the midst of a global information revolution which is leading not, as its proponents claim, to more 'choice', better quality media and more perspectives on the world, but to an ever-contracting group of Earth-encircling corporations mediating the stories that shape our world. We become consumers not just in goods, but in ideas, philosophies, ideologies. They entertain us, we sit and listen – but not until we've paid them. Stories have always defined the way societies and cultures see themselves. Now the lens through which we view the world is owned by CNN and our fairytales are told by Disney, with merchandise tie-ins at Burger King.

This, at its starkest, is the privatisation of imagination. To counter it, activists posit an alternative that requires all of us to take back the colonised space within our minds. Be your own media. Write your own news. Define your own space, both public and cultural. Tell your own story, lest it be told for you; packaged and sold in a global mall where everything, from running shoes to democracy to the tales your granny told you, is a product with a price tag attached.

5 **the penis gourd revolution**

'If the mountains and nature are harmed, our mother is hurt as well. The mountain we see as our mother is sacred. It is where the souls of men go when they die. We keep this place holy, and worship it in our traditional ceremonies.'

TOM BEANAL, AMUNGME TRIBAL LEADER

'In a country of mountains, why shouldn't one be sacrificed in the name of progress?'

SPOKESMAN, PT FREEPORT INDONESIA

Two lanky, sunburned, six-foot Englishmen are nervously leading a troupe of war-painted, whooping five-foot tribesmen through a thatched arch into the centre of a roadless village in the highlands of New Guinea. The mountains that encircle them on all sides are layered with untouched rainforest and hung with ribbons of cloud. Before them jog two painted men, bones through their noses, dried white mud patterned on to their lean torsos, feathers of hornbill and bird of paradise in their matted black hair. They dance ten steps forward and five steps back, motioning ritually with hardwood spears. On each side of them dance two ancient women, bare-breasted, similarly painted, wearing nothing but grass skirts, swaying their hips and thrusting sticks at the sky.

The whoops and whistles grow louder as the two white men reach a semicircle of village leaders drawn up to greet them. They halt, and the warriors behind them sit down as one. They remain standing, awkwardly, in the high, thin sunlight, trying to look honoured.

Slowly, painfully, one of the men in the centre of the semicircle begins to cry. It starts with a forced sniff and graduates to a circling, howling sound, the tears flowing freely. Soon, the thirty or so men and boys with him are crying too; an unearthly rolling barrage of sobs and wails punctuated with words and phrases in their distinctive highland language. The sound punctuates the short grass, the dewdropped ferns and the low, round thatched huts that dot them on all sides.

Three minutes later, the crying stops, eyes are dried and we are officially welcome, and honoured, guests in this remote Lani village, two days' walk from the nearest track. It's moving, in a way that neither of us has ever been moved before.

'Wow,' I say out of the side of my mouth, to Steve. 'That was . . . strange.'

'They haven't finished yet,' he replies, out of the side of his. And they haven't. Galile, our friend, guide and translator, steps between us. The villagers are moving off towards another clump of people arriving through the gates, carrying bows and arrows, spears – and four live pigs trussed up and strung on to wooden poles, carried across the shoulders of eight lithe tribesmen.

'Now,' says Galile, 'you must kill pig.'

'Who, me?'

'You must both kill pig. With bow and arrow.'

'Shit, Galile,' I say, 'I can't kill a pig.'

'It is traditional. To welcome you into our tribe.'

'But I'm a vegetarian. Anyway, I'd miss.'

Galile turns to Steve, who is standing next to me looking equally uncomfortable.

'I think I'd miss too,' he says. 'Do we have to? Really?'

'OK,' says Galile, 'they will kill pig. But we must eat it. And now you must watch.'

Two pig carriers approach us with their struggling load.

'You must take the pole,' Galile instructs us. Steve and I struggle with the pole, and the extremely unhappy pig, and heave it on to our shoulders as instructed. Then, at Galile's prompting, in unison, we say 'Wa, wa, wa, wa, wa . . .' – the ubiquitous highland word for both thank you and hello. The hundred-strong crowd bursts into riotous applause and another round of whistling and uncanny animal noises. Now I really do feel honoured.

Then an old man, wearing nothing but a *koteka* – the cultivated gourds which highland tribal men wear as sheaths on their penises – kneels before us and thuds four arrows nonchalantly into the hearts of the unfortunate animals. They flap about frantically for a minute or so, then subside into stillness.

A village elder rises, bone-creakingly, from the crowd, and addresses us in Lani, as the pigs are gleefully carted off around the corner to where the women are building earth ovens.

'Now,' Galile translates, 'he says you are Lani family and Lani tribe. He says this is your village and any time you want to build house here, land is yours. Anywhere in jungle forest, you may build your house, and live with your tribe.' Everyone grins, and so do we.

'But first,' says Galile, 'we must get free.'

When the Netherlands claimed sovereignty over half of the planet's second-largest island, New Guinea, in 1824, they were just one of the nations taking part in a colonial scramble for territories all over the 'East Indies'. Across the sparkling archipelago that now makes up the state of Indonesia, the Dutch government had been relying for its territorial plunder on the work of the *Vereenigde Oost-Indische Compagnie* – the Dutch East India Company – a state-sponsored multinational corporation that made the targets of today's activists look like a bunch of social workers. With the power to colonise new territories, make treaties and issue currency, and with its own private army, the Dutch East India Company succeeded in two hundred years in colonising most of what is now Indonesia, and seizing control of its lucrative spice trade. The market had come to the East Indies.

Over in what the Europeans called New Guinea, meanwhile, no one had really noticed. This vast, forested island had little to offer the European colonists. Passing by in 1526, the Portuguese explorer Jorge de Meneses named it 'Ilhas dos Papuas' – 'island of the fuzzy hairs'. A later Spanish explorer, deciding that its inhabitants looked a bit like those of Guinea, in Africa, on the basis that they were black, named it 'New Guinea'.

Those inhabitants, who would later come to know themselves as 'Papuans', had been there for at least 40,000 years, split into over a thousand separate tribal groups, each with their own language (a fifth of all the world's languages are still found in New Guinea, some spoken by fewer than 500 people). They lived, as most still do, in tiny highland villages, swamps and rainforests, subsisting on sweet potatoes and sago. With 600 plant species, 200 bird species and 200 reptile species found nowhere else, home of the bird of paradise and with some of the last great intact rainforests on the planet, Papua was, and remains, a place apart.

Life only really began to change for the Papuans after the Second World War, when the European colonisers began to leave. The Dutch East Indies were to become a new nation-state – Indonesia. But the Dutch wanted West Papua to become an independent state. The black, Melanesian Papuans, the departing Dutch argued, had as little in common with the fair-skinned Asiatic Muslim Indonesians as they did with the Europeans. They were a different race, living in a different ecological zone, with a different culture and different values. They should have their own country. In 1949, the Dutch ceded sovereignty of the Dutch East Indies to the new nation of Indonesia – but excluded West Papua from the deal.

But the Indonesians were having none of it. Their first president, Sukarno, wanted his new nation to be the greatest in Asia. Everything the Dutch had owned, he said, should now be Indonesian. Indonesia and the Netherlands broke off relations. On 1 December 1961, the Dutch formally ceded independence to West Papua. A new Papuan flag – the Morning Star – was raised as its people, only recently aware that they inhabited what the Europeans called a 'nation' at all, proclaimed their independence. Celebrations were to be short-lived. The UN, under pressure from the US, Indonesia's newest ally, refused to recognise the new nation or the Dutch action, and in 1962, an Indonesian invasion force parachuted into the forests.

From then on, the outcome was in no doubt. Though the UN intervened and promised the Papuans a referendum on independence, the Indonesians, with what was to become their trademark brutality, forced a 'representative' group of 1,000 tribal leaders to 'unanimously' vote, at gunpoint, to become part of Indonesia. In 1969, West Papua – or 'Irian Jaya', as the Indonesians were to rename it – became Indonesia's twenty-sixth province.

The next thirty years were to prove the most brutal in Papuan history. Under their new dictator-president, General Suharto, who toppled Sukarno in a coup in 1967, the Indonesians embarked on a campaign to 'Indonesianise' the new province and to wipe out Papuan culture. Those who resisted this ethnic cleansing were murdered, tortured or 'disappeared' with a horrific ferocity. Officially, more than 100,000 Papuans have been killed by the Indonesians since occupation; unofficially, the figure is said to approach 800,000.[1]

But as with all colonial occupations, there was another reason behind the Indonesians' ferocious campaign to gain control over West Papua: resources. It is the glory and the tragedy of the Papuan people that their land is positively dripping with just the kind of things that make the global economy tick. Timber, oil, gas, copper, gold: it was all there, in abundance. Anyone could see what was coming next.

Even before it took control of West Papua, Indonesia had been negotiating with the American mining company Freeport, which wanted to open up what looked like a vast copper deposit in West Papua. In 1969, Freeport moved in. In, too, came the Anglo-Dutch oil company Shell, and a clutch of other mining and oil prospectors. The Indonesian government, thousands of miles away in the capital, Jakarta, laid out some maps of West Papua on a table and drew lines on them to designate the forestry 'concessions' – taking up much of Papua's vast primal rainforest, second in size only to the Amazon – which they were going to hand out to logging companies. Within a few years, West Papua had been doubly colonised: by the Indonesians, and by some of the biggest, and most destructive, corporations of the age.

Today, West Papua is Indonesia's most polluted, ignored, exploited province. Its tribal people have become second-class citizens in their own ancestral land. Indonesia and its friendly multinationals take $500 million out of the country every year. The Papuans see virtually none of it. They are a people at the very tip of the global economy's sword: the point where the resources that the rest of us use every day are taken, by force if necessary, from the people they belong to.

Betrayed by the world's silence, the Papuans have been left to sink into a slow, acquiescent extinction. But they have other ideas.

West Papua's crumbling capital, Jayapura, is a colonial town. Most of its shops, time-warped hotels, noodle bars, industries – even the schools, the hospital and the museum of Papuan culture – are owned and operated by Indonesians. It is a grotty, malfunctioning place, sweltering in the malarial lowland heat between the end of the highland mountain ranges and Pacific beaches studded with the wrecks of Second World War landing craft. Not the sort of place you'd come for a holiday, which is why nobody does.

Except me. Officially, I am a tourist. Try and be anything else in West Papua and life gets difficult. Since the occupation, the Indonesian government has maintained a strict policy of keeping outsiders away from any part of West Papua they don't want the world to see. A year before my arrival, a Swiss journalist was thrown into a Papuan police cell for 'illegal journalistic activity', then deported – though not before he had witnessed some 'unspeakably shocking' scenes in prison: Indonesian police torturing suspected Papuan separatists with clubs, staffs, bamboo whips, boots and fists; blood spraying the walls as they beat three Papuans to death over a period of hours in front of his eyes.[2]

Needless to say, I can't afford to let the authorities know what I'm really here for. So I'm here to see the exotic indigenous culture. Even this means a visit to the police station, and an application for a *surat jalan* – a visitor's pass – on which the police will write the names of the places you are officially allowed to visit this month.

I am sweating from a combination of nerves and heavy, thirty-five-degree heat as I stand before a fat policeman in Jayapura's steaming police station. He doesn't seem to have noticed.

'How you like Indonesia?' he asks, as he bangs out my *surat jalan* on a typewriter that would probably get a favourable reception on *Antiques Roadshow*.

'Very nice.'

'What you do here?'

'Just tourism.'

'Tourism? Here?'

'Er . . . yes.'

'Just as long as you not work. Not doing any journalism maybe, any bad things like this. You engage in any activity like this, you go to jail. Five years. I just warn you.'

'No, no . . . just a holiday. You know, many interesting tribes, forest, er . . . animals.' I gesture vaguely at the ceiling and wonder if I have any incriminating notebooks on me.

'You want tourism, my friend, you should not be here. You should be in Bali. Many beaches, nice girls, *Bintang* . . . you know. Why you come here? This place full of savages. Bad place. I would be in Bali if I could. My job, you know.' He grins, sadly. Less than a year later, when a terrorist bomb killed dozens in a Bali nightclub, he was probably more grateful for his posting.

'Enjoy yourself in our country.'

The irony of Jayapura, and all the other Papuan towns, is that while the Papuans lose economic power, control over their own destiny, and their cultural identity to the Indonesian occupiers, many of those 'occupiers' don't get much from it either. Thousands of miles from home, in a 'backward' land they don't understand, many of the migrants came here through the Indonesian government's programme of 'transmigration' – a massive state effort to shift people from Indonesia's overcrowded central island, Java, to 'underpopulated' outer islands like Papua. Many transmigrants were given no choice by the government about whether to move – when they did, they found themselves dropped on to 'farms' carved out of the forest, with no running water or electricity, and patchy land that dried up within a few years. But the programme (which is now being wound down) had the pleasing effect of both ridding Java of people for whom there was not enough land to support, and 'Indonesianising' West Papua.

But there is another irony, too, in Jayapura. While this Indonesian town, in a Melanesian land, is a symbol of the ethnic cleansing that the Indonesian government has been inflicting on the Papuans, the Indonesians are undergoing their own version of ethnic cleansing: their culture and values whipped from under them by the powerful iconography of Western consumerism. TV ads show smiling Javan families sitting down in jeans to dinners of packet noodles. Computers in the two local Internet cafés are run on American software in the English language (or would be if they worked). Outside the slowly collapsing cinema, a six-foot mugshot of George Clooney twinkles down at the Muslim women in their veils and long white dresses. Outside the school, kids – Indonesian and Papuan – mill about dressed in uniforms straight out of middle America, right down to the baseball caps. While the Indonesian government is busily wiping out the identities and culture of the Papuans, Papua's Indonesian migrants are busy trading theirs for a photocopied Americana that they will never experience.

I am here to meet my contact, Amunggur,[3] a key figure in the Papuan resistance. I have come to West Papua, at his urging, to see how a tribal people are resisting the forces of globalisation. Amunggur has told me that the Papuans – some of the most 'undeveloped' tribal people anywhere – are just beginning to engage with the global movement and its concerns. He thinks they need to, and quickly.

There has never been an international popular movement that has included, involved and taken up the concerns of tribal people. For centuries, the fate of such 'savages' has been to be passed over, ignored or exterminated in the name of progress. Throughout the twentieth century both right and left, empire-builders and International Socialists, champions of either labour or capital, tended to see the remaining tribal peoples in the forests and the mountains and plains as awkward, embarrassing impediments to a glorious industrial future.

This movement is different. Indigenous concerns have been at its heart from day one. Because it is a movement that was born in the 'developing' world, because of its culture of diversity, because land and cultural identity and giving voices to the overlooked are key to its concerns, tribal people have played a key part in it. In

India and Bangladesh, thousands of *adivasi* tribal people have gathered to oppose dam-building projects, protest against GM crops being grown on their land and fight for their rights and cultures. In Nigeria, tribal groups in Ogoniland and elsewhere have fought for years against Shell oil's destruction of their communities, and against the global economy that allows them to do it. Amazon tribes fight logging and land theft, and join up as they do so with Thai hill tribes, Maoris, North American Indians, Ecuadorian tribes, Colombian forest people, Australian aborigines and many others in taking their concerns to the global level, linking up with each other and influencing the ideas, direction and values of the growing global movement.

Amunggur has been all over the world trying to forge these links, and to persuade his people that they are worth making – and has become *persona non grata* with the Indonesian government as a result. His people, he explained to me, when I met him before I arrived in Papua, had been fighting the symptoms of globalisation for years: now they were beginning to turn their attentions to its causes.

I am here to find out if this is true. If anyone can show me, it has to be Amunggur. The only trouble is, I can't find him.

For two agonisingly hot days I have been tramping the streets of Jayapura, looking in all the places he promised I would find him and finding only taxi drivers, market traders and half-naked old men trying to sell me pig-tusk good luck charms, carved wooden ancestor poles and conch shell necklaces. After two days of poking into corners, asking dangerous questions and roaring around dirt tracks on the pillions of motorbikes driven by Papuans who are sure they know where to find Amunggur, but then turn out to be thinking of someone else, I am about to give up and go home. Then, by sheer luck, I meet an old man who claims to know where to find Amunggur's cousin and, amazingly, turns out to be right.

Galile is short and stocky, with a brief beard and the trademark Papuan features: broad, flat triangular nose, heavy brow topped with a mat of short, tightly curled black hair, and a mouth which breaks into a delightfully wide, guileless grin when he is told what I am here for. He shakes my hand for what seems like a full five minutes, then ushers me into his weathered, clapboard house and closes the door behind me. 'Many spies,' he confides, furtively, sitting himself cross-legged on the floor. 'When in Jayapura, you must be careful. Some Papuans betray their country; paid by Indonesians, in *rupiah* or whisky. Pheeew! We must be careful.'

I am desperately pleased to have found Galile, for it turns out that Amunggur is not even in the country. 'He in big trouble,' says Galile, seriously. 'Police and army all look for him. He is trying to tell the world about Papuans and their suffering. He is brave man, and if police get him' – he runs his finger across his throat in a motion that anyone in the world would instantly understand. 'Pheeew!' he says again. 'Bad trouble. He cannot come back to Papua until it is safe. I not know where he is now. But I can help you talk to the people. Anything I can do for you, I will do it.'

Galile is Amunggur's cousin, but he might as well be his brother, his brother-in-law, his best friend, his son. In Papua, none of these words mean much; everyone is 'family' – in the loop or outside it. Right now, Galile is hundreds of miles from the forest village he grew up in, working and studying in Jayapura – 'for the future'. But his new surroundings have not divested him of the patterns of life he was born into, among which the importance of family – extended families, numbering in their hundreds – is paramount. At heart, Galile remains a Papuan tribesman.

Now, though, he is sitting on dark floorboards, swatting fat, heavy mosquitoes and smiling at me disarmingly, openly, trustingly, as if he has known me for ever.

'So,' he says, 'what you want to do?'

I tell him.

The Papuans' resistance to their occupation takes several forms. For decades after the Indonesian takeover, the only form of organised resistance came from the *Organisasi Papua Merdeka*

(OPM) – the Free Papua Movement. The OPM, formed in 1970, is a broad-based social movement to which almost everyone in West Papua, if you get them alone, will admit to 'belonging'. To the rest of the world, though – those few who are listening anyway – the letters 'OPM' mean the organisation's armed wing: a mysterious and determined bunch of guerrillas who live, Robin Hood-like, deep in the forests, moving their camps regularly to escape army manhunts and occasionally emerging to attack a mine or kidnap a few unsuspecting foreigners. OPM guerrillas talk the talk of hardened soldiers but, small in numbers and armed with little more than spears, knives, bows and arrows and the occasional stolen gun, they have never been more than irritating crumbs under the bedclothes of Indonesian rule.

In the last few years, though, things have changed in West Papua, as they have in Indonesia as a whole. General Suharto ruled Indonesia unchallenged for over thirty years, but in 1998, in the financial maelstrom that was sweeping South-East Asia, popular resentment finally bubbled to the surface and swept him from office. Two short-lived presidents followed him, then, in 2001, in what she no doubt saw as poetic justice, Megawati Sukarnoputri, daughter of the man Suharto had deposed in 1967, became president of Indonesia.

Taking advantage of a new, tentative climate of openness in Jakarta after the dictator's fall, the Papuans began to call openly for independence. In 1999, for the first time since 1969, they publicly raised the symbol of their national hopes – the banned Morning Star flag – without widespread retribution from the Indonesian authorities. Then, in May 2000, they held the biggest public show of national aspiration that had ever been allowed. Three thousand delegates came to the Papua People's Congress in Jayapura, some of them hiking barefoot through the mountains for weeks to get there, to demand independence and to set up a new organisation to work towards it – the Papua Council. The Council, made up of 500 tribal leaders, was exactly what the Papuans had never had –

a respectable, non-violent lobby group calling, openly, for independence. The Council's executive, the oddly named 'Presidium', announced that it would work alongside the OPM and others, united in pursuit of *merdeka* – freedom.

When I arrived in West Papua, six months after the People's Congress, it seemed as if the Papuans had their best chance ever of real change. In Jakarta, the government had noticed it too, and had come up with a dual strategy to dampen down demands for independence.

First, it had offered the Papuans something called 'special autonomy' – more control over their affairs within Indonesia, including changing the province's name from 'Irian Jaya' to 'Papua', creating a Papuan parliament with indigenous people in its ranks and giving West Papua some use of the revenues generated on its soil. Secondly, in case this didn't work, ministers in Jakarta drew up a secret plan to crush demands for independence at the grass roots. They included using the army to train pro-Indonesian militia and buying off potential separatists with government jobs. So far, neither has worked: the Papua Council, the OPM and other organisations working for independence have dismissed the special autonomy powers as an attempt to buy them off. Only *merdeka*, they say, will satisfy them.

What form it will take is a question I am going to put to the newly formed Presidium. It's not a good time to be talking to them, though. Barely a fortnight before I arrived in West Papua, the Presidium's leader, the charismatic Theys Eluay, had been murdered by the Indonesian army – apparently as part of that plan to destroy the independence movement. Despite the resulting turmoil in the Presidium, however, Willy Mandowen has agreed to talk to me. Willy is middle-aged, cunning, highly educated, well travelled and very influential. He is one of the key thinkers and strategists in the Presidium, and if West Papua ever becomes the independent nation that so many of its people want it to be, Mandowen will undoubtedly be one of the key figures in its government.

I perch myself on the edge of a sofa in Willy's living room as he tells me that the Presidium would govern the country in a very different way from what has gone before.

'You see,' he says, quietly, 'we don't want to get independence, and then find that capital is regulated by someone else. We are aware of this threat. How will we tackle it? By ensuring that tribal leaders play a full role in any government. So a company may want to open up a mountain for mining, but if the people and their culture say "no, it is our mother", then no. Papuan customs will check our government.'

I ask if he really believes that the customs of tribal people could take precedence over resource extraction and the enormous power of the global economy.

'Well, yes, it could,' he smiles. 'From a just point of view we can't allow so-called "developed" countries to continue dominating smaller countries through regulations and things like the WTO. This is just a new form of colonialism. And what is so developed about these places? When I walk through New York, Sydney, San Francisco – even Jakarta – I see very high, tall, empty buildings and most people moving to the suburbs to escape. Why don't you build small houses which are healthy? Why make a city a place of waste – all steel and having to fight over the price of oil? In Papua, we have enough space to live healthily – not like you. We want fish from the coral reefs and meat from the jungle, not fish that has been in a refrigerator for a month.'

'Do you know,' he goes on, 'that in America they have this television programme – *Survivor* I think it is called – which spends millions putting people into the jungle for a week? In LA, I have seen jungles created in hotel lobbies. Why should I develop into the sort of country where people want to become like me again? We must have a clear vision, and that vision must be to localise globalisation. This is Papuan development. We don't need to be American. Development for the world should be like building a house. Here is the window, here are the bricks, here is the roof. All these materials are different and are made by different people.

All contribute to the finished building. Similarly, countries must be made up differently, to contribute to the whole world.'

A world, in other words, with many worlds in it. Talking to Willy, as to Amunggur before him, I realise just how far across the world this thinking about globalisation, economics, independence and power has spread, in such a short time.

Meanwhile, Willy has a plan, he says, to rein in corporations. If a company wants to work, or invest, in West Papua there would be strict rules under which it could do so – rules decided at community level. Local communities would have the final say over whether corporations came in to work on their land. If they did, it would have to be in a way respectful of their customs and way of life, and the community – and the Papuan government – would have to receive the benefits. Finally, each corporation operating in West Papua would have to contribute money to a trust fund, controlled by local communities, with community leaders deciding how the resulting money would be spent to the benefit of their communities.

It sounds good. If it worked, it probably would be. But there's something I want to ask Willy about – a rumour I have heard that could make the difference between the success and failure of such ambitious ideas. I have heard that the Presidium is being funded by some of West Papua's biggest multinational corporations; precisely those corporations which people like Amunggur and the OPM – and Willy, in his milder way – say are responsible for the raping of this nascent nation. There is Freeport, Shell, the loggers – corporations whose atrocious environmental and human rights records speak for themselves. Now, there is also BP, the rebranded oil company which claims it is moving 'beyond petroleum'. BP wants to drill for liquid petroleum gas in Bintuni Bay on the western tip of West Papua, but it wants to do it, it says, in partnership with the people. Mindful of the mistakes made by others, BP is keen to avoid attacks by the OPM, condemnation from environmentalists and nasty leaks about human rights abuses on its turf.

'Yes,' confirms Willy, with no hint of a conflict of interest in his tone. 'BP and Freeport help pay for transport and meeting places and accommodation costs for the Papua Council. Other companies have approached us too. We are in intense communication with BP.' Willy's idea about corporate trust funds, on further investigation, turns out to have come straight from the oil company, who use the same model elsewhere. I ask him if he sees a conflict of interest. 'No,' he says simply.

Some Papuans are already beginning to get uneasy about this sort of talk; and I have heard all this somewhere before. I arrived in West Papua from Johannesburg, where I had asked the ANC government why their plans for national reconstruction had crumbled before the might of the market. Now, here, I can already see the corporations that control the Papuans' destiny hedging their bets; trying, it seems, to gain a hold over those who might one day have the power, and the popular support, to hem them in, control them, even expel them. It is a sobering sight. Unseen, yet-to-be power is gathering itself around Willy and his friends in the Presidium like gnats around a twilight brook. Will they be able to handle it, or will they be sucked in, as so many others were before them?

It could be, of course, that I'm getting carried away. Perhaps BP is just trying to help; engaging in 'stakeholder dialogue', as the latest business jargon has it. But John Rumbiak doesn't think so. Rumbiak is head of ELS-HAM, a leading Papuan human rights group, and he is worried about corporate involvement in the Papuan struggle.

'My strong critique of the Presidium,' he told me, when I spoke to him after meeting Mandowen, 'is that if you don't have very clear values – what you are fighting for and against – you're going to repeat the same mistakes once you have your own state. In many ways this struggle is not against the Indonesians, it is against a system and its values. Replace the Indonesians who run that system with Papuans, without changing the system and the values, and you have the same problem.'

Rumbiak doesn't like what the Presidium – so early in its life – is getting itself into. 'What worries me,' he said, 'is the naïveté of some of my Papuan brothers. They don't know the track record of these companies, or what they want. Recently, I spent two hours in London with John Browne [BP's Chief Executive]. He said to me, "Of course we have done things wrong in Colombia and other places, but we don't want to do the same in West Papua. We want to be good neighbours." And I said, come on – you're not a humanitarian organisation, you're not a church, you're a business. You want the gas, you want money money money. You have a culture of money and our culture is different.'

In West Papua, the presence of corporations, the way they operate, their disregard for the people they affect and the 'culture of money' they bring in are crucial in fomenting resistance both to what they do, and to what they stand for. It's one thing to know this, though: it's quite another to see it with your own eyes.

Walter Goodfellow was the sort of explorer that only the British could produce. He arrived in West Papua in 1910 to lead an expedition to its highest mountain. To get there, he and his right-hand man, Dr Alexander Wollaston, decided to plough on foot through the hundred miles of steaming swamp forest that separated the shore from the mountain ranges. With an army of 400 foreign guides and coolies who, like them, had never set foot on the island before, they met with obstacle upon obstacle as their underprepared and overburdened expedition trudged through the malarial mires.

'Heavens, how it rained!' wrote Wollaston, later, of the rainforest. 'Can this forest, with its horrible monotony and impregnability, be equalled by any other in the world?' After a few weeks of trudging through the horrible monotony of one of the richest ecosystems on Earth, trailed by a morose army of porters, Goodfellow died of malaria. His successor as expedition leader, Cecil Rawling, stumbled across some members of the local Ekagi tribe and, rather than asking them how to get to the mountains, decided instead to take them prisoner, announce that he had 'discovered' them, and christen them, for reasons best known to himself, 'Tapiro pigmies'.

When it became clear that they would not reach the mountains, the expedition turned back and sailed dejectedly for home, taking with it, as compensation, a collection of 'ethnographical objects' in the form of the corpses of hundreds of rare birds, mammals and reptiles.

Twenty-six years later, Dutch geologist Jean-Jacques Dozy did make it to the mountains, where he began sketching and taking samples of what he saw. He was intrigued by two vast, emphatic peaks, which he named 'Grasberg' and 'Ertsberg' – grass mountain and ore mountain. The latter, as the name suggested, appeared to be rich in copper ore.

Nobody thought any more of it until, in 1960, Forbes Wilson, a geologist from the New Orleans-based Freeport mining corporation, arrived in West Papua. He had come across Dozy's reports, and had persuaded his company to send him to this remote landscape to follow up an excited hunch. And what a hunch. In Ertsberg, Wilson confirmed what Dozy had only suspected – the largest above-ground copper deposit ever discovered.

One morning in 1960, Wilson's group of geologists emerged from their tents to find their camp surrounded by pointed sticks topped with skulls and snake skins. Taboo poles. The local Amungme people had visited them in the night. Nervously, they made their way down to the tribe's village to talk. They were met first with a hail of arrows and then, when a translator was hurriedly found, with a simple message: this is our land, this land is sacred, we do not want you here.

But the men from Freeport were pioneers, entrepreneurs. They weren't about to see their company's future hampered by savages. So they gave the tribal leaders a few metal axe heads, which they stared at in wonder, took some kids up for a spin in their helicopter and promised that any more white men who turned up would have plenty more such goodies for the Amungme to play with. It bought them the time they needed to find what they wanted. Then they went home. But they soon came back.

Fifty years separated the expedition of Wilson from the expedition of Goodfellow, but in many ways, nothing had changed at all.

The first thing you see when your unstable, rusty prop plane touches down at Timika airport, a few miles from the spot where Walter Goodfellow and his doomed expedition struck off into the swamps, is a giant sign above the 'arrivals lounge' (a hut) painted with a riot of national flags, celebrating the construction of the world's biggest copper and gold mine here by workers from two dozen nations. Forbes Wilson's dream has come true in West Papua – and more so. After his geologists reported their findings to Freeport headquarters in the early 1960s, the company began to talk to the likely new owners of the country in which Ertsberg nestled – Indonesia. In 1967, a full, and mysterious, two years before the Papuans officially 'decided' to become part of Indonesia, Freeport became the first foreign corporation to sign a contract with the Suharto regime.

It moved into West Papua and began mining Ertsberg in 1973. By 1988, by which time the black rock pillar had been reduced to a deep hole, Freeport's geologists made another discovery, which knocked even the metal miracle of Ertsberg into a cocked hat. The nearby Grasberg mountain contained the largest gold reserves, and the third-largest copper reserves, anywhere on the planet.

The story of what Freeport did – and continues to do – to the people and the environment around the Grasberg mine is emblematic of what the corporate invasion has done to the Papuans. The figures alone are staggering. In 2001, the Grasberg mine produced more gold in three months than most gold mines produce in a year. Every day, Freeport shifts 700,000 metric tonnes of rock: the equivalent of moving the Great Pyramid of Cheops every week. PT Freeport Indonesia – a subsidiary of the US-based multinational Freeport McMoran – provides a fifth of Indonesia's entire tax base and accounts for half of West Papua's GDP. In

2001, the pay of Freeport's chief executive, 'Jim Bob' Moffett, squeaked in at just under $7 million (not including an extra $4 million or so in stock options).[4]

Freeport Indonesia employs 9,000 workers, of whom at least three quarters are non-Papuans. The Indonesian government has requisitioned almost a million hectares of tribal ancestral land for the mine and its surroundings. Thousands of families have been 'resettled' without compensation to make way for the mine, which operates in an area of 3.6 million hectares, and uncounted numbers have been killed by Indonesian soldiers, paid by Freeport to guard the mine site from disgruntled locals. The company has violated, according to the mine-monitoring group Project Underground, at least eight of the human rights contained within the UN declaration of human rights. By the end of Grasberg's life, Freeport expects to have dumped three billion tons of waste rock into the valleys surrounding the mine – twice the volume of earth extracted during the construction of the Panama Canal. It has, according to observers, damaged 30,000 hectares of rainforest in the last three decades, and every day it dumps up to 200,000 tons of mine waste, laced with acid and heavy metals, into the sacred Aikwa river, from which local people used to drink and fish.[5]

It is facts like these which have made the Freeport mine the lodestone of Papua's struggle. Freeport – a corporation which the *Far Eastern Economic Review* has called 'the most maverick American multinational in the world today'[6] – is central to OPM resistance, central to the Papuans' resentment of corporate invasion and central to the clash of worldviews which the global market has brought to these people.

In the late 1980s, Timika was a nondescript village, home to a few hundred inhabitants. Today, it is the fastest-growing town in Indonesia, with a population of 110,000, less than a third of whom are Papuans. The result of this rapid urban explosion is depressingly apparent: Timika is a dump. It is a box grid of rubbish-strewn roads, black, greasy, open sewers, tin-roofed noodle bars, breeze-block hotels and chaotic rickshaw ranks. Most of the shops are

Indonesian; the Papuans are reduced to selling their bananas, durian fruit, melons and sweet potatoes from plastic sheets laid out by the roadside, next to grey pyramids of mine waste which are dumped, seemingly randomly, throughout the town. Packs of motorbikes hunt along the dirt roads, skidding to avoid dogs and schoolchildren, and belching black smoke into the dripping forty-degree heat.

Galile and I arrived at the airport with two friends we picked up in Jayapura: Gubay, a member of the Alliance of Papuan Students (AMP), a pro-independence group for the young, and Steve, a fellow Englishman working to raise the profile of the Papuan struggle back home. We soon found ourselves in the back of a jeep driven by four of Galile's 'family' – he had never met any of them before, but they were hugging and laughing like long-lost brothers in seconds – through verdant gardens to the door of one of the tin-roofed houses built by Freeport for its employees.

These four men are members of Demmak, which translates roughly as 'penis gourds assembly' and claims to be an umbrella group representing all the tribes of West Papua. Since it started in 1999, Demmak has made progress, particularly in persuading the Presidium to stick to its radical guns – partly by hinting darkly that it would be more than happy to take over the Presidium's role if it started to look like it was selling out the people. The Indonesians, sensing danger, have responded by banning it.

Demmak members, like OPM soldiers, are *persona non grata* to the Indonesian government, and, of course, to its friendly corporations. So it is with great pleasure that our hosts inform us that, not only are they in contact with Freeport employees who can get us, undercover, into the mine, but that they can arrange a clandestine meeting with an OPM guerrilla who would usually rather kidnap journalists than answer their questions. With any luck, they may even be able to persuade him to come to us.

Six o'clock the next morning, and we are ricocheting around the interior of a Freeport jeep like jumping beans in a tin can, being driven up bone-shaking, foggy mountain roads towards the mine. Freeport's Grasberg site is a miracle of engineering, built with pioneering techniques and technologies in one of the most inaccessible places on Earth. The mine itself – the open-cast hole that used to be the Grasberg mountain – is one of the biggest in industrial history, a place with a kind of arrogant, awesome beauty.

To the Papuans, though, there is no beauty here. What Freeport didn't know when they first arrived in West Papua – and what they later learned but ignored – was that the mountain they called 'Grasberg' was a holy site for the local Amungme tribe. Amungme mythology tells of a woman who sacrificed herself in the midst of a famine to save the lives of her children. She asked them to kill her, to cut up her body, to throw her head to the north, the right side of her body to the east and the left side to the west, and to cast her feet south towards the river. The next day, the children awoke to find a great mountain – Grasberg – where their mother's head had been. Where they had thrown her body and feet they found gardens full of fruit and broad expanses of hunting land. Today, the remaining Amungme still live on what they see as their mother's torso – the place nearest her milk, where children can sleep in her lap and where her people can be comforted by her embrace.

To Freeport, the mining of Grasberg is a miracle of modern technology. To the Amungme, it is, quite literally, the slicing off of their mother's head, and the spiritual equivalent of drilling for oil under the altar of St Peter's.

On the way to the mine, we stop in at Kuala Kencana, the model town which Freeport has built for its employees and their families, at a cost of $500 million. It is the most surreal sight in West Papua. Smooth lawns, a great church, a mosque, libraries, a shopping mall, gyms and acre upon acre of housing, have all been carved out of virgin rainforest and filled with clean-shaven consumers, wandering around in trainers with plastic shopping bags. Suburban America has come to tribal New Guinea. We drive down a road which reminds me of California; all curved drive-ways, square pastel houses, post boxes, litter bins, hosepipes (in a rainforest?).

Kuala Kencana's crowning glory is its shopping mall, built, with no sense of incongruity, on the former hunting grounds of the Komoro tribe. Hemmed in on all sides by tall, elegant rainforest trees, its supermarket is a halogen-lit, buzzing hive of activity: trolleys, carrier bags, checkouts, bleeping barcode scanners, piped music and American-style uniforms. Blink, and you could be in Texas. Galile, who has never been here before, looks slightly ill; there is a look on his face which speaks of wonder mixed with dis-taste. Steve is laughing out loud at the absurdity of it all, and getting some odd looks from the happy shoppers.

There is no doubt that Freeport is proud of Kuala Kencana. The company points out that its employees here get clean, spacious homes, running water, regular wages, shops, gyms, health care and schooling. There is no doubt, too, that the few thousand people who live in Kuala Kencana (of whom most, like the major-ity of the people Freeport employs, are Indonesian) enjoy a materially richer life than most Papuans. But even leaving aside the fact that this has only been provided for a select few, by means of mass dispossession and environmental vandalism, the Freeport model of 'development' bears closer examination. It tells us a lot about the assumptions on which the wider globalisation project is built.

For the company's attempts to provide for their workers and some of the local people are culturally loaded with heavy ammu-nition. For the men (and the few women) of this very American company, 'development' is about providing a carbon copy of the Land of the Free for the lucky people of less enlightened nations. This is not simply a matter of the design of the houses and the clothes people wear; it's also about the worldview that comes with it. A worldview that ensures that even when Freeport do try their hand at a bit of 'community development' they tend to make a hash of it.

One example: pigs. Pigs are central to Papuan highland culture. In every village, pigs mingle with the people and are killed and eaten only on special occasions such as a war feast or the return of a long-lost family member. If a man wants to marry, his fiancée's family will expect to receive ten pigs as a dowry. If one tribe messes with another tribe's pigs, the men will paint themselves for battle. Pigs are central to war, marriage, status and wealth. It's even possible to pay for a plane ticket in the remoter highland areas with a couple of good pigs.

Freeport, though, didn't like the Papuans' pigs. Not only were they smelly and flea-ridden, they were also distressingly inefficient. So after rebuilding some Papuan villages with nice, square tin-roofed houses, rather than the traditional but 'scruffy' round, thatched huts, they decided to help the Papuans with their pig problem. In one village, Banti, they built a pig shed on the outskirts, rounded up the animals and locked them into it. In other places, they exiled the small, black, bristly indigenous pigs altogether and imported fatter, faster-growing, pink American animals ('not as tasty', grumbled one local villager to me). In one fell swoop they had knocked away the central pillar of Papuan village culture – one which had stood for centuries. It took the hurt corporation a long time to work out why their kindness had not been received with the gratitude they expected.

Across the world, the cultural conflicts engendered when multinational corporations meet traditional peoples, who simply do not think the same way, often give birth to physical conflicts as the people resist both economic and cultural colonialism. This is what Freeport has brought to West Papua, and it is far from unique. In Indonesia alone, half of the country's international mining operations were shut down, destroyed or evacuated as a result of community resistance between 1999 and 2001.[7]

This is, to reheat an overcooked phrase, a genuine clash of civilisations, and, while it is not unique to West Papua, it has led the people here to question, and begin to rethink, the whole concept of 'development'.

'Development' is now an idea so ubiquitous that it is rarely, if ever, questioned – to question it is to be against the poor, against progress, against the future. In fact, 'development' is a late arrival in human history. It wasn't until 1949 that US President Harry Truman decided that the world could be divided up into 'developed' – Western, industrialised, consumerist – and 'underdeveloped' areas – everywhere else, where 'greater production is the key to prosperity and peace'.[8] At a stroke, Truman had decreed that the purpose of progress and the aim of history was for every civilisation in the world to become like the West. The world has never looked back.

In theory, this 'development' should be about improving the material standard of living of everyone on Earth – providing them with enough to eat, clean water, health care and all the rest, and dragging them from the slums which the expansion of industrial capitalism had itself dumped them in. In practice, it has often amounted, in the words of American historian Emily Rosenberg, to a deeply ideological project which uses 'the rhetoric of peace, prosperity, and democracy to promote Americanising the world in the name of modernisation'.[9] In short, turning 'them' into 'us'. Coincidentally, this is not a million miles away from the Victorian notion of the White Man's Burden – the moral duty of the advanced races to help lift the savages out of the dirt.

It rarely looks like this to its promoters, of course, but whatever the truth, the Papuans want a rethink of what 'development' means before they decide that they will meekly adopt it as their national *raison d'être*. Why, say many, should they follow the path which the powerful define as 'developed'? Why should they allow rich nations to snatch their resources at bargain prices, use them as cheap labour, set their terms of trade, guide them on a path of the West's choosing? Why can they themselves not define what 'progress' is?

'We refuse any kinds of development,' say the OPM, at the extreme of the debate; 'religious groups, aid agencies or governmental organisations. Just leave us alone please!' While others are not so isolationist, Papuan resistance is increasingly defined by a determination to re-think the model of top-down, industrial urban 'development' that has long been a sacred cow of both left and right. It is a re-think that is going on all over the world.

We drive on, up between the grey crags, past power plants, pylons, a steel workshop, a vocational training centre. We also pass a military base. When Freeport moved into the region in the late 1960s, Suharto sent his troops to help them secure what they needed. Under Indonesian law, tribal land could be seized by the government, with no compensation, in the name of national development. Almost a million hectares of ancestral lands were requisitioned for the Freeport mine and surrounding developments, and in order to prevent any of the uppity locals from trying to get it back again, Suharto sent in the army.

Today, Timika is the most militarised region in Indonesia, and ever since the Indonesian invasion, military atrocities have been regular and sickening. In the past, the military have strafed mountain villages from British-built Hawk jets, napalmed the highlands, dropped suspected separatists from helicopters back on to their villages as a warning to their people and, just a year before my visit, thrown them from warships to the sharks in the Pacific. In that same year, 2000, Wamena, the tiny capital of the highlands, descended into war when armed police attacked the Papuans for raising the Morning Star. Nearly forty died, and ninety were injured. Galile found himself in the local hospital, sewing limbs back on to Papuans whom doctors had refused to treat.

But while the soldiers in West Papua are ruthless in defence of their motherland, they are equally determined when it comes to protecting the interests of multinational corporations. One reason is clear: the soldiers are keen to supplement their meagre pay with handouts of corporate cash – or 'off-budget funding' as it is more professionally known. Thus it is that, according to an academic expert on the Indonesian military – herself later arrested and imprisoned by Indonesia for researching another separatist revolt in the province of Aceh – Freeport has paid the military in Timika a lump sum of $35 million, with promises of a further annual bonus of $11 million, in exchange for 'security' around the Grasberg site. It has been estimated that at least a third of this money has gone straight into the pockets of the top brass.[10]

According to a candid source within the Indonesian government, this 'security' regularly involves deliberately inciting community anger around the mine, thus providing an excellent excuse to quell it with violence.[11] Often, such violence has the added bonus of providing entertainment for the bored troops. One ex-Freeport employee reported that soldiers around the mine would 'shoot tribals for sport and get pictures of themselves resting a foot on the chest or head of the kill, like trophy hunters'.[12]

If ever there were a military–industrial complex, this is it. Yet Freeport is not alone. Abuses like those in and around Grasberg can be found at mines, dam sites, logging concessions and oil patches all across the 'developing' world; they are the true price of the copper in our electric wires and the gold around our necks. This is the side of the system that we are not supposed to see, and with good reason. For the wheels that keep the global market rolling are often oiled with blood.

An hour or so further on, high up in the mountains, we round a corner and see ahead of us, framed by weeping rocks, Freeport's final mega-development: Tembagapura – 'Copper Town'. A squat, grey collection of high-rise blocks, machinery sheds, workshops, bars and not much else, Tembagapura is where the mine's manual workers live during their shifts. Hunched below the corpse of Grasberg, it looks like a particularly grim Soviet township somewhere in deepest Siberia.

But Tembagapura, to everyone's frustration, is to be the end of our journey. We stop there to pick up some food, and when we pile back into the jeep it has decided to give up the ghost. Two hours of pushing it up and down slopes, poking around beneath the bonnet and making futile calls on walkie-talkies get us nowhere. It's dead, and we're not going to make it to the pit. Steve and I are horribly disappointed.

We spend the rest of the day in Tembagapura, in the room of a Demmak miner, lounging on dirty bunkbeds watching American films on satellite TV with a gang of bored pit men. In the evening, we catch a miners' bus back down to Timika. Like so many others before, Grasberg has seen us off.

The next day, there is compensation. We are sitting in the Demmak gang's kitchen, eating bananas and rice for breakfast, when a message arrives from the forests: the OPM will see us. A thrill shivers through the room. It is rare for the guerrillas to talk to outsiders. We will be meeting, we are told, the 'operational commander' of the Timika branch of the TPN – the OPM's armed wing. His name is Goliar Tabuni, he is the rebels' chief military strategist for the region and he has seen, in his decades as a forest outlaw, his fair share of action. His most recent kidnapping was in June 2001, when two Belgian journalists were snatched. In return for their release, the OPM wanted an international platform to demand freedom for West Papua. They didn't get one, because nobody paid the slightest bit of attention to them. So they released the Belgians anyway, unharmed.

Sadly for the OPM, most of its sorties are similarly fruitless. Goliar Tabuni's ramshackle army have launched numerous kidnappings, attacks on army bases and raids against the Freeport mine, and have always been met with crackdowns by Indonesian troops. Their most successful attempt to shut down Freeport was in 1977, when the OPM sliced through the mine's slurry pipeline and briefly shut down the site. The government responded by strafing highland villages with warplanes, and torturing and killings thousands of suspected OPM supporters all across the highlands.

It might seem that the OPM are alone in such actions: a small bunch of extremists (there are no figures, but there seem to be a few thousand guerrillas at most) roaming the woods with stone age weapons. But the professed support for their actions by the Papuans is almost total. In and around Timika, such support may be spurred on by the fact that the idea of Papuans driving out a mining company that is destroying their lives is not an impossible dream. In fact, it has been done.

The nearby island of Bougainville, owned by Papua New Guinea, contains a copper reserve almost as big as that of Grasberg – the Panguna copper mine. Like Grasberg, this deposit was turned over in the 1960s to a multinational mining company – in this case, Rio Tinto – without the permission of the tribal people who actually owned the land. Like Grasberg, the mining company was supported by troops, and the environment and the local culture were ravaged.

Unlike Grasberg – so far, anyway – the tribes fought back, and won. In 1988, locals rose up against the miners, storming the mine and blowing up its equipment with the company's own dynamite. The Papua New Guinea army was sent in, and soon driven out again by the tribes. The Australians – the Rio Tinto subsidiary which owned the mine is an Australian company – arrived to help with soldiers and gunships, and the conflict escalated into civil war, with the Bougainvilleans declaring independence from PNG. Almost a decade later, in 1998, a peace agreement was reached, and negotiations began on independence. The miners have gone, probably for good. The OPM looks on in awe.

I was rather hoping for a dangerous and clandestine trek into the forests to meet the OPM in their jungle camp, but it seems the guerrillas will not be indulging my fantasy heroics. Goliar and his men will be coming to us – 'too dangerous for you', says one of our hosts. Too dangerous, more importantly, for the guerrillas, who are some of the most wanted men in Indonesia.

They are also, apparently, superheroes.

'Goliar,' says one of our hosts, with a very straight face, 'is seven foot tall. He has a very big beard – big like *this*' – he stretches his arms out on either side of him, to full length. 'When you see him your hair will stand on end.'

'It's true!' says another. 'He has done many magical things. Once the Indonesians put him in prison, and he escaped by slipping through the bars. Then he flew back on a plane, but the Indonesians couldn't see him, because he made himself invisible.'

'He can walk across the whole country in two days.'

'He flies!'

'No, he walks on the leaves of the trees. Nobody can see him!'

'He is a magic man!'

I look at Steve, who is translating all this for me.

'Are they having us on?'

'No, they mean it. They seem to believe it – well, maybe not all of it, but they believe the OPM have special powers.' I discover later that this belief is widespread. Trained OPM soldiers are said to have the spirits of the forest fighting on their side. Indeed, nature itself is often an ally – mosquitoes and snakes, say the Papuans, will bite the OPM's enemies but not the guerrillas. She-demons of the forest tempt Indonesians into the trees and kill them. Even some of the Indonesian soldiers believe in the unearthly powers of people like Goliar Tabuni.

They arrive after dark. Two jeeps pull up outside, their headlights causing a flock of birds to rise, squawking, from the orange trees. Our hosts scamper around the lounge, arranging chairs, preparing coffee, straightening the rugs.

'When they come in,' says Steve, 'we all have to stand and shake their hands and be very serious. It's like meeting the Queen.'

Outside, car doors slam, and we all stand, expectantly. And then, they come. From the forests, their feet bare, their hair wild, their clothes torn and caked with dust, three figures pad up the porch steps and through the screen door towards us. Past a shelf full of fake Wedgwood china plates, past family photographs, past cheap sofas covered in cheap chintz, they come. We smile, in a serious kind of way, as they move along the line shaking hands, then sit down on three plastic chairs lined up for them directly below a framed photograph of two sickeningly cute kittens in a wicker basket.

None of them are seven feet tall, after all. Like most Papuans, in fact, they are all about five foot in height, and their beards are pretty standard. Goliar Tabuni has a deeply lined face, cut-off denim shorts and bare feet with angled toes that look anything but human. His neck, biceps and wrists are strung with coloured beads. He wears a Freeport T-shirt. There is a wary intensity in his eyes as he scans the two white boys facing him – not unfriendly, but questioning.

On Goliar's right, in a filthy MTV T-shirt, identical shorts, even more beads, conch shells and bracelets and with a broad headband pushing his dreadlocks back from his face, sits his deputy, who barely says a word all evening. On his left sits a deep-black man-mountain, a major, we are told, who glowers at us from under the brim of a wide green hat as he leans, wordlessly, on an enormous axe. A two-foot knife of cassowary bone is strapped to his right bicep. I decide to ask my questions politely.

Introductions are made, names are named, and we get down to business, as our visitors explain to us what they are doing with their lives, and why.

'We,' says Goliar, grandly, 'fight for freedom. Nothing else. There is nothing else. Some people ask us why we fight, and we say, what else can we do? Yes, there are other ways – diplomacy is important, but fighting is important too. The Indonesians come here and they see that our land is sweet, like milk, and they want it for themselves. They have not been interested in diplomacy, they have taken our land and killed our people. And so, we fight.'

This seems reasonable. In any case, I am not here to argue, especially not with the man-mountain fingering his axe blade six feet from my nose. But I do want to know how they keep it up. It all seems so – well, hopeless.

'We are a strong people,' says Goliar. 'Our food and our culture make us strong. We will not give up. But I will tell you something, my English friends. We need weapons. We have so little. I will show you something.' From a knitted, rainbow shoulder bag, he pulls what looks like a Second World War revolver. Its barrel is stuffed with a red handkerchief. He waves it around, disconcertingly.

'This,' Goliar announces, 'is our only gun! This is all. I have been in the forests for twenty years. Shall I tell you how many Indonesians I have killed? I have killed 3,606 – with axes, spears, knives, arrows – and this. With one bullet, I can kill eight people. All Indonesia knows how dangerous I am! But it is not enough.' It sounds more than enough to me, but the major and the deputy are nodding their assent as Goliar leans towards us, conspiratorially.

'We want to know,' he says, 'what you activists are doing in England. Can't you get us guns? We don't need many. Get us some guns, and we will drive these Indonesians and these corporations out of here.'

Steve and I exchange looks.

'I have seen a film!' announces Goliar. This seems startlingly unlikely. 'Yes, a film. This man, Rambo. He has these arrows which he can set on fire. Have you seen these things? We want those!' There is general assent from the military command on this point. The major's eyes light up excitedly.

'We all agree,' continues Goliar, 'that England has the best weapons. On the television, we have seen you killing these people in Afghanistan. You have planes that can hover. We want those, and we want to know if you can get them for us. We have come to ask you for help.'

Everyone is sitting around the visitors in a circle on the floor, listening to the conversation in awe. The air in the room is hot and heavy, tropical rain is crashing down on to the red tin roof, huge rats are pounding across the flimsy ceiling panels at regular intervals, choirs of tree frogs are chorusing wildly in the trees outside. And we are being asked to be gun runners.

There is a short pause.

'Er,' says Steve. 'Well, we're not fighters. We don't know where to get guns. But we can try and tell people in England what is happening in Papua, which we hope will help you to get free. We think that if the world learns what is happening here they might begin to help you.'

Goliar sniffs, to hide his disappointment. The major sits back in his chair, sighing sadly, and I feel suddenly guilty. These bedraggled warriors have walked for miles to beg from people they have never even met. They have spent twenty years in the woods fighting a genocidal modern army with sticks and stones. It all seems so futile. Maybe if I just had a few teeny guns to give them . . .

Further discussion of the armaments issue is curtailed when a boy carries in, from the kitchen, a tea tray loaded with sugared doughnuts, china cups, sugar, milk and a blue teapot, containing coffee. Everyone helps themselves – the guerrillas with a delicacy of touch that suggests a finishing-school education. The three wanted outlaws sit delicately sipping coffee from china cups under a picture of a pair of Athena kittens. They seem to be enjoying the doughnuts.

We don't have much time left, so we ask them about the corporations in West Papua. What does the OPM think of them, and what should be done? Goliar's answer is bracingly unsophisticated.

'Corporations?' he says. 'If we can, we will kill them. The OPM has already said this: we want no more companies here. We have already warned these people to go. Why should these corporations be able to come here and take our land and our resources? Freeport are killers. If we could, we would close them down. When we get free, we will. The OPM will be making decisions about these things. We will be the government. We will make the choices. If I want you in the government, Mr Paul' – he points at me – 'I will put you in the government.' I'm flattered. The major grins impishly at me from under his hat. He has doughnut sugar all over his beard.

Really? I say. But what about the Presidium?

'The Presidium,' sniffs Goliar, 'have never given us anything. In our culture, if you have food, you share it with everyone. The Presidium are the sort of people who keep their food to themselves.' In Papua, this is a serious insult. 'We have no cars, no guns, no money,' Goliar says. 'The Presidium have all the money they need. They are not pure, or where would they get it from?'

Steve and I exchange looks again. Then we tell them that the Presidium's funding comes from the very corporations that the

OPM apparently wants to drive into the sea. Goliar's eyebrows raise, very slowly.

'These companies,' he says, deliberately. 'Who are they? When we get free, we must get free from them too. Freedom is not just about Indonesia. I have heard that there are people in other countries now who say this too – that these corporations must go. I have heard there are many people in the world now fighting these corporations. Well, the OPM have always said this, and we will fight with them. Freedom for us from these people of money who destroy our land. That is all.'

There is more talk, there are group photos (the guerrillas grin like children when Steve shows them their own images on his digital camera) and then, Goliar and his men have to leave. Before they do, he pours himself another coffee and addresses us.

'I knew you were coming to Timika,' he says. 'I could see you in the plane overhead. I knew that you wanted to see me, and so I came to you. There was no need for anyone to ask me.'

The room has gone very quiet.

'If I wanted,' he goes on, 'I could be in Papua New Guinea tomorrow. You may have heard about my abilities. It is all true. The forest gives them to me, and they are secret. Not even my brothers here know' – he indicates the two desperadoes polishing off the doughnuts on either side of him. 'When my time comes, I will pass these secrets on. But not yet. You must know this: we Papuans – we are not like everyone else.'

Silence rings like a morning bell for a long five seconds. Then the rebels rise. They are heading back to the forest. On his way to the door, Goliar glances down at the tray and sees that someone has left the lid off the teapot. Neatly, he drops it back into place with his thumb and forefinger. He smiles.

'Goodbye, my friends,' he says. 'You will come back.'

The next day we say goodbye to our Demmak friends, and catch a plane out of Timika. I have less than a week left in the country, and Galile wants to take Steve and I into the interior – to see 'the real Papua'. He is going to take us to his highland village – his true home. It is to be an unforgettable experience.

Galile's village is in the remote, forested highlands, a two-day walk from the nearest track. With a procession of family and friends in tow, we strike off into the forest. We climb gentle, forested hills, to the hooting of hornbills and – occasionally – birds of paradise. We ford wide, shallow rivers, rip our clothes on thorns, strip off and plunge into crystal rock pools when the heat gets too much. We stop to swing on low-hanging vines, howling like Tarzan and praying for them to hold. We trek past trees with trunks like cathedral columns, their branches reaching in supplication to the heights of epic rocky gorges.

We slap at mosquitoes, and pick hopeful leeches off our boots at ten-minute intervals (the barefoot Papuans slice them off their feet with machetes). We are given sweet potatoes by women who pass us on tiny jungle paths, bowing as they walk under the weight of packed string bags. Great grey and green peaks, sheathed in mist, reveal themselves to us through breaks in the forest cover – the spine of New Guinea, rolling on towards an unseen sea. Crickets, cicadas, frogs and an orchestra of birds sing us to our destination.

We stop overnight in a tiny clutch of *honay* on the banks of a river guttering through a wide green gorge, and the next day are escorted to our destination by men from the settlement, their bows and arrows and spears on their shoulders. They keep our spirits up with home-grown tobacco leaves, sweet potatoes – *erom*, as they are known to the highlanders – and boiled water. When we reach breaks in the forest cover, the men line up and sing to the mountains, the trees and the spirits that inhabit them. Their ancient chorus of celebration and worship merges with the mountain winds. Galile looks at Steve and I, smiling wildly in the highland air.

'This,' he says, 'is what we fight for!'

We reach Galile's village late in the day. He has warned us that we will be greeted with a welcoming ceremony – and we are. Afterwards, the pig roasting in the earth oven, Galile and I stand in the centre of a clutch of *honay* and watch the last wisps of twilight being drawn into the dark forests, gazing in awe at a rainbow halo around a great, full moon. The sky is pinpricked with stars from horizon to horizon. I have never seen anything like it.

Eventually, the pig comes. Sitting in a Galile's father's *honay*, steaming meat laid out on banana leaves on the floor, Galile and I are eating and talking. Galile is in thoughtful mood as he gnaws on a pig bone. The light of a single candle is patchworking the four people in the *honay* with us. I am having trouble with the more unsavoury bits of my pig, but Galile has no such qualms.

'I want to know, Paul,' he says, slurping the marrow out of a thigh bone, 'what you think about this. Our culture, I think, is special, and I think we must fight for it. You think so? I think it very different to other cultures but I have not been out of Papua. I think we must keep this culture.'

'I think you should, too.'

'Papuan culture very different to English culture?' he asks.

'Well, yes, you could say that. You know, Galile, I think the important thing is for you all to get a real picture of what the West is like. This stuff you see on the films — we don't really live like that. You have to get both sides of the story before you decide how you want to run your country.'

'What do you mean?'

'Well, I mean that you have to know what it will cost you. Everything has a price. You could gain many things if you wanted to try to live like us, but you'd lose a lot of what you have. You can't do both. Listen, just one example: there are about seven million people unemployed in America.'

'Pheeew!' His eyes widen.

'And something like two million without homes.'

'Without homes? What you mean without homes? Where do they sleep?'

'They sleep on the streets. And they eat rubbish, from bins.'

Galile is speechless. He has lost all interest in the rest of the pig; an indication of the seriousness of the subject.

'But I think everyone in America and England is rich!' he says. 'Everyone has cars, jobs, big houses, much money . . .'

'Well, they don't. And listen – something else: no land. I can't even afford to buy a house where I live.'

'But my family have three houses.'

'If I wanted to buy a house the size of yours in England, guess how much it would cost me.'

'How much?'

I wish I had a calculator. 'Maybe about three billion rupiah.'

Galile nearly faints into the fire. A toothless, topless old man sitting across from us grins through the flames and waves his rolled tobacco leaves at us to indicate that he hasn't got a clue what we're talking about but he's enjoying listening to it anyway.

'Paul,' says Galile, very seriously, 'I want to know why you live like this.'

'That's just the way it is. We have plenty of things you don't have, which a lot of people in Papua probably want. But some of the things we have you're lucky not to have. If you want to live like us, you'll have to have some of them, and things will change a lot. It's a kind of cost–benefit thing, I suppose.'

'What else you have?' he asks, sounding as if he doesn't want to know.

So I tell him about old people's homes and rehab clinics, Prozac and cardboard cities, motorways and climate change, genetic engineering and landfill sites. He looks as if I'm having him on. I'm beginning to feel cruel. But I have to tell him one last thing.

'Do you want to know something else?'

Galile steels himself.

'Our pigs live in factories.'

'*Factories?*' This is the killer blow. Had Galile been sitting on a chair, and not on the grass-strewn floor, he would, at this point, have fallen off it.

'Why?' he pleads.

'Because it makes economic sense. It makes them cheaper to buy. So do the chickens and the ducks.'

There is a tingling silence, broken only by the contended slurping of the village dogs gnawing on bones outside.

'Now my head is spinning,' says Galile, slowly. 'They never tell us *any* of this.' He looks at the dejected remains of the pig, but his mind is elsewhere.

'Right,' he says.

In my six weeks in West Papua I met a lot of people like Galile: wide-eyed, open, ill-informed about the modern world and, despite having every reason to be otherwise, instinctively trustful of strangers. The Papuans are a strangely beautiful people: they will take you under their wing with little or no introduction; invite you into their house, sit with you silently, smiling at the world and doing nothing in particular. Their conception of time, work, purpose, life and society is so different from that of the modern world that it's sometimes difficult to cope with. Naïveté, or perhaps innocence, is part of what makes them who they are. But innocence should not be confused with ineffectiveness. For what the Papuans lack in guile, they make up for in determination. And until they are free, they will never give up. This is the other national trait that I saw everywhere I went: a quiet, fierce obsession with 'getting free'. Ask a Papuan when they will be free and they won't be able to answer: ask them *if* they'll be free and the answer never varies. And this, despite the OPM's stone-age weapons, despite the Indonesians and their brutal repression, despite the world's ignorance of this most forgotten of struggles, is what gives me hope. 'Papua is the next East Timor,' Amunggur told me several times. I think he might be right; I think that the Papuans will be free, and I think that when they are they will want more than their own nation-state made over in the world's image. They will want their own, Papuan, future, built on their own values, rejecting much of the pain that globalisation has already brought them, following their own path, defining their own 'development'. They will want the Papua that all of them keep alive every day inside their heads and hearts. Their time will come.

PART 2

many yeses

'The storm is here. From the clash of these two winds a storm will be born. Its time has arrived. Now the wind from above rules, but the wind from below is coming . . . When the storm calms, when rain and fire again leave the country in peace, the world will no longer be the world, but something better.'

SUBCOMANDANTE MARCOS, 1994

6   the end of the beginning

'I know what they're against but I have no sense of what they're for.'

TREVOR MANUEL, SOUTH AFRICAN FINANCE MINISTER, CONFUSED BY THE MOVEMENT, 2000

'Bad capitalist! No martini!'

BANNER, WORLD SOCIAL FORUM, 2002

It's too much. I can't decide, and I can't take it any more. I can hardly move, in any direction, and I need to sit down. The high entrance chamber of the university building is rippling with thousands of souls from hundreds of countries; a vast, heaving, multicultural, multicoloured fire hazard, and all going somewhere. All except me. I had been planning to go to a conference, in one of the large lecture halls, on 'financial capital control'. It doesn't sound thrilling, but it does sound important. At the same time, though, in another hall, is another conference, on transnational corporations, which sounds good too. And another, somewhere else, on international trade. Then there are the seminars. A group of landless farmers are holding a session on 'food sovereignty and trade' at the same time as several groups of campaigners are holding one on 'ending global apartheid: dismantling the World Bank and the IMF'. There's one on biodiversity, another on participatory budgeting and another on activist tactics.

All this, of course, is before I even consider the workshops – hundreds of them, all at the same time, often miles apart. There are at least seven I want to go to this morning: one on public services, another on education, one on 'new social movements', another on 'culture and globalisation', one on sustainable agriculture, another on radical democracy, one on abolishing the WTO . . .

It takes me a good five minutes to stagger through the throng and heave myself into the sunshine outside the building. I weave my way past a puppet show and an Amazonian Indian handing out leaflets, negotiate myself a cup of coffee with my three words of Portuguese and slump down on the grass, overwhelmed. It's nine in the morning and I already want to go to bed. But there's no time for that. Like the 60,000 other people who surround me, I'm here to change the world, and I've only got a week to do it.

There comes a time in every activist's life when he or she has to answer a question. After the elation and emotion has died down and the tear-gas wafted away; after arguments have been repeated a dozen times over, and campaigns have been kicked off against the aspects of globalisation that they object to – from the erosion of democracy to over-consumption, from environmental destruction to privatisation, from corporate power to colonialist development models – there comes a point when the question becomes unavoidable. *Fine*, it runs, *I know what you're against, but what are you* for?

Put that way, the question is hard to answer, because put that way it assumes the existence of precisely what so many activists are so keen to stave off – one way, one plan, one manifesto, one Big Idea. Nevertheless, it's an important question. It's important because, unless activists can begin to answer it, they're going to have a lot of trouble explaining to the rest of the world what they're up to and what they're after – and if they can't explain it to others, chances are they probably don't know themselves.

Critics of the movement have, for some time now, assumed that it is incapable of answering this question. It is incapable because its ranks consist of a grim alliance of lank-haired soap dodgers, ill-informed if well-intentioned liberals, malicious lefty ideologues, protectionist reactionaries and fearful Luddites, all of them based in the West and all of them with too much time on their hands. They don't know what they're for, because they're not for anything; they're just against anything that scares them, even if they're not sure why. In his recent globalisers' manifesto *Open World*, former WTO employee Philippe Legrain exemplifies this line of 'thinking', railing at 'college kids who have rarely ventured beyond their middle-class suburbs' talking 'arrant nonsense' about a global economy they don't understand and have no alternatives to.[1] 'The protest coalition,' declares *The Economist*, singing from the same hymn sheet, 'can hang together only if it continues to avoid thinking about what it might be in favour of.'[2] This song is sung so often in the Church of Global Capitalism that the choirboys are beginning to lose their voices.

I hope that Part 1 of this book has helped torpedo one of the most widespread myths about this movement – the suggestion that, as the former Deputy Managing Director of the IMF, Stanley Fischer, puts it, 'The critics of globalisation come mostly from the rich countries.'[3] With any luck, Part 2 will help shoot down this second piece of misinformation – one which is extremely helpful to those beneficiaries of the status quo who propagate it so widely. The myth that the movement has no answers, no alternatives – nowhere to go from here.

As I'm rapidly finding out, the truth is, if anything, at the other extreme. It is January 2002 and I have come, with those 60,000 other people, to the Atlantic city of Porto Alegre, the Gaucho capital of southern Brazil. It is the second World Social Forum, and for six days all of us here will be dedicating ourselves to answering that all-important question: what *are* we for?

Just two days in, though, exhausted, sipping my coffee to keep myself going, the mêlée of activity that is the World Social Forum is assaulting my senses. The whole event is as exciting as it is overwhelming – and occasionally frustrating – and I am beginning to think, treasonably, that far from not having any alternatives, this movement has too many of them.

All around me, people, organisations, ideas and realities are rubbing shoulders on a grand scale. US unions mingle with African fisherfolk, Japanese economists, Brazilian artists, Ecuadorian landless people, Israeli peace campaigners, Nicaraguan intellectuals, French debt campaigners, European politicians. From 8 A.M. until late every evening meeting halls, 3,000-seat lecture theatres, tent cities, stages, classrooms, gyms and churches all over the city are filled with thinkers, rebels, dissidents and dreamers. A 155-page programme, the size of a thick tabloid newspaper, lists everything that is going on – you can hardly get through it in the week available. The ideas, the theories, the proposals and the programmes are coming thick and fast: too fast to keep up with, and too thick to get my head around. It's tough just keeping up.

The World Social Forum is still young and still bold, and is unlike any other international event around. It was conceived in the late 1990s, when a group of Brazilian activists decided that the movement they could see rising around them needed somewhere it could come together and hammer out its own agenda. With the support of others in France, a coalition of Brazilian unions, debt campaigners, peace activists, economists and landless farmers got together to make it happen. The government of Porto Alegre, run for a decade by the left-wing Workers' Party (PT), agreed to host the gathering, and in January 2001, the World Social Forum was born. The organisers expected about 2,000 people; 12,000 came.

There was a symbolic reason both for the gathering's name and its dates. It was, and is, held at the same time as the annual World Economic Forum in Davos, Switzerland. The WEF, a private corporation set up in 1971 to bring the world's power elite together, makes the G8 look like a model of openness. Funded and run by 1,000 of the world's biggest corporations (to qualify for this honour, a company must have an annual turnover of at least a million dollars, and pay a membership fee of around $15,000) attendance is by exclusive invitation only. Its winning combination of corporate big cheeses, leading politicians, 'thinkers', important media players and a handpicked, well-behaved and tiny clutch of 'civil society representatives' spend a week in the stunning surroundings of the Swiss Alps, taking full advantage of what the WEF calls 'unique networking opportunities with other world leaders'.[4]

'Men of the same trade,' observed economist Adam Smith over 200 years ago, with timeless accuracy, 'seldom meet together even for merriment or diversion but their conversation ends in a conspiracy against the public.'[5] He could have been describing the World Economic Forum. For three decades now, those 'unique networking opportunities' have made Davos one of the most influential control centres of the neoliberal project.

The World Social Forum is a riposte to all this: not a protest against it, but an alternative forum, positing an alternative future; a conspiracy of a wholly different shade. This year, the World Economic Forum (theme: 'Leadership in Fragile Times') has switched its location, for the first time, from Davos to New York. The organisers say that this is in a spirit of 'solidarity' with the stricken city – a magnanimous gesture which also has the convenient effect of reducing the likelihood of the kind of vast demonstrations that besieged Davos's mountaintop retreat in 2001.

What is on display in Brazil is evidence of just how far this movement has come in one short year. The second World Social Forum is bigger, more complex, more sophisticated and more significant than the first, and is also proving something of a global inspiration. Already it has spawned a host of similar positive gatherings on several continents: wherever activists meet now you are likely to find a 'social forum' debating ways and means of changing the world. In the last year alone, a European Social Forum has been held in Italy, an African Social Forum in Ethiopia, and an Asian Social Forum in India. Mini forums have sprung up in Genoa, Monterrey in Mexico, Buenos Aires in Argentina, Durban in South Africa, Beirut in the Lebanon and in Washington and New York, with many more coming soon. They rarely garner the media attention that a good tear-gas and cobblestones punch-up with the police does – positive agendas don't make such good copy as 'violent protest' – but they are likely to define the future of this movement in a way that street showdowns like Seattle defined its past.

This year's event at Porto Alegre, like its predecessor, operates on principles I can almost recite by now with my eyes closed: opposition to 'the domination of the world by capital', the desire to build a world based on the principles of human rights, democracy and social justice, rather than on 'a process of globalisation commanded by large multinational corporations'; and a plurality of participation. This last point means, of course, that no one person or organisation is in charge of the WSF or can speak for it; that no 'final declaration' will be issued that everyone will be expected to agree with and that no political parties or single ideologies will be allowed to hijack it.[6]

I've been looking forward to the World Social Forum for months. This, for me, is something big, something new and something wholly different. Unlike Seattle, unlike Genoa, unlike Prague, Porto Alegre is a mass gathering of people who come not to react to something else, but to push a positive agenda forwards; to scheme and to dream. The test now is what that agenda is made of, and how it can help me to answer certain questions I've been storing up on my travels. How co-ordinated, for example, is this movement; and how co-ordinated does it want to be? What ideas is it coalescing around, and are they the same ideas I've seen developing from Chiapas to Cochabamba to Soweto? If so, how can they be applied on a global scale? How will it reconcile some of its internal tensions? And how can it make itself heard, just five months after 11 September 2001, in a new world of revenge and war and uncertain futures?

The slogan of the World Social Forum – so ubiquitous that by the end of the week I never want to hear it again as long as I live – is a simple one: 'Another world is possible'. At first it seems trite. Then, after a few days of seeing it written on everything from banners to coffee mugs, it occurs to me that its effectiveness depends on its pronunciation. Not 'another world is *possible*', but 'another world *is* possible'. Not an expression of desperation, but one of defiance – and of hope.

I'm sitting in an uncomfortable moulded plastic chair on the first floor of a university building listening to a respectable American MBA and ex-Harvard economist explaining how to abolish capitalism. David Korten – middle-aged, bearded, shirt and tie – has a career history as conventional as establishment economics gets:

Ph.D. and MBA from Stanford University Business School, training in 'organisation theory and business strategy', business studies
teacher at Harvard. All of this makes his belief, brought about by
twenty years' working on development projects in Asia, that the
economic model he had been taught to promote was causing more
problems than it solved, very hard to ignore. His 1995 book *When
Corporations Rule the World*, still probably the best summary of the
arguments against the corporate economy, has since become one of
the movement's primers. Now he is impressing upon an intrigued
audience the need to do away with everything he grew up believing in.

'We've been conditioned to believe,' he is saying, mildly, as I
take my seat, 'that there are only two economic systems – a state
socialist system in which governments own all the assets or a "capitalist" economy. "Capitalism" is a word which emerged in the
eighteenth century to describe a system in which a few control
production to the exclusion of the many. The crucial point to
understand is that capitalism and a true market economy are not
the same thing. In a true market economy, many small firms,
rooted in real communities, trade and compete with each other.
Under capitalism, large, rootless transnational corporations with
no responsibility to anyone but their shareholders destroy real
market economies and monopolise production. Let's be clear
here – the idea is precisely to abolish capitalism, and with it the
institutional form of the limited liability corporation.'

What I'm hearing is a curious but not an unusual paradox: a
believer in market economics who hates capitalism. There are a
fair number of these milling around the corridors of Porto
Alegre: people who believe that small property, rooted markets,
accountable companies and equitably distributed land are the
basis for stable economies and stable societies, and who believe
that the current model of supposedly 'free' trade – 'free' from any
social obligations or responsibilities – destroys that as effectively
as any socialist regime. It's an interesting approach – though
one that plenty within the movement reject as 'reformist'.

Korten is trying to explain how it might work. Someone, reasonably, has asked him what strategy could be pursued to achieve his aims.

'The strategy,' he says, '. . . well, there already exists a network of thousands and thousands of real, locally rooted markets and communities. There always has done. So the strategy would be to strengthen and promote these as you pull apart the large corporations.' He holds up a copy of a report he's been preparing with some of the other people on the platform with him. All of them are from the San Francisco-based International Forum on Globalization (IFG), a thinktank staffed by wonks like Korten which likes to 'think the unthinkable' on globalisation. The report contains some suggestions that the delegates over at the World Economic Forum would find most discomfiting.

'In here are some bold but workable proposals,' says Korten. 'The World Bank is in the business of maintaining external debt. Let's close the World Bank and replace it with an international clearing union to get rid of those debts. The IMF is in the business of entrenching poverty through structural adjustment. Let's replace the IMF with an international finance organisation to help countries control financial flows, maintain trade balances and ensure that investment is actually useful for people. The WTO is in the business of regulating governments so that they don't regulate corporations. Let's replace it with a UN-mandated organisation to regulate corporations, track and prosecute corporate criminals, hold corporations legally and financially accountable and impose an enforceable code of conduct for all transnationals, which must include a ban on corporate involvement in politics. Let's unify global governance under a restructured UN, and ensure that economies work for people's needs, and not the other way around. Let's eliminate corporate welfare, promote clean energy, institute land reform, promote sustainable farming. All this is possible, workable and practical.'

It's a hell of a wish-list but, as Korten says, it's a workable one. How to make it happen, of course, is another matter. That, as ever, comes down to political will: and that comes down to a wide-spread and forcible demand for real change.

'These are big and bold changes,' says Korten, 'but with real power behind our demands, they are practical and possible. And that power comes through building this movement, and through changing public opinion. I've been working on these issues for a long time, and I can see things changing. The people in the World Bank used to laugh at me ten years ago when I came out with this stuff. I'm meeting a bunch of them tonight to talk about why we think they should be abolished, and they're not laughing any more. Their legitimacy in the eyes of the world's people is being worn away. And when your legitimacy goes, your system usually follows.'

When I file out of the room an hour or so later, I feel invigorated. You didn't have to agree with Korten's ideas to see that there was real creative thinking in the air as he expounded them. After so many protests and rebuffs, after putting up with so much rubbish from defenders of the status quo, it's refreshing to see that this young movement can have big ideas all of its own – it's refreshing to be setting the agenda, rather than rejecting it.

Does it want them though: Big Ideas? Aren't they supposed to be part of the problem, not part of the solution? One of my worries before I arrived at the World Social Forum was that it would be used as a platform for people and organisations who were convinced they had the One True Way to solve every problem on Earth; convinced that the way out of our current mess could only be another grand enterprise, a new Big Idea. Would the Forum be co-opted, as the old Workers' Internationals were, by an intellectual elite, a vanguard of ideologues pushing their Utopian visions on the backs of a mass movement?

This question made me nervous before I arrived, but it's making me progressively less nervous the more I see. For what I thought, and hoped, was true of this movement as a whole seems to be true of Porto Alegre: no one here is willing to be pushed around any more. If Lenin's ghost is here, it must be disappointed.

Still, big questions remain. Autonomy, economic independence, local democracy – all these could perhaps be foundation stones of a new political worldview, but they can't be all it is built of. How will they deal with global financial architecture, with trade flows, with international conflicts? How will they deal with climate change or global environmental destruction? How, in other words, does probably the most international political movement in history apply its principles internationally without losing their essence, and without losing the lust for diversity and democracy that makes it what it is?

Korten's approach gives some idea of how this might happen: institutions and approaches that are international in scope and outlook, but often also local and specific in much of their application. A 'New New World Order' which looks forward to a world of co-operation and internationalism, but which is rooted too in participatory democracy and community control. Can it work? We don't know; not yet. But ideas like this – like many of the ideas coming out of Porto Alegre – are both big and small, global and local. Most importantly, they are liberating rather than prescriptive. So the IFG's proposals, for example, don't prescribe one economic or social model for all, but they do remove the worst of the obstacles – illegitimate corporate power, iniquitous debt, skewed terms of trade, the power of the markets, corrupted democracy – which stand in the way of people changing their societies for the better.

That, at least, is the theory. Whether what is happening elsewhere will back it up is for me to find out. If, that is, I can find my way around.

Fortunately, I'm not alone. My girlfriend Katharine is here, too, so we can get lost together. It's the next morning and we're both sitting on the grass in an area of the university campus that has been given over to food stalls run by agricultural co-operatives selling cuisine from the four corners of the world. We've managed an early start, but already the crowds are beginning to build around us. There's a student dressed exactly like Che Guevara, right down to the red-starred beret and scraggy beard; a couple of NGO leaders, shirts tucked in, delegate badges prominent; an Indymedia journalist filming three Indian women holding a banner protesting against the Narmada dams; two Belgian farmers; a Malaysian academic in T-shirt and jeans; a gaggle of law students; a French MEP. We're basking in the morning sunlight drinking fresh orange juice, flicking through the programme and deciding how to use our day most productively.

'What,' I am saying, 'is "Fisco's little store", and why is it listed under "workshops"?'

'Why don't you go along and find out?' says Katharine.

'Because it sounds stupid. Sounds like something you'd find at the Edinburgh Festival.'

'Let's go to this one instead, then – "another socialist world is possible". I must have missed the first one. We could ask them when it was.'

'Or what about "A people's capitalism"? Bet that one's popular.'

'Or "The interdependence of all beings"?'

'"Recycling residue: an alternative to social integration"!'

'"Relax and multilogue: a space of silence and extended language"!?'

'"Cartography in the new millennium"! Hold me back!'

This could go on for some time. It's one of the wonders of the World Social Forum that anyone can turn up and do a workshop, meeting or event on any subject they like, and nobody will try to stop them. It's deliberate, it's multitudinous, it's diversity at work. My democratic heart is warmed to see a space being created in which people can, indeed, relax and multilogue without being oppressed by anyone else. I just have no intention of going anywhere near it.

Instead, I go to a packed and popular press conference. Noam Chomsky, mild-mannered Massachusetts professor, dissident thinker and owner of what may be the largest brain in the West, is one of the Forum's biggest draws. Later, he will almost cause a riot when thousands cram the halls and corridors of the university, forcing a last-minute change to a bigger room which still won't begin to accommodate the numbers who want to hear him quietly expounding his refreshingly egalitarian opinions. A mildly disturbing cult of personality has hung around Chomsky for years, but he never seems to notice. This morning, in the Porto Alegre town hall, under vast, pompous stone columns, classical murals and heavy chandeliers, he is telling the press what he thinks of his government's 'war on terror'. He's also telling them what he thinks of the World Social Forum, and of the movement it represents.

A local reporter has asked him if all this World Social Forum stuff isn't a bit, well, pie in the sky. What alternatives has it come up with, and what examples can the professor give of any countries that have actually made them work?

'Well, you could have come to me two centuries ago,' responds Chomsky, 'and asked, "Can you give me an example of a society that functions without slavery, or with a functioning parliamentary democracy or with full women's rights?" and the answer would have been no. Following on from that, the response should have been "right, well let's go ahead and create such societies", and people did. The people here – many of them have come with alternative programmes proposed in great detail and explicitness on issue after issue. They can work, and they should be pursued. There is plenty to be excited about, if you have the vision.'

Another journalist pops up. What's the state of the anti-globalisation movement these days, she wants to know. Chomsky does a little frown.

'I think,' he says, 'that we should be careful not to call this an anti-globalisation forum. Every progressive popular movement's goal throughout history has been to create a movement of solidarity which is global – in the interests of the people of the world. This meeting is about ways and means of transferring leadership from centres of power to the general population, and that's a global ambition. In my view, this is the only globalisation forum – there's an anti-globalisation forum taking place right now in New York which is trying to prevent this development. I believe that it is unlikely to succeed.'

It's only a couple of hours later, sitting in one of the university's cavernous but packed lecture halls – steel roof beams hung with spotlights, hundreds of people wearing simultaneous translation headsets, Indymedia journalists videoing everything that moves from the edges of the room – that I realise that Chomsky is not alone: that something wider is going on at Porto Alegre. Speaker after speaker, delegate after delegate, is working to reposition the way the movement is seen by the wider world.

Up on the stage this time it's a conference on international trade. Speakers from Malaysia, South Africa, Belgium, Mexico and the USA are putting out proposals to change the terms of international trade, which they say favours the rich. So far, several proposals have been widely agreed upon: abolishing or radically reworking the WTO; subordinating trade agreements to UN treaties on human rights and the environment; developing global policies to protect local markets and national industries; stopping any new trade round; removing agriculture from the WTO agreements to prevent further destruction of small farms by colossal agribusinesses. Hector de la Cueva, of Mexico's Alianza Social Continental, talks of 'neoliberalism's disastrous effects on Latin America', and of his organisation's efforts to create a continental alliance focused on ending external debt, refusing any more IMF or World Bank 'adjustments', taxing financial transactions and protecting small farming. Martin Khor, of the Third World Network in Malaysia, and one of the global movement's most prominent economists, is even more stark.

'We should not be negotiating with the WTO,' he says, simply. 'We should be working to delegitimise it and build popular support to prevent any new agreement liberalising trade in services. This organisation should be rolled back, not negotiated with.'

The next speaker is Lori Wallach, an American trade lawyer from the watchdog organisation Public Citizen and the woman who probably did more than anyone else to expose and thus destroy the ill-fated Multilateral Agreement on Investment in 1998. She is small, blonde, fast-talking and brilliant, and she knows how to hold an audience's attention. In her hand she is holding a very, very thick document.

'These,' she says, 'are the WTO agreements. And this' – she heaves another vast tome up on to the podium – 'is NAFTA. This is a framework for corporations to sue governments in closed trade tribunals. There are people here today from all over the Americas – well, how many of your MPs or representatives know that NAFTA, and the proposed Free Trade Area of the Americas, will declare your zoning laws illegal trade barriers? In other words, that your government could have to *pay* corporations for the right *not* to site toxic waste dumps next to your schools? How many of your MPs know that there are over 2,000 multilateral agreements in the world designed to safeguard workers and the environment – a huge body of public interest laws that put people first, from UNICEF codes, International Labour Organization laws . . . and that all of these are subjugated to NAFTA, the IMF and the WTO?' She is talking at breakneck speed. Disturbed murmurs are coming from sections of the audience.

'We don't like it?' says Wallach. 'It's not working? No problem.' With a flourish she lobs both documents over her shoulder, where they land in a heap on the stage. The disturbed murmurs morph into laughter. But Wallach is making a serious point.

'We have always been told,' she says, 'that what they call globalisation is an inevitable process. What we have done as a movement is to clearly demonstrate that it is not – that it is something manufactured by a specific set of interests and sold to us as something irresistible. Their problem is that all the evidence is now coming in, and we know what these agreements do, what this model does. This evidence comes as great pain, but that pain is also our strength as a movement – because more people can see what this model is doing to them. Neoliberalism *doesn't work*. They tried it – it tanked. They promised a lot – they didn't deliver.

The data is in. Time to move on. What we must now do as a movement is make it move on. That means that we have to be clear what we are for – and clear that we are a positive movement.' Chomsky was saying the same, and Wallach is getting a lot of nods from the audience.

'Two things that we need,' she races on. 'A two-pronged strategy. We must build a demand for change across the world, and we must build a consensus about what we're *for*. When I say change, I mean *real* change. This is not a movement for marginal reforms. This system, neoliberalism, is gangrene. It's cancer. There is a growing recognition that corporate globalisation's one-size-fits-all model isn't working. We, as a movement, have the momentum. The proponents of the status quo know this, and this is why they are striking back. They have a very clear propaganda war running against us, and we can see the points they make – they have their own two-pronged approach. Their first strategy is to say this process is inevitable, it's evolution, you can't buck it – the ten commandments came down from Mount Sinai and included the statutes of the WTO. If that doesn't succeed in making everyone give up, their second strategy is to say that these protesters, this movement against our system, is just a movement of people in rich countries. Trouble is that what NAFTA and the WTO are now doing to the West, the IMF and World Bank have been doing in the south for decades – which is why this movement came from the south first. They'd rather people didn't hear that story. But they are in trouble, and they know it. But we have to be clear, too, what we are for – we can't fall into their trap.'

Wallach is a performer, and a convincing one. All eyes are fixed on her.

'Our movement is at a turning point,' she says. 'They label us "anti" – we have to shake off the label. We're *for* democracy, *for* diversity, *for* equity, *for* environmental health. They're holding on to a failed status quo; *they're* the antis. They are anti-democracy and anti-people. We must go forward as a movement for global justice. Thank you.' She walks back to her seat without bothering to pick up the documents she threw to the floor. The applause is long and loud.

This is brilliant, rabble-rousing stuff. It's also clear how Wallach's point is much the same as Chomsky's, and how both of them are saying something that people here have been, and will be, saying all week: this is not a movement of 'antis' – it's a movement of 'pros'. We've been rehearsing the nos on the world stage for three years, since Seattle. Now let's get going on the yeses. Come to that, let's re-examine those nos and ask ourselves whether they might not be yeses too. After all, the many things this movement says no to, stands up against, tries to prevent or take apart are in themselves barriers to the sort of world it wants to see.

This is an argument that economist Nicola Bullard, from the Thai NGO Focus on the Global South, put to me one evening during the Forum when I bumped into her in the lobby of a crowded hotel.

'So many people here are rehearsing these arguments,' she said, 'it's great. As a movement we're being overwhelmingly positive. This old cry "you have no alternatives" is such a semantic trick. It turns what are actually positive arguments into negative ones. For example, unconditional cancellation of Third World debt – that's a specific measure, you could call it "anti-debt", but it's actually an overwhelmingly positive alternative. If it were to happen, it would create a space for so many alternatives to flourish. Money spent on servicing that debt could be spent on basic health care, education . . . economies would be freed up from a lot of reliance on export, a lot of pressure from the Washington consensus. That's a positive measure – a huge positive change.'

Creating a space. Lori Wallach said that too. David Korten's proposals for reforming the world economy were aimed at creating a space within which those many worlds could flourish. This, it seems, is what a lot of Porto Alegre is about. It's another two-pronged strategy: remodel the global economy to allow local and specific alternatives to flourish without being destroyed from above by the steamroller of unaccountable economic power. It's not one or the other, it's both – maybe a Big Idea after all, but one that, this time, is premised on giving birth to a million small ones.

The next morning my head hurts. Katharine and I bumped into a few friends the previous night and spent longer than was probably wise drinking *caipirinhas* in a field by the sea which has been rigged up with a stage, stalls and all the accoutrements of a mini-festival. The result is a substantial hangover.

I'm late anyway, and was delayed even more by crossing paths, as I rushed down one of a hundred corridors, with some old friends: George Dor, Virginia Setshedi and Trevor Ngwane, heading in the other direction towards a meeting of African social movements. It's great to see them, and we spend at least ten minutes hanging around exchanging tips. George is finding the whole thing as exciting and occasionally bewildering as I am. Trevor is having a relatively quiet time compared to last year, when he was connected up, via video link, to the World Economic Forum in Davos, to engage in an impassioned debate with global financier George Soros. Virginia keeps asking me if I'm planning to go dancing. Which I'm not.

One snatched coffee later, and I'm in another hall (they all melded into one some time ago) listening to people focusing on another key theme of the forum: privatisation. The global corporate resource grab that is one of the defining factors of the globalisation process is a key concern here. From water to seeds to land to infrastructure, a worldwide process of privatisation of public and common resources is currently going on on an unprecedented scale. It is inherent within the globalisation process; a necessary prerequisite for the expansion of an economic system which needs private property like a fish needs water. Activists say that this resource grab – which often ends up as a redistribution of wealth from the poor to the rich – is one of the major causes of the poverty and powerlessness that the globaphiles say that their system will abolish.

In this particular meeting speakers from Russia, France, Britain, the US and Costa Rica are assailing the topic of 'intellectual property'. Again, the WTO is in the firing line: its TRIPS agreement on 'intellectual property', which caused so much controversy in the case of the South African AIDS drugs, is also, say the speakers, giving a green light to the corporate control of life itself.

TRIPS is one of the WTO's key agreements – and one of the most controversial. It came about as a result of lobbying by a committee of self-interested corporations, including Monsanto, DuPont and General Motors,[7] and is designed to tighten the corporate noose around ownership of products, processes and information itself. It requires all WTO member countries to adopt a harsh US-style patent regime, meaning that a patent or copyright taken out in one WTO member country automatically becomes valid in them all. The agreement is used by corporations to justify everything from preventing the development of cheap software, denying affordable medicine to millions of desperately sick and poor people, selling expensive, copyrighted textbooks to 'third world' schools and preventing the spread of basic technologies which have traditionally been copied from industry to industry and country to country as part of the development process.

The motivation, as ever, is simple: monopolies over information, as over products, resources or markets, mean fat and virtually guaranteed profits. They also mean control. Information shared, on the other hand, is information wasted, as far as the market is concerned; no profit, no point. Curiously, the one thing that neoliberals are supposed to be firmly set against is monopolies, which break every rule in the free market handbook. But, as I have learned over and over again on my travels, market theory and market reality are rarely the same thing.

The most controversial aspect of TRIPS, though, and the one that is exercising the delegates today, is its role in the 'patenting of life'. TRIPS allows the patenting of not just products and information, but living things: seeds, new strains of plant, even genetic information. Corporations, arguing that under patent law a discovery is the same thing as an 'invention', have in recent years slapped patents on plants, medicines and foods used for thousands of years by Amazonian Indians, varieties of Mexican corn grown in Chiapas for centuries, seeds developed and used by entire Indian villages and even strands of human DNA. There is a name for this, and today everyone is using it: 'biopiracy'.

In 1997, in perhaps the notorious example of biopiracy to date, a Texas-based corporation, RiceTec, Inc., claimed 'ownership' of basmati rice. The patent on basmati, a staple of the rural economies and national cuisines of India and Pakistan for centuries before Europeans even got there, officially granted RiceTec control of twenty-two varieties of the rice, developed in India and Pakistan by local farmers. RiceTec apparently had no intention of informing those farmers, let alone paying them, for their work, and every intention of selling its own 'basmati' all over the USA and elsewhere. An appeal by the Indian government later led to a modifying, but not a withdrawing, of the patent.

Biopiracy's potential for harm is huge: it could lead, as it already has in some cases, to widespread patenting of traditional seeds and crop varieties by multinational corporations, which farmers will then have to buy back from them. A profitable game, but one of which this conference is having none. People here, at the very least, want all life-forms removed from the TRIPS agreement. More want TRIPS trashed altogether. Speakers are calling, as a matter of principle, for every country to be able to develop its own patent laws as it sees fit. The patenting of life is firmly rejected, and calls go up for global rules to ensure that certain areas of life, knowledge, technology and information remain permanently free from corporate buccaneering.

'TRIPS,' says one speaker, 'is about transferring resources and knowledge from south to north, from rich to poor. It is the privatisation of everything left that remains, and it must be fought. It is against everything that we value.'

Here, again, I am seeing a clash not just of viewpoints but of values. TRIPS outrages so many people because its effect – and probably its intent – is to help eliminate the existence, and perhaps even the very concept, of something that has been at the heart of the vast majority of human societies through history and, for many, still is: the commons.

In rural areas all over the world, and in many urban ones too, the commons are still the foundation stone of community life. Common land, shared seed, common access to water, genetic reserves, forest land, public space in village and town: all this, under the rule of global capital, is up for sale. Seeds are to be genetically altered, patented, then sold back to farmers. Land is to be enclosed, divided, titled and then charged for. Public water is to be bought up, forests fenced off, animals, plants, even gene lines laid claim to by those who have the money and the reach to do so.

This is the commodification of everything, and it is an issue at the heart of the clash between the proponents of globalisation and those who resist it. The stance of those here – and there are many of them – who are doing that resisting is a fundamental one: common resources are the natural heritage of mankind, and communities have the right to decide what is done with them. There are certain areas of life, say most of the delegates at Porto Alegre – from the world's biological heritage to its airwaves, from seeds to water, from the atmosphere to public services like health and education – that cannot and should not ever be privatised or commodified. It's not a bargaining chip, it's a principle, a line in the sand, a rallying point – and one which, in coming years, may come to define this movement more and more.

Applying it on the ground, of course, is less straightforward, but the conference on intellectual property is only one of the Forum's attempts to translate principle into proposals. Throughout the week, there are others. Later that day there's one entitled 'Water: our common heritage', in which delegates, including a representative of Cochabamba's *Coordinadora*, insist that 'water is a fundamental resource for life, and therefore is the common heritage of all . . . it cannot be privatised, nor converted into a market product'. A declaration is issued, signed by twenty-four NGOs from across the world, proposing a moratorium on destructive dam-building, an end to water privatisation, bans on certain chemical pollutants and new, strict legal obligations on corporations to protect any water sources they use. To oversee all this, they suggest the creation of a 'world water parliament' which would oversee the promotion of locally managed, sustainable water delivery systems, accessible to all.

Meanwhile, in yet another small, overcrowded university back room, a group of scientists, farmers, economists and biotechnology campaigners from more than fifty countries is launching the Porto Alegre Treaty on the Genetic Commons. It calls for an international treaty to ban biopiracy and patents on living things and recognise the Earth's gene pool as a 'shared legacy' which cannot be privatised, in perpetuity. It will be introduced, say its proponents, into national parliaments around the world in coming years, in an attempt to get it a footing in law. One of its proponents is the Indian physicist, environmentalist and writer Vandana Shiva, another of the movement's big hitters. 'Biopiracy is morally repugnant,' she insists, to widespread agreement. 'It is theft, the rich stealing from the poor. Genetic resources, plants, the fruits of the land – all these are basic, common goods, and they must be protected as such. Corporations have no right to any of this, and we have to say so loud and clear. It is quite simple: the commons are ours.'

For the next few days, the Forum's main events follow the same pattern. Workshops, conferences and seminars (am I the only one who hasn't worked out the difference?) provide a huge intellectual menu of proposed solutions, alternatives and ideas – some of them ever-so-slightly mad, some of them unconvincing, but the majority well thought-through and potentially workable. Filipino economist Walden Bello, another globally recognisable dissident intellectual, who can never resist a bit of rabble-rousing, tells audiences that 'Davos and the World Economic Forum are on their way down' and that 'we are seeing a crisis of legitimacy for the global elite'. He suggests that the world should accept this fact and follow it up with a restructuring of its economy – abolition of the WTO, new regulations on the behaviour and influence of corporations, a reworking of the global financial architecture to prevent destructive currency speculation.

Arguments are held about how to rein in corporations: with laws or consumer pressure or both? The idea of a tax on international financial speculation, which has been around for years, gains more ground. Everyone agrees on the abolition of Third World debt. Environmentalists argue that 'sustainable development' is an oxymoron: a meaningless term used widely by corporations and governments to avoid for as long as possible the fact of how un-'sustainable' our economic model is. Farmers and indigenous people agree with some NGOs that radical land reform is a prerequisite for social justice. A group of hopeful peace campaigners are promoting the idea of a 'war budget'. They are holding a 'World Assembly' to debate better ways of using the $800 billion that the world spends on arms every year.

Elsewhere, economists are reworking an idea that has been kicking around in the environmental movement for decades – redefining Gross Domestic Product (GDP), the standard measure of economic growth, and thus, wealth. GDP, they point out, simply measures the amount of goods and services a nation produces in any given year – not whether producing them actually improves society as a whole. Chopping down a rainforest and turning it into toilet paper boosts GDP. So does cleaning up an oil spill, or an increase in the sale of rape alarms. So did the epidemic of panic-buying of weapons, gas masks and 'self-defence kits' in post-September 11 USA (Wal-Mart alone saw its gun sales rise by 70 per cent[8]). All this is 'growth', but hardly progress. Measure development by other means, they say, including environmental health, social cohesion, income equality, poverty rates, employment and so on, and the picture worldwide – and particularly in the 'developed' countries – is not one of endless progress, but increasing decline since the 1970s. It could be a metaphor for what made people come here in the first place.

There are six days of this. It's useful; it's important, perhaps even vital; it's sometimes inspiring, often challenging, occasionally exciting. But it can get a bit much. There are only so many talks you can sit through, lecture halls you can visit, corridors you can wander lost down, ideas you can take in. Fortunately, there is more to the Forum than this. Outside the official conference-workshop-lecture circuit there are spaces for just about anything else you could want, many of them more reminiscent of Genoa, Prague or Seattle than a United Nations development conference, and consequently more fun.

There are marches, naturally – one practically every day, supporting the Palestinians, opposing the IMF, calling for land reform, colouring the streets of the city with flags, banners, drums, laughter, bombast, music and slogans. One of the biggest is held by the international small farmers' union, Via Campesina, who are here in their thousands, camped out in a local gym with members of Brazil's Landless Workers' Movement. Meanwhile, a major focus of alternatives to the alternatives available in the main forum is the 'Carlo Giuliani Youth Camp', named after the protester killed in Genoa by the police. The youth camp, which looks, smells and sounds like a Brazilian Glastonbury festival, has hundreds of tents, food stalls, merchandise sellers and its own programme of events. It's altogether more earthy than the main menu provided inside the venues; videos are shown of the protests at Genoa, workshops on direct action techniques are held, meetings spring up to discuss the 'sell-out' that is the 'reformist' Forum, and provide alternatives to the alternatives it offers.

On show here, inevitably, is the classic split, based around the fundamental question that every dissident movement has always suffered from and probably always will: reform or revolution? You're wasting your time, say the 'revolutionaries' to the 'reformists', with ill-concealed contempt. Negotiating with governments, tinkering around at the margins, rewriting a treaty here, regulating a corporation there – it's the system that's the problem. Capitalism must go! Meaningless cant, say 'reformists' – time to grow up. Even if you could 'overthrow' 'the system' history suggests that your chances of building a better one from scratch are pretty slim. The real issue is building the political will for serious change. 'Reformists' often get shirty about being called reformists at all, and refuse to accept that such clear lines have to be drawn in the sand. 'Revolutionaries' refuse even to discuss the matter, and instead spend their time in tents plotting the inevitable overthrow of everything. This debate – rarely useful, usually frustrating, often artificial, always systemic and never likely to be resolved – will run and run.

But it's not the only internal division on show here. There is another, which may turn out to have more long-term significance. A surreal introduction to it came from the youth camp, where Katharine and I were waiting one morning to meet a friend we'd been trying to find for a couple of days. He arrived late because he'd been arguing with a man selling red T-shirts with pictures of Stalin on them.

'Do you realise,' he had said, pointing at the merchandise, 'that this is the greatest mass-murderer of the twentieth century?'

'Don't blame me,' said the man. 'I just sell T-shirts.'

The T-shirt man had apparently assumed that, since this was a gathering of dissidents, it must be a gathering of socialists and/or communists – probably not an unfair assumption in South America. Stalin being a communist, the T-shirts probably seemed a good bet. Unfortunately, the T-shirt man was not the only one at Porto Alegre to assume that changing the world meant disinterring the worst of the twentieth-century left.

All week, representatives of what might be called the 'old left' have been roaming the campsites and corridors of the World Social Forum. Communists from Greece, socialists from Spain, a ragbag of hard-left parties from all over Latin America and the inevitable gaggle of vocal Trots from Europe. There are workshops on 'building a socialist world', a lot of shouting and red flag-waving, pamphlets and lectures explaining that all this talk of autonomy, radical democracy and local control is reformist claptrap, no substitute for a workers' revolution. All pretty harmless in itself, but representative of a tension that is more important than it might look and which goes to the heart of what this movement is, and wants to be.

For while there is much common ground, there is also a fundamental difference between this new politics of resistance and the old politics of the revolutionary left. It is the difference that Marcos discovered in the mountains of Chiapas; it is, again, about power and attitudes to it. Traditional hard-left politics is about seizing state power, either through revolution or through electing a 'workers' party'. It is about vanguard politics, it is usually anti-democratic and even the working class that it claims to represent is so changed from the days when Marx and Engels wrote their gospels that even some of their modern adherents have trouble defining who's in and who's out.

Radical political movements have long been renowned for dissipating their energies on People's Front of Judea-type squabbling rather than attacking their common enemies. This movement, at the moment, is rather different. It is so frightened of shattering its often fragile unity, or developing a hierarchy that would enable the more powerful and influential activists to push all the others around, that there is an almost pathological fear of airing differences in public and potentially 'splitting the movement'. It explains, for example, why it is frowned upon to publicly criticise the Black Bloc even though most people disagree with what they get up to. The old left/new movement division, though, is different; sometimes the battles can get quite vicious.

In Britain, for example, these arguments focus on that rusty nail in the side of every political activist, the Socialist Workers' Party, which has developed a reputation for latching itself on to every radical cause around like an embarrassingly flatulent relative at a family wedding. Immediately after Seattle in 1999, forward-thinking SWP members were clear that the new movement they could see developing was in need of 'direction' and 'leadership' from them. 'Mass movements don't get the political representation that they deserve,' wrote one, in the SWP's magazine, *Socialist Review*, 'unless a minority of activists within the movement seek to create a political leadership, which means a political party . . . The first precondition of influencing future struggles is to be involved in them – deeply, organisationally involved . . . The movement is still under construction and socialists can shape it so long as they are wholeheartedly a part of it.'[9]

Quite what this poor movement has done to 'deserve' leadership from the SWP is unclear, but some activists are obviously less grateful than they should be. 'It must be really confusing,' wrote one, in an open letter to an SWP spokesman who had claimed that a movement of millions was no substitute for mobilising 'wider class forces', 'to wake up in the middle of the first organised and even televised global movement and discover that people in it neither speak your political language nor share your dogmas on how the movement should be, who should "lead" the struggle and on what they should be struggling for . . . How come you people have discovered the global anti-capitalist movement only when it became visible to all? Where were you six, seven or eight years ago when many of us were building that movement?'[10]

In some cases, these splits have tipped over into battles between scattered groups of campaigners and the UK's most visible 'anti-capitalist' grouping, Globalise Resistance. Globalise Resistance was set up before Genoa by two members of the SWP, and has since mushroomed into a well-organised, well-funded and increasingly dominant left-wing grouping. One of its founders, Guy Taylor, insists it is 'constitutionally non-ideological'. Its members, he says, include 'socialists, anarchists, Christians, environmentalists and many people who wouldn't give themselves a label'.[11] Other activists accuse Globalise Resistance of being a kind of fifth column, designed to sneak a hierarchical, dogmatic left-wing ideology into a movement keen to find new answers.

A group of influential anarchists in Brighton responded to this with a pointed pamphlet entitled *Monopolise Resistance?*. 'If it was just a matter of the SWP having pointless marches and shouting themselves hoarse inside police pens it wouldn't be a problem,' they wrote. 'They've been doing that for years and nobody's noticed. The problem is that they are actively conning people . . . Globalise Resistance exists mainly to increase the influence of the SWP within the anti-capitalist movement.' They quote a Globalise Resistance spokesperson overheard in Genoa: 'Remember, we're the only people here with an overall strategy for the anti-capitalist movement. So I want five people to go out with membership cards, five to sell papers and five to sell bandanas.'[12] (The role of the bandanas in the overall strategy has not yet become clear.)

Whatever the truth about an organisation which, if not a direct lovechild of the SWP, certainly shares the same poster designer, this battle between new approaches and old has already had negative results. A long-discussed UK Social Forum, for example, has never taken off, partly due to a fear that Globalise Resistance, its socialist allies and their agendas will dominate the event. And these are not parochial squabbles: they are repeated across the world. A movement inspired by *Zapatismo* and radical democracy that speaks a new language, promotes new ideas and wants no party or vanguard to lead it can never make its peace with dogmatic statists from the Utopian left, convinced that 'power' must be 'seized' at state level, by them, for 'the workers', whether anybody else likes it or not.

The discussions, debates, arguments and ideas on show at Porto Alegre represent, when looked at in this context, something significantly different. A new attempt at a different type of politics, and one which is slowly crawling out from under the long shadow of the twentieth-century left – packing away the old ideological kitbag and unwrapping new tools. It's a hard struggle; often the language and the methods are not yet available to describe what is happening. These paths, unlike the six-lane motorways of state socialism or revolutionary communism, have not yet been widely trodden. But the journey that has begun is perhaps more important than many realise.

The next day, I'm reminded again of this division. Brazil's Workers' Party – the PT – are co-organisers of the Forum, and despite promises not to, they are finding it hard to resist using it as a vehicle for electioneering. Later in the year, Brazil faces a presidential election: at the moment, the PT's candidate, the former metalworker known popularly as 'Lula', is ahead in the polls (in November 2002 he will win the election, becoming Brazil's first elected left-wing president). This morning he has turned up at the Forum to give a speech, surrounded by cheering party appa-ratchiks. It suits Lula to be seen with this international gathering of forward-thinkers. He is, after all, a politician. In the central hall, the loudspeakers are vibrating to the promises of an inevitable people's victory, and it's getting right on my nerves. This wasn't what I came here for. Judging by the muttering crowds outside, I'm not the only one.

But then the PT win me over. Not that they need to, since I can't vote in Brazil. But after a couple of hours in the conference room of the São Rafael Hotel, I have been given a picture of local democracy in action that seems to offer intriguing possibilities for the future. The PT have governed the city of Porto Alegre since 1988 and their tenure has led to real changes. State-wide, the PT have self-consciously kicked back against what they openly call 'the neoliberal model'; they have suspended privatisations, guaranteed public service provision levels and channelled support into agri-culture and micro-enterprises. They are trying to build a system of what they call 'decentralised social welfare' through locally based literacy movements, adult education programmes, housing and workers co-ops. Most interestingly though, in Porto Alegre itself, the PT has embarked on an ambitious experiment to hand back some of the running of the city to the people who live there.

Porto Alegre's 'participatory budget' is trumpeted by the PT as a future for urban democracy, and 'people's economics', and they may be on to something. In the hotel, a summer-skirted woman from the Porto Alegre government is explaining how it works. 'People's participation in the city used to be confined to the act of voting every few years,' she says. 'Now they decide on how their money is spent in their city, through a democratic process.' The PT are, of course, keen to trumpet their achievements, but it seems they do have something to trumpet; the people of Porto Alegre control the way their money is spent on their city to a degree that I have not come across anywhere else.

The woman from the government explains how the process works. In 1989, the PT removed the power to decide on the city's budget from the usual councillors and technocrats in City Hall and began a process of popular consultation, which has evolved annually to iron out glitches that appeared along the way. Currently, budgetary priorities are divided up by themes – environment, transport, taxation, culture, health, education, etc. – and for each theme there is a regular public conference in each region of the city. Any citizen can participate in these conferences, which debate how much money should be spent on that theme, and how. Each conference then elects a delegate, who puts forward the decisions made by their electors before electing a clutch of budget councillors who put the budget together according to the broad choices made by the citizenry. Finally, after months of being kicked about, touched up and debated, the proposed budget is voted on by the people of the city – only if they approve it will it go ahead.

It's a long and complex process, and not without its flaws, but it does give the people of Porto Alegre a significant degree of real control over how their money is spent. According to the PT, the participatory budget has meant changes in the way the city is run, as citizens adjust it to suit their priorities. Since it was introduced, they say, it has been used to pave 25,000 kilometres of roads, provide 96 per cent of homes with clean running water, steadily increase sewage provision, set up family health clinics, work towards eliminating child labour and expand the number of infant schools. The idea, clearly, is that the money is spent on what people want – not what politicians think they want, or want themselves. And it is proving popular – so much so that the model is being extended not only to 500 towns across Rio Grande do Sul, but to other Brazilian cities which the PT controls, including Rio de Janeiro. Other cities across the world are watching it closely – so are plenty of other people at the World Social Forum. It is an example of an alternative approach that can be seen in action, rather than simply envisioned on a stage. And it works.

The last full day of the Forum has just ended. Tomorrow morning there will be a closing ceremony, and then the crowds will begin to disperse. Tonight, thousands of us are down at the grass arena by the sea again for a closing concert; speakers (the charismatic Lula is at it again), bands from around the world, fireworks, food, drink and a full moon in a black Atlantic sky. Katharine and I and a gang of friends are on the *caipirinhas* again, sitting on the grass, revelling in the recently announced news that the president of the World Bank, James Wolfensohn, who wanted to come to the Forum and give us all a talk on how neoliberalism is abolishing poverty, has been turned away. They have turned us away with tear-gas and armoured cars so many times; now we turn them away with a polite refusal. We are worrying them, and this time, the agenda and the momentum are ours. It's a golden moment. While we enjoy it, we are being serenaded, for about the four hundredth time this week, with the official theme song of the World Social Forum. The bouncy, Eurovision-type chorus, in Portuguese, goes *'Aqui, um outro mundo é possível!'* – 'Here, another world is possible'. It's horribly tacky. It's also catchier than it sounds, and after a few *caipirinhas* you can't get it out of your head.

It's just over six months since I was in Genoa; it's just over two years since Seattle, and it seems to me now that something has already ended here in Porto Alegre, and that something else has begun. I have a feeling – and I've talked to plenty of other people that have it too, but can't quite explain why – that this movement has reached a turning point: that it has reached the end of the beginning, that somehow, now, it moves into phase two. The ideas and the energy that came out of Porto Alegre were astounding; more than I think I had expected, and more exciting than most of the world seems to realise. This movement has a long way to go, a lot of tensions to resolve, a lot of wrinkles to iron out, questions still to be asked and answered. Where it will end up is anybody's guess. But it is going somewhere, and it looks like being the right direction.

As for me, lying on the grass with a drink in my hand – I am watching the fireworks beginning, silhouetting the lighthouse down on the shore with starbursts of red and green and white. And I am thinking: this is a time to be bold. Something is in the air; a tide turning, a paradigm slowly shifting. I don't know quite what it is, but somehow it seems that we, here in Porto Alegre, hold the future in our hands; that we have wrested it from the delegates over in New York, and claimed it for ourselves. And that now, anything could happen. And somehow, for some reason that, again, I can't quite explain – somehow, I know that it will, and that it will be something big.

I'll drink to that.

7 land and freedom

'The most dramatic and far-reaching social change of the second half of this century, and one that cuts us off for ever from the world of the past, is the death of the peasantry.'

ERIC HOBSBAWM, 1994

'Either Brazil finishes off the *sem terra,* or the *sem terra* will finish off Brazil.'

BRAZILIAN STATE PROSECUTOR, TRYING TWO LANDLESS PEOPLE FOR MURDER, 2000

The policeman has seen me. I knew he would. He's seen me and he's shouting at me to stop walking, to turn around, to come back to the road where he's standing. He wants to know what I've got in my bag, and he wants to know now.

I can't understand a word he's saying. I don't speak Portuguese, and he doesn't speak English. So for all I know he could be shouting at someone else. Or he might just be saying hello. Or asking me the time. Or singing. I keep walking towards the fence. Being an ignorant foreigner has its uses.

On the other side of the fence, dozens of peasant farmers are gathered, watching me. They're only about six feet away. The policeman is still shouting; louder now. I still can't understand a word of it. All I have to do is keep walking, keep walking, keep . . .

Two feet away from the wire, just as I think I've made it, the policeman's hand lands firmly on my shoulder. He marches me back to where I started from, next to the three patrol cars that are parked outside the blockaded country estate that is being occupied by the people on the other side of the fence. The policeman is shouting at me and gesturing at the white carrier bag I have in my hand. I open it and show him the contents: *bacuri* fruit, a local delicacy in this part of northern Brazil. He shakes his head and takes the bag from me. Daniella, my translator, arrives.

'Tell him the fruit's just for me,' I say.

'There are ten of them in the bag,' she says. 'He doesn't think your appetite's that big. And he doesn't believe that you don't speak any Portuguese. I'm explaining to him that English people don't bother learning anyone else's languages because they're lazy.'

'Thanks very much.'

As Daniella negotiates with the cop, I look over at the people gathered on the other side of the fence, who are still watching the spectacle. They are leaning on the wire, following my progress:

wrinkled old men in straw hats, women in flip-flops nursing babies, barefoot kids with worm-swollen stomachs, young, dark-skinned topless men in jeans and sandals. I shrug my shoulders in their direction and some of them grin. Since they invaded this land, claiming it for themselves, saying they had nowhere else to go, the police have been (illegally) trying to starve them out, and won't let anybody take any food in. Even, as it turns out, a few *bacuri*.

Daniella has finished negotiating with the policeman.

'They're not going to arrest you,' she says, 'but they don't like you.'

'That's OK. I don't like them either.'

'You might have made some new friends, though,' she says, gesturing at the onlookers. We walk back towards them, over to the fence, minus my bag of *bacuri*. People nod at me, smiling. An old man insists on shaking my hand. Someone parts the wires for us, and we squeeze through.

The north-eastern state of Maranhão is one of the poorest and most corrupt in Brazil, and the land that these families are occupying, like much land in the state, is part of a *latifundio* – a vast landholding owned by an absentee landlord. This land, say the occupying families, has not been used for years. They, meanwhile, are poor and landless. So why shouldn't they have this land? And if they take it, is it theft, or is it justice?

The people occupying this estate are not alone in asking this question. All over Brazil it has been asked, with increasing regularity, for the last twenty years. And all over Brazil, for the last twenty years, people like these have answered it for themselves. These families are all members of the *Movimento dos Trabalhadores Rurais Sem Terra* – the Landless Rural Workers' Movement, or MST. The MST began life in 1984, as a reaction to the plight of Brazil's increasing numbers of landless people. Almost two decades on, the MST has resettled over 300,000 poor, often destitute, families on over 21 million hectares of land. Its model of land reform from below has turned it into the biggest social movement in Latin America.

One reason for the remarkable rise of the MST is straightforward. In this enormous nation, bigger than the USA and covering nearly half of South America, less than 1 per cent of the population owns almost half of the land. Much of this is owned by absentee landowners, who rarely, if ever, actually farm it.[1] According to the MST, 60 per cent of Brazilian farmland lies idle while 25 million peasants scrape by in temporary agricultural jobs and millions more go hungry in the slums of Brazil's teeming cities.[2] Brazil is pipped to the post – just – by Paraguay as the country with the most unequal land distribution in the world. And globalisation, it seems, is making it worse.

The MST seeks to change all this. And it long ago gave up asking anyone's permission.

Daniella and I arrive at the newly occupied farm in a convoy of cars and vans which left the MST's local office in the state capital of São Luís an hour or so before. The convoy has come to bring food and support to the people who occupied this land twelve days ago, in the face of a local government which is keen to see them gone.

We pull up at the main farm gates in a cloud of red dust. The landscape is vast and empty: flat, wide open country; wire fences, scrub grass, unbounded fields and tall, elegant *babasul* palms reaching into a huge sky. A cluster of black and yellow police cars are parked on the dirt road. The main track to the farm buildings has been blocked by the settlers, who have strung barbed wire across it and built a temporary shelter of poles and black tarpaulin, which crackles slightly in an almost imperceptible breeze. Across the blockaded gate hangs the MST's emblem – a red flag adorned with a rough map of Brazil and a man and woman holding a machete aloft in a gesture of rural defiance.

Arriving in the convoy with us, among others, is Helena Burros Heluy, the only representative of the Workers' Party (PT) in the

Maranhão state assembly. In this state, at least, the PT – in the sole form of Helena – are the only politicians prepared to take the MST and their concerns seriously. 'There are three attitudes among state politicians to the MST,' she tells me later. 'One, make a point of ignoring them. Two, vehemently oppose them. Three, deliberately show them in a bad light to the public at large – call them thieves, terrorists, that sort of thing. Landowner control here is almost total. But the MST is a serious movement, with serious national concerns, and real credibility, and this will not do.'

Helena gets out of her car and moves across the red dust road towards one of the policemen guarding the entrance. He is wearing, like his colleagues, a black bullet-proof vest. A small gaggle of local journalists gathers around her. I join them.

'I want to go on to this land, to see how the people are,' she tells the policeman. 'Will you allow me in?' The policeman looks nervous. Helena is a well-dressed, determined, middle-aged woman with authority, and she is not about to be fobbed off.

'I'll have to radio my commander,' he says. 'After all, you are a deputy in the state assembly, so we don't want to infringe your civil rights.'

'So if I wasn't a state deputy it would be acceptable to infringe my civil rights?'

The policeman smiles, wanly.

'And tell me something,' says Helena, pressing home her advantage, 'why won't you allow food in to these people? You do realise this is illegal?' He shuffles a bit in the dust.

'Just my orders,' he says. 'From the commander.'

'The police commander has no authority to give such orders,' insists the deputy. 'Tell me who really gave the orders.' The policeman looks at the ground and stops shuffling. He knows when he's beaten.

'They came from over his head,' he mutters. 'From the state government.'

After that, the policeman is only too happy to take out some of his impotence on me, when I decide to see how strict the food blockade is, and whether an ignorant foreign visitor can get away with breaching it. The answer turns out to be no. But within a few hours of our arrival – and, more significantly, of Helena's intercession – it turns out not to matter. The food blockade is suddenly and mysteriously lifted, and we are allowed to take the food we have brought with us on to the settlement.

Inside the estate, a collection of white farm buildings with tiled roofs and blue wooden porches are bustling with activity. People are out exploring the land, testing its readiness for planting, exploring the extent of their new domain. Old men sit on chairs under the open skies, chatting. A radio plays to a woman sewing on one of the porches. Children, shoeless and topless and smiling, throw dust at each other, or follow me around curiously, demanding that I take their photos. People keep slapping me on the back, or grinning at me as they pass, and saying things that, according to Daniella, translate virtually every time as something like, 'Hey, friend, got any *bacuri*?'

At the centre of the complex of buildings, inside an open-sided enclosure with a neat thatched roof, apparently built as a cattle market but never used, hammocks are strung up from every available beam. A line of people snakes around the edge of the building, holding plates and forks, queuing to reach the two steaming iron pots of beans and rice that contain their lunch. Several people invite us to eat, but they have little enough as it is without me taking it.

Half an hour later I find myself sitting on one of the porches, in a wickerwork chair, surrounded by people. Children are crawling around the floor scribbling on the tiles with chalk at the direction of a young woman who is apparently childminding for much of the camp. Another woman sits on a chair at the edge of the porch, breastfeeding, wearing a red MST cap backwards. In front of the porch is a dirt track that runs from the blockaded entrance off into the depths of the farm. The white and blue fenceposts that edge it are strung with MST flags, staking their claim to this liberated land; this republic of the poor.

On the porch with me sits Anildo de Morais, one of the MST's state co-ordinators. He has dark stubble and dark skin, and wears what most people here are wearing; flip-flops, shorts, a T-shirt and the ubiquitous MST cap.

'We have been waiting eight months for the government to tell us which of the farms in this area were not productive, and whether any of them would be given to us,' he tells me. 'For eight months, three hundred landless families were camped on a roadside nearby waiting to be given land, and the government gave nothing. So we decided not to wait any longer, and to take this land ourselves. The occupation was quite simple. The families got on to lorries and buses, and we all came here. There was one night watchman on duty, and he just opened the gate and let us in. It was all peaceful. Next day, the farm manager arrived from the city with about fifty heavily armed police. They started pushing us around and pointing their guns at our children and old people, but we didn't react. The manager came in and went to his house and took out some suitcases with things in and left. Then we built the barbed wire fence to stop them driving their police cars in, so they just sat outside all day and night to intimidate us.' Around us, on the porch, people begin to nod.

'On the third night we were here,' interjects a woman, 'they spent the whole night with their sirens on! Very loudly, so we couldn't sleep!' There are more nods.

'Anyway,' says Anildo, 'the farm owner went to the local courts, and yesterday the judge said that within fifteen days, we have to leave this land, by court order. Which means fifteen days to challenge the court order. We have a lawyer working on it. We are hopeful. We will tell the court what we told the police: if you throw these people off this land, where will they go?'

A white-haired man leaning on a fencepost a few yards from the porch doesn't know where he would go, but he's glad he came here. His name, he tells me, is Arnoldo, and he's forty-seven. He was a farmer until 1983, when a bigger farm bought his land, and he was forced to move to the city in search of work. He hated it.

'I work the land,' he says. 'That's all I have ever done. I have never had a boss, I have always been my own person. I worried all the time when I was in the city. I never had a job there and I don't understand the city. Ever since we left our land we suffered. And then we came here.'

It looks hard here, I say. What if you're thrown off? What about the police? Is it worth it?

'It is risky,' says Arnoldo, 'but I don't have any worries. It's a hard life, but it's what I know. And one day we will win over these people who don't want us to work peacefully on our land; who take it away so we can't work. If we all unite, then we will be able to avoid any problems.' He talks quietly, matter-of-factly. Curious boys skulk at his elbow, staring at me then looking away, giggling, when I catch their eye.

'Here,' continues Arnoldo, 'there is a lot of solidarity. If there is anybody in need, we help them. We have already planted some vegetable gardens, and some rice and corn. I have left my wife and children in town until it is safe here; then they can come too, and we can be a family. My wife is worried, she knows I could even lose my life. But I tell her it is worth it. Ever since I was thrown off my land I haven't been able to find real peace.' His lined, brown face breaks into a smile under his wide-brimmed straw hat.

'Here,' he says, 'I have found peace again.'

Land – what it produces, who lives on it, how it is organised, how it is owned, the cultures that spring from it – is one of the fundamental pillars of human society. An estimated 53 per cent of the world's population is rural – though within a decade it is predicted that, for the first time in human history, the numbers living on the land will begin to be eclipsed by the numbers living in cities and towns.[3] Even when this happens, though, the world's urbanites will be as dependent on the land and what it produces as they ever were.

For those who live outside the rapidly expanding urban sprawl, now as in the past, access to enough land to feed your family, and/or to produce food for sale, has always been one of the most effective ways to enable people to live secure, independent lives. Loss of, and lack of access to, land, on the other hand, has always been and remains one of the biggest causes of poverty.

Peter Rosset, co-director of the Institute for Food and Development Policy, based in California, is one of the world's foremost authorities on land and land reform. He currently lives and works in Chiapas, where the struggle for land was central to both the original Mexican Revolution and the Zapatista uprising. Back in San Cristobal, five months before I got to Brazil, I had talked to him about the global context of land access, land reform, and land rights.

'We've been saying for decades that you can't have any kind of sustainable or broad-based development that will really address issues of poverty or political democracy if you have an extremely inequitable distribution of land,' he told me. 'In rural areas, people who are landless or land-poor – people who have land that's too small to support their families – are basically marginalised from the national economy. Firstly they don't have the resources available to feed themselves or their family. Secondly, that forces a level of poverty on them that's so severe that they're not a part of the market. And if they're not a part of the market then nobody addresses their concerns. It's inequality that leads to that situation. The poor have no significant political or economic power.'

On the other hand, said Rosset, ensuring that land is fairly distributed – and undertaking radical land reform, if necessary, to make it that way – can be one of the best ways to improve people's lives.

'Historically,' he went on, 'countries that have had more equitable land distribution than others have developed faster and in a more broad-based and inclusive way over the long term – over hundreds of years. In the shorter term, say from the end of World War Two to now, the very few countries that really did accomplish expropriation and redistribution of quality farmland for most of the very poor people are the countries that have had economic miracles; Japan, for example, or Taiwan, or South Korea.'

Brazil never had the sort of revolution that brought land reform to so many Mexicans, and never underwent the traumatic post-war upheavals that led the Japanese or Korean governments to begin handing land back to their people. Partly as a result, it is still run to a large extent by a landholding elite, and has the second-most unequal land distribution on Earth. This is nothing new; the country's heavily concentrated land-ownership pattern is a legacy from the days of the Portuguese Empire. But the rush to join the global market is exacerbating the situation.

Brazil opened up its agricultural markets to competition in the 1990s. The Zapatistas, for one, would have recognised what happened next. In came the subsidised products from foreign agribusiness farms, out went much of the Brazilian government's support for its own agriculture, and into the city slums went a steady stream of small farmers, unable to compete with some of the wealthiest and most voracious agribusiness corporations on the planet. Between 1985 and 1995, the number of small family farms in Brazil dropped by a fifth, and the number of people employed in agriculture fell from 23 million to 18 million – the biggest decline ever in such a short time.[4]

Taking advantage of the new regime, multinational corporations began moving in on the fundamental basis of farming: seed. Seed production is crucial to agriculture and any company that can control it has its competitors – not to mention farmers – over a barrel. It also has an opportunity to focus production on a few key species and introduce new technologies – genetic modification, for example. Sure enough, in came Monsanto, DuPont, Dow, AgrEvo and other biotechnology giants: by 1999, they controlled 90 per cent of Brazil's seed market. 'We are going back to colonial times,' noted Brazilian economist Horacio Martins, 'when our economy was controlled from abroad.'[5]

President Fernando Henrique Cardoso, Brazil's man-at-the-helm from 1994 to 2002, liked to see himself, along with Tony

Blair, Bill Clinton and German Chancellor Gerhard Schröder, as one of the creators of the 'Third Way', that slippery political attempt to triangulate between an increasingly rampant market and the needs of society. There was, said Cardoso, no alternative to globalisation. 'It's the law of the market,' he told a farmers' leader who came to plead with him to do something about the country's rural collapse; 'it's inexorable.'[6] Brazil's rural future would be to specialise in a few export crops, grown on large, cost-efficient farms: soya, coffee, sugar cane, cotton. This would bring in the foreign currency which would allow Brazil to service its debt and develop. By 1999, with this policy in full swing, Brazil was earning itself around $5 billion from soya exports alone. Unfortunately it was spending another $7.5 billion importing food – mostly rice, beans and maize – that it had traditionally grown itself.

Since becoming a member of the WTO, of course, Brazil had little choice in the matter. The WTO's Agreement on Agriculture requires countries to continually lower tariffs and subsidies, enforce minimum import levels on various crops, and introduce no new protection or support for their farmers. This last rule does not, however, apply to existing support. In other words, under the WTO's Agreement, Europe and the USA are allowed to continue massively subsidising their farmers as they have done for decades – but 'developing' countries like Brazil are not allowed to introduce similar protection themselves.

In rural Brazil, as a result of all this, several trends are converging. A small number of large farmers have benefited from the new market regime. Around 90,000 of them, it is estimated – less than 2 per cent of all Brazil's farmers – account for over 60 per cent of agricultural income. These are the big exporters. The rest are not so lucky: millions of them, according to one of the Brazilian government's top advisers, are in big trouble. Over 80 per cent of Brazil's farms could go under as a result of globalisation. Many already have; steady streams of people are being forced off the land, unable to compete. Over 4 million flooded into the cities between 1996 and 1999 alone, often ending up in the filthy slums that surround Rio de Janeiro, São Paulo and other such megacities. 'There is no way,' the government adviser, Guilherme Dias, warned his bosses in 2000, 'in which these producers can survive a transition as violent as the one we're going through . . . such is the scale of the social problem created by this transformation that the country's productive structure is threatened.'[7]

Many of the small farmers who remain, precariously, on the land are reduced to the status of hired hands – contract labourers producing seeds for American multinationals, chickens or pigs for giant meat companies, tobacco for European smokers. The expansion of vast soya monocultures to feed increasing global demand for this crop, which is used mainly to feed cattle for Western consumption, is gradually edging into the Amazon basin, taking parts of the world's biggest and most diverse rainforest with it as it goes.

Finally, and perhaps most bitterly of all, Brazil's immensely concentrated land distribution is concentrating even further. Between 1992 and 1998, the proportion of land taken up by farms of over 2,000 hectares increased from 39 per cent to 43 per cent, and the number of very large farms – over 50,000 hectares – almost doubled, to cover almost 10 per cent of all farmland.[8]

Enter the MST. In the early 1980s, when what was to become the Landless Workers' Movement began to coalesce, Brazil was still ruled by the military dictatorship that had seized control of the country in 1964. That coup had put paid to widespread hopes that the left-wing government it overthrew might put a serious national land reform process in place from above. All that remained, it seemed, was to initiate one from below. This, with a military junta in power, was a risky business; but so was starving to death without land. Though globalisation had not yet begun to bite, mechanisation was forcing families from their farms and concentrating land in the hands of fewer and fewer people.

In 1979, in Rio Grande do Sul, Brazil's southernmost state, a group of landless families, with the help of sympathetic supporters in the Catholic Church, decided to act. With nothing to lose but their lives, they invaded a local estate and claimed it for their own. Nationwide media attention made it difficult for the government to send in the troops, and the occupation, miraculously, survived. Within a year the state government had formally granted the land to the families. Inspired by this victory, other landless people across Brazil – the *sem terra*, as they began to call themselves – started to invade land too. In 1984, a group of a hundred *sem terra* from thirteen states got together with trades unionists, church workers and others to turn this burgeoning social movement into a national force, and the MST was born. 'Land for those who live and work on it' ran their slogan. Nobody, including those involved, had any idea what this new political force was about to unleash.

'There are three things that every man should do in his life,' says Sebastian Batista to me, as he walks me around the edge of his cornfield. 'He should write a book, plant a tree and have a child. I have done the second and third of these. You are doing the first. And there are plenty of trees here you can help us plant, so we will both have done two out of three.' Sebastian is a big, serious man, with short black hair, wearing jeans, a blue jumper and cowboy boots. A knife is attached to his belt. He and his wife, Nazare, are among about 500 formerly landless families who have created an enviable life for themselves on one of the MST's earliest settlements, Itapeva, in São Paulo state. Itapeva was idle land when Sebastian and others invaded it in 1984, the year that the MST was born. Back then, there was nothing here. Today, it is an object lesson in how land reform from below can give new life to those who have nothing.

São Paulo is a long way from the Amazon rainforest, but the rain, when it comes, seems like it belongs there. It is vast, instant, sheeting, and it drives us to seek shelter. Inside Sebastian's low, wooden house, a soggy dog is sheltering underneath the porch, dripping guiltily on to the wooden floor, and an old man is leaning on a wall eyeing the sky with a quiet satisfaction. 'Good for the crops,' he says. Inside the kitchen, Sebastian sits down and begins to tell me about Itapeva.

'We came here when the MST was just beginning,' he tells me, 'but it wasn't until 1995 that the government formally recognised our right to this land. Eleven years of struggle, but it was worth it. I was brought up on a farm around here, but then I went to the city and became a metalworker. I lost my job, and had nothing, so I decided to come back to the land; that's when I joined the MST. When we first took the land, we lived for a year under black plastic. All of us – families, children, the old people. It was hard.' Nazare ambles in through the door. She has been outside, in the rain, picking ripe plums off the tree in the garden. She piles them up on the table in front of us.

'Now we have good homes, and much more,' says Sebastian, as we both start on the plums, which are delicious. 'Tomorrow, you can see. At the moment we are growing corn, beans, rice, soya and wheat. We have pigs, and we produce honey, cheese and milk. Some of it we keep, some we sell, though it is very hard to sell these days.'

'The soil!' interjects Nazare, from the other side of the room, where she is preparing dinner. She is a kind, friendly woman with curly black hair whose hospitality knows no bounds. She has insisted on feeding me and Daniella and putting us up for the night. 'The soil here is wonderful. Beautiful red earth – anything you plant, it grows. In some places in Brazil the land is terrible; all the people can do is graze cows. Here, we can throw any seeds on to the ground, whatever they are, and they will just grow!'

'The MST,' says Sebastian, 'is very important. It allows people to start to do things for themselves. If you vote, you change nothing. We could have Jesus Christ as president, and he'd still have to do all the deals that politicians do. He would still not be in control. Unless the people can start to do things for themselves, and unless we can change our way of seeing things, nothing will change – in Brazil or anywhere.' He drops a plum stone on to the concrete floor.

'The MST help you to think. They teach illiterate people to read and write. They teach people how to work together. We have schools, land, homes, and all of it we have got because we stood up and we fought for it. In the old days, church people used to say that if you were poor it was God's will. The MST say, if you are poor, it is because someone is exploiting you. One thing I have learned since I joined: Brazil is a very rich country, and there should be a place in it for everyone. But if you want that place – that place which you deserve – well, then you are going to have to fight for it.' He finishes another plum.

'None of us will get rich here,' he goes on, 'but we have what we need, and what we want. We have enough. Everybody should have enough in Brazil; and they could. But I will tell you the most important thing that the MST has given me.' He looks me straight in the eye.

'The most important thing,' he says, 'is my dignity.'

Itapeva is a big place: 17,000 hectares of land, studded with houses and communal buildings. Like other MST settlements it is run as a co-op and is an interesting combination of common and private land. The settlers have each been allocated a piece of land of almost equal size – about seventeen hectares each, Sebastian tells me – within the whole. None of the families have their own land titles, however, because this would allow them to sell their land and break up the settlement. The landscape, like that of Maranhão, is broad, flat and expansive.

The next morning I am being given a tour by Jamil Ramos, one of the MST co-ordinators on the site who is unsurprisingly keen to show me the best of the settlement. Jamil is balding, with a goatee beard and an MST T-shirt, and the first thing he wants to do is show me the radio station.

'*Radio Camponesa*,' he explains, which translates as 'farmers' radio'. 'We set it up ourselves, and we broadcast to the whole community. We play traditional country music that is being lost, and we broadcast debates, politics – many things. Whatever we want.'

The radio station is based in a low building with antennae on the roof. We are shown into the studio, a small, square room with a large mixing desk taking up most of the space, and revolutionary murals on the wall behind it. A random collection of people are hanging around, there is no lock on the studio door, and as a young, lithe man behind the decks broadcasts to the *sem terras*, kids play around on the floor, fiddling curiously with CDs and being half-heartedly shushed by their mothers, who are gossiping in the next room.

I thought I might interview the DJ; ask him what the radio station does, and why, and what it means to the community. It turns out, though, that he wants to interview me; through Daniella, naturally. He hands me a very large microphone and quizzes me on air about what I'm doing here, what I think of Itapeva, how I like Brazil. 'Do you have any message for the heroes of the MST?' he asks me, in conclusion, and politely listens while I stumble about trying to say something inspiring, hoping Daniella's translation sounds better than the original.

The next stop is the herbalist. Itapeva has a women's co-op which produces herbal products from a pot-pourri of herbs grown in a special plot behind their office. 'Lucia the herbalist', as she is known, takes me outside to her herb garden. It has been bucketing down all morning, and in a brief gap in the rain she shows me around the neat plot, picking sprigs for me to sniff and explaining their purpose. Inside the office-cum-clinic, Lucia explains that the main function of their work is health care.

'There are no doctors in Itapeva,' she says, 'and the nearest one is in the town, a long journey away.' Lucia, and the nine other women in the co-op, make up for much of that lack of medical attention with their herbal medicines. They have allergy creams, headache remedies, lotions for skin problems, disinfectants and more, all made from the contents of their garden. They even, Lucia tells me, proudly, make a type of flour with added calcium, which is used to make bread for young children and people with osteoporosis.

'Most people are very healthy here,' she says, 'and many problems can be solved this way.' Then she sells me a bottle of home-made herbal shampoo and some MST-recipe mosquito repellent, which I don't feel able to refuse.

An hour or so later, my tour complete, I find myself eating, probably faster than is polite, a plate of delicious home-made cheese, and drinking strong home-grown coffee, in the house of Ilda Martins da Souza, a 56-year-old woman with lively eyes, a wide, firm smile and a house full of grandchildren who run in and out of the room and roll across the floor together as she speaks. Ilda was, she tells me, one of the original occupiers of Itapeva.

'For two years,' she says, 'we lived on a roadside before we got this land. And it was worth all of it. Look around you. Yet since I got involved with the MST, I have learned that it is not just about getting land, but about understanding how to live in a different type of society. Since I came here, I have seen a real transformation in people – people making an effort, understanding that we can live in a more egalitarian society. This is what made me fall in love with the MST, and what brought me out here. The more I got involved, the more beautiful things I found out.' As she speaks, her grandchildren, Nina and Marco, catapult themselves from nowhere on to her lap. She tousles their hair and tells them to go and fetch more food from the kitchen.

'Of course,' she goes on, 'not everything is perfect. The MST is not perfect, and neither is Itapeva. There is still a lot of work to do, here and elsewhere. This is a continuous struggle, and there are tensions. For example, when we were camping out, waiting for land, there was total solidarity. When we got the land, when the government came in and granted title, when people got their houses – then it was less easy. People's opinions change; some get more selfish. But still, this is much more of a brotherly society than I have ever seen. It's in this struggle that we come to firmly believe that there is a way out for Brazil – there can be a new way forward.'

Nina and Marco march back in with more coffee and cheese. Outside, the rain is pounding down again, on to Ilda's tin roof. I ask her what it's like being a woman in the MST.

'Better!' she says immediately. 'In Brazil, men are in charge. In the MST, it is much more equal. Early on in the MST's life, women would come to all the initial meetings, before an occupation. They would come for years, and say they had a husband, but he never turned up at the meetings. When they got their land and their house, the first thing that would arrive would be the husband. This made some of us very angry. Then the government would come in and write the contract for ownership of the house, and the contract would be made out not with the woman, but with the husband! In *his* name!' She snorts, derisively. 'Some of these men,' she goes on, 'would then try and sell the house, and the women would be homeless again! We have put a stop to that. In the MST now, we do not allow this to happen. The women's role is very equal. Here, both people in couples can really contribute in a way that I have not seen elsewhere.'

Most importantly though, Ilda thinks that what the MST stands for is something that can apply outside the settlements – perhaps even outside Brazil. She makes this point several times, until she's sure I've got the message.

'People have to work for their own transformation,' she says. 'People often think of this in terms of consuming: "There are good things out there and I want them; I have to buy them." Then people just get attached to small things, and forget about the bigger things in life. It makes you dependent on people who sell you things, or on the government to give you schools or roads or hospitals. People have to lose their fear of struggling – not in the sense of fighting or violence, but in the sense of addressing their own problems, and making their own answers. On your own, this struggle will not work. Learn solidarity, and struggle together, and it does. We have all seen that. There is a lot of good in all of us – together, we can spread it. This is creating solidarity.'

Ilda heaves her determined grandchildren off her lap again, gets up and walks across the room. I'm horrified to discover that I've managed to stuff both plates of cheese down my throat in under fifteen minutes but Ilda doesn't notice, and probably wouldn't mind if she did. She's looking out of the window, where the rain is still battering down, running in rivulets across the red roads and the green verges.

'People die,' she says, suddenly. 'It's such a shame. They go to heaven, they say, but why would you want to?' She looks at me, smiling again, the rain still drumming on the roof.

'I am only going to heaven,' she says, 'if they can guarantee that heaven will be like this.'

The MST's head office, in the smog-hung megacity of São Paulo, could be any office anywhere. Apart from the framed, black-and-white photos on the walls – famous, stark and beautiful shots, taken by photographer Sebastião Salgado, of life in MST settlements – it is a comfortable, unexceptional, officey sort of place: pot plants, photocopiers, a receptionist, a water cooler; a million miles away from Maranhão and Itapeva. It's a comparison which the MST's critics have not been slow to highlight, and one which can grate: dirt-poor farmers living under plastic at the suggestion of an organisation run by non-farming urbanites with regular salaries. Some have accused the MST leadership of manipulating the landless for their own political ends; an accusation which assumes something of a lack of intelligence and guile on behalf of rural people. It is true, though, that the MST's leadership, some of whom see the organisation as a political project to transform Brazil, can clash with the grass roots, for whom the overwhelming priority is everyday life, and improving their material lot.

I am here to talk to one of the MST's leading lights, Neuri Rossetto, a man who sees no contradiction between these two goals. Neuri is one of twenty-three people on the MST's national directorate, which is elected by delegates from the settlements at regular national conferences. He is a middle-aged man in glasses who has been involved with the MST for many years and has seen it transform itself, slowly and sometimes painfully, from a movement for land reform into what Ilda wanted me to see it as in Itapeva – a broad-based national movement for change.

This, says Neuri, is the aspect of the MST's work that is most overlooked. It is also, he says, probably the most important for the future.

'You could say the MST has gone through three phases in its development,' he tells me, as we sit around a big wooden conference table drinking coffee. 'The first phase, in the early 1980s, was the movement arising. The second phase, from about 1985 to 1995, saw us consolidating and growing. We are now in a third phase – perhaps the most difficult one. I call it the "confrontation of models". To put it very simply, we have realised that you cannot imagine a traditional model of land reform under the kind of capitalism we have today.' He shrugs, almost imperceptibly.

'We want the landless to have their bit of land,' he says. 'That was the reason for the birth of the MST. But the problem is that within the current economic model there is simply no *need* for small farmers – no need for *most* farmers. Small farmers are being penalised by the market, and this has got a lot worse since 1995, when the government really began to introduce neoliberal measures into the countryside. Even during the military dictatorship, agriculture was supported by the government – the annual budget was about $18 billion. Under Cardoso's government, it's gone down to less than half that amount.' The results, he explains, have been an attack on small farmers and small landowners from virtually every side.

'There has been a big advance in agribusiness control,' he says. 'Four or five big companies control almost all of our agro-industries. How can our settlements compete? We are told that we must enter the market – even if we want to, we can't. Three big companies control the whole dairy market, for example. Three of our bigger settlements went into dairy production for a while but there was no way they could compete. If the dairy companies that controlled the market didn't like their prices, they would just go elsewhere and there was no alternative. Prices are so low, and there are no subsidies, that much of agriculture is simply unviable. Now we are importing everything in this country – potatoes from Belgium, coconuts from Malaysia, animal feed – all things that we can grow, that we don't need to import. Neoliberalism in the countryside has done all this.'

Cardoso's government was more than aware of this problem, and its claim to have done something about it makes Brazil's land problem more complex, and more interesting. Cardoso and his combative agrarian development minister, Raul Jungmann, boasted for years that they had instituted 'the world's biggest programme of agrarian reform'. Government figures – contested and argued over on all sides – claim that the Cardoso government, between 1994 and 2001, settled over 500,000 families on around 18 million hectares of land, much of it requisitioned from big landlords.[9] It cost the government an estimated $6.5 billion. The result, according to Cardoso's former adviser on land reform, Francisco Grazino, was 'the largest and the worst land reform programme in the world'.[10]

There are many criticisms of the government's policy. The MST, according to Neuri, has two crucial ones. First, he says, the numbers are deeply suspect. Those 500,000 families, he tells me, are previously landless people who were granted land titles by the government – but they include many of the people settled on occupied land by the MST, and then granted titles by the government. In other words, many of the people that the government claims to have given land, were actually given land by the MST.

'Some people in government,' says Neuri, 'used these figures to argue that the MST should not exist – that we are not needed, the government was handing out land. The opposite is true – if we had not pressured the government through our occupations, their land reform would not be happening. And much of what they say they have done has been done by the MST.'

The wider criticism, though, is shared not just by radical reformers like the MST, but by critics on all sides of the debate. It is, simply, that giving people land, even in a halting, imperfect and far from comprehensive way, becomes almost meaningless when your economic policies make it practically impossible to survive on it. This is the government's problem. But it is also the MST's.

'Yes,' concedes Neuri, 'this economic model doesn't *need* land reform – it can do without it. So we help someone fight to get a piece of land, and two years later he realises it's economically unviable and he can't stay on it. The psychological blow to people is huge. So what can be done in the face of this system? What does land reform mean in this world – in this system? How can Cardoso talk of land for the landless when his policies remove more people from the land every year than the MST and the government combined can give land to? We need to address this confrontation of models. This is the MST's challenge at the moment.' He takes a deep breath, and emits a very audible sigh.

'It is a very, very big challenge,' he says, 'but we must try and meet it. We have to keep organising the rural population to demand land reform, but we are also working with other organisations on what we call a "popular project" for Brazil. Together we are looking at this crucial question – how can we organise the country so that the basic needs of the population are met?'

This 'popular project' could turn out to be a significant leap forward for the MST. First announced at their fourth national congress, in 2000, it proclaims the MST's ambition to be a national, political force – and, effectively, its realisation that constructive land reform without wider social, political and economic change is an impossibility. It is the organisation's biggest challenge to date.

'The popular project is in its infancy,' says Neuri, 'but its aims are to get to the roots of the current problems, to elaborate solutions, and to advance mass organisation of people to pursue those solutions. To do this, we are allying with other popular movements, with trade unions, with progressive parts of the Church, with leading individuals and with others who wish to join. We are building a national mass movement for change.'

As yet, there is no manifesto; but there are some stated goals, some of which the MST laid out at the 2000 congress at which the project was announced. There, 11,000 delegates from twenty-three states called for the suspension of foreign debt repayments, refocusing of the public budget on health, education and agriculture and defaulting on a recent IMF loan, given to Cardoso's government to help it through a financial crisis, to allow Brazilians to 'retake the reins of economic policy'. These actions, say the MST, would allow for an ambitious reworking of Brazil's agricultural model.

First, of course, the MST wants meaningful land reform. But, understanding that this would not be enough in itself, it looks to a refocusing of agriculture based on providing for the country's needs before focusing on export. Family agriculture should be strengthened through guaranteed prices and rural credits, agricultural co-ops promoted to make market access easier for small farmers and government bodies dealing with rural affairs restructured. Research into agricultural technology should be shifted away from biotechnology and other such corporate fixes, towards developing technologies compatible with Brazil's soil, landscape and family farms.

The overall effect, runs the theory, at least, will be to stimulate a model of agriculture based on small and medium-sized farms, which will in turn stimulate national food security and poverty relief. This, says Neuri, is known as 'food sovereignty'.

'Every nation,' he says, 'has the right to grow food for itself, to decide how it will farm, what it will grow, what it will import and export. Food is not just another commodity, like training shoes or cars – it is part of what makes societies grow and survive. Food sovereignty is a vital principle. So, for example, agriculture should be removed from the WTO, removed from all free-trade agreements, and the people should decide their own farming models, based on their cultures and needs.' The MST is far from alone here – food sovereignty is a concept that is increasingly promoted by farmers and activists all over the world. At the World Social Forum, a half-day conference was held on the subject, at which delegates agreed it was a principle with global application, and a human right. This, too, was evidence of the landless movement's wider political ambitions – the MST was one of the founders of the World Social Forum.

These are the MST's long-term ambitions – ambitions which it hopes its popular project can build support for and ambitions which, it seems to me, demonstrate an interesting combination of practicality and strategic thinking. Wherever I have seen the MST at work, this has been the case – impressive, on-the-ground organisation, spurring its members on to think bigger, and think beyond what they have already achieved. There is a lot more to be done, but the process is under way.

On the ground, some results are already clear. Beyond the obvious achievement of giving land, and a living, to millions who had nothing, the MST has, for example, instituted health-care projects across its settlements, training health agents, creating AIDS education projects and promoting medicinal herb projects like that at Itapeva. It also has an ambitious programme of popular education going on in its settlements. An initial demand that government provide schools on settlements for MST children has blossomed into a semi-autonomous education project, in which the MST trains its own teachers, and institutes mass popular education and literacy programmes for both children and adults. The systems are far from comprehensive or perfect, but the MST is making strides in forging a new type of popular education, with some government help. The MST claims that 150,000 children attend elementary classes thanks to this work, and that 1,200 MST-trained educators have taught 25,000 landless adults to read and write. The next step, they say, is the creation of an 'MST university'.

It is precisely such work that highlights the MST's broader aims – aims they now hope to transfer to the national stage.

'In Brazil,' says Neuri, 'it is quite possible for all people's needs to be met if we can organise together and create a system that works for all. We put those needs into four big categories: land, work, housing and education, and we say that we must democratise all of these needs, and make them available to all the people. We need to democratise the land, democratise capital and democratise education. We have to tear down the fences that surround all these three things. This is a huge challenge, and we do not yet have all the answers we need. But we must organise to face it – organise families to take part in the task of transforming the model.'

'Every man,' says Osmar Brandaó, 'should have a piece of land.' He looks across the broad cornfield that rolls down the hill from his garden towards his pumpkin patch on the other side of the hill. The sun is coursing across the shifting yellow stalks.

'A man without land is incomplete,' he says. 'But how you treat it determines whether it makes you happy.' Osmar, like so many other people I have met on MST settlements, smiles a lot; he is clearly, obviously, openly content. I have seen this everywhere and it has been, for me, an eye-opening sight. Osmar is a blond, blue-eyed man in his thirties. We are sitting talking in battered cane chairs under the shade of tall trees in his garden, while his children and his manic black dog play around us. Osmar has come in from working in his beanfield to talk to me.

'I don't use poison on my land,' explains Osmar. 'I don't use chemicals. Before I came here I used to, but then I started talking to the technicians from the MST and learning what it actually meant for the land. And I asked myself: do I actually want this poison washing into my rivers? Do I want my children to eat the food I am growing with chemicals or do I want to do it the natural way? So now I have gone organic.' He says he doesn't regret the decision.

'I do find organic farming is harder work,' he says. 'A lot more weeding, for example. But I also find this is more worthwhile, and I spend a lot less money on buying chemicals. A lot of things change when you go organic. I am much more conscious about the land and how it works than I was when I used sprays for everything – about the micro-organisms in the soil, about the birds and creatures and human relationships with the soil. Where I used to live, people used a lot of poison – you didn't see one bee, you didn't see any birds singing, and a lot of my friends had health problems . . . here it is different. All of us here – we can see the results.'

Osmar is not alone: all his neighbours in the MST settlement of Hulha Negra, in Rio Grande do Sul, not far from the border with Uruguay, farm organically. I have already been given a tour of the settlement: the co-operative farm shop; the warehouse, stacked with huge straw bales, home to a roaring threshing machine; the wide fields bounded by slippery mud roads; the packaging room, where a small group of teenagers are glueing seed packets. Other farmers have explained to me how they sell their vegetables at a new MST farmers' market in the nearby town of Bagé; how they are learning to treat their cows with home-grown herbal medicine; how their health has improved since they gave up using pesticides. Like Osmar, they are part of a relatively new attempt within the MST to find a new type of solution to the economic – and the ecological – problems that farmers in Brazil face.

In his low, square, concrete office, half an hour or so up the road, Artemio Parcianello is explaining why. Artemio is a seed co-ordinator for the MST's regional seed co-operative, Cooperal. He has already shown me the vast and chaotic collection of plastic bottles crammed with every conceivable type of seed which takes up most of the space in his office, and a set of painful-looking tubey devices which, he proudly informed me, are used for inseminating cows.

The MST settlements in the Hulha Negra region nestle in the middle of some of the best land in Brazil. All the biggest national seed companies, and many multinationals, grow seeds in the region, and when MST settlers first arrived here in the 1980s, they began growing seeds for the big companies to tide them through. But it didn't take long for them to encounter familiar problems.

'After a couple of years,' explains Artemio, 'we realised that the seed companies' way of working clashed with our values – they selected certain families to work with over others, played people off against each other, discarded certain workers. This did not fit with what the MST stands for. And there were other problems. Even if we wanted to, we could not compete in the markets with our produce, and we were at the mercy of the companies.'

Enter João Rockett. I met Rockett at his house in Bagé, before I visited Hulha Negra. He is a talkative, enthusiastic agronomist, who may yet help to transform the MST; he is the man who introduced the settlers in Hulha Negra to organic farming.

'I believe the MST's best chance is to go organic,' he said. 'There is a growing market for it, it is inexpensive, it is healthier, and it allows them to have control over their own production that the seed companies will not allow. But they are slow. Many people on many settlements want to go organic. The leadership, though, is slower. They are being pushed by the people on the ground. Many people in the top levels of the MST are old political warriors. There is something of a division between some of the people in head office and those on the ground. They think that land reform and political change, nationally, is more important than sustainable agriculture. But there is no contradiction. And the interesting thing is that the young people are a lot more interested in organic farming than many of the older ones, and the settlements are pushing the leadership towards it. So I think things will change.'

What João and Artemio both agree on is that going organic could, potentially, solve a number of problems for the MST. First, it provides them with a unique product to sell – a niche market, as an economist would call it. They can never compete with the multinational corporations in terms of volume, technology, cheap labour or sheer muscle; maybe, instead, they can produce what people increasingly want: organic seeds and organic food. This economic solution is also an ecological solution; one which rejuvenates the environment and people's health, and costs a lot less in inputs for farmers. *Agro-ecologia*, as it is known, could provide a decentralised, ecological and non-corporate alternative model for many of Brazil's farmers.

The MST's seed company, Cooperal, broke its contract with the big multinationals a few years ago, Artemio tells me, and instead set up a deal with a new company that the MST had set up and developed – Bionatur. Bionatur is an organic seed company, created, owned and controlled by the MST. It produces organic seeds grown by settlers, and sells them to the world's growing legion of organic farmers. When Rockett helped set up Bionatur, twelve farmers began by growing a few carrots and onions, as an experiment. Today, over fifty families grow more than twenty seed varieties, which are sold nationally and internationally.[11] And the project is growing.

There is another side, too, to the MST's ecological progress at Hulha Negra. Many of the people in Artemio's office wear caps or T-shirts with 'No transgenics' and 'I am not a lab rat' printed on them. Like so many others around the world, MST activists are increasingly engaged in a campaign against genetically modified foods. Since 1999, the Brazilian supreme court has maintained a ban on the growing of GM foods in Brazil, pending studies into their safety – a ban that the Cardoso government, lobbied hard by Monsanto and other biotechnology companies, long wanted overturned. Ironically for the government, the ban has actually been rather good for Brazil, even in conventional economic terms. Brazil is the world's second-biggest soya exporter, and since the first and third biggest – the USA and Argentina – both grow GM soya, Brazil has been able to cater for growing European and world demand for non-GM food. Its share of the world's soya trade has increased from 24 per cent to 36 per cent since the ban.[12]

For the MST – which, with Greenpeace and other environmentalists, has taken part in the destruction of GM crops – the main concern is, again, corporate control. Quite apart from the possible health and environmental dangers of GM crops, they are, as any farmer can tell you, a key means by which corporations can gain control over farmers – selling them GM 'packages' of seeds and pesticides which they will need to buy every year, creating dependency and using seeds, in Artemio's words, as 'a means of controlling farmers'. It is yet another reason that many MST farmers are keen on going organic; and it is something else that connects them to a global movement within which ecological and economic concerns are intertwined.

Just before I left Hulha Negra I had been sitting under a shady tree with an old farmer called Natalino. He was lean, tanned and bearded, with a cataract in one eye. We were sipping *maté*, a Brazilian national drink, from the hollowed-out gourds that are used to contain it. Natalino was telling me how much happier he was here than before he arrived, telling me how he milked his cows, what he grew, how he was learning to read and what his hopes were for the future. As he did so, he used a word I had heard from many lips recently: 'contentment'. Contentment, said Natalino, was what he had gained since he had occupied this land.

'Peace,' said Arnoldo in Maranhão. 'Dignity,' said Sebastian in Itapeva. 'Heaven,' said Ilda, his neighbour. 'Contentment,' said Natalino. Every time, the words were in their eyes as well as their mouths. And every time, they were expressing something that no economist could measure, and which no activist could campaign for – something impossible to quantify, which can never be turned into statistics, but something which must be at least half the point of everything we all do.

In all the settlements I visited, and among all the people I talked to, that real, unfakeable contentment – that happiness, that new chance, that security, that human dignity – was clear to see. The contentment of people whose lives had clearly improved, and whose independence and pride had been rediscovered. And the contentment, too, of those who live on the land.

People who are even prepared to discuss this are often accused of romanticising rural life. The debate about globalisation, after all, should be about poverty statistics, growth rates, economies of scale, hidden paragraphs in international treaties. It should be measurable, hard, statistical. Romantic sentimentality has no place in the modern world. Living on, and from, the land is hard; hard in a way that urbanites are usually unable to grasp. It must, then, surely be the case that what rural people want to do is get off that land as fast as possible; get into the cities, wash the mud out from under their fingernails, grab a latte, get a job, buy a suit, *be like us*.

This is how the globalisation debate is so often played out. And, applied to the land, it is a debate which is strung with ironies and contradictions. It is certainly true that, all over the world, kids in poor countries dream of leaving the land and living like the TV tells them that everybody in the West does; a lifestyle that approximates to that lived by the cast of *Friends*. Meanwhile, in the West, hypertense city-dwellers dream of exchanging their soul-destroying nine-to-fives for a place in the country with roses round the door.

But there are darker ironies too. Crusaders for the global market have long accused those who even discuss rural alternatives to city life as being middle-class dreamers lulled by a bucolic fantasy, condemning 'the poor' to scratch a living on the land while they kick back in their centrally heated homes. 'We' would deny 'them' 'choice' – the right to choose to be like us. And yet, this 'romanticism', as I discovered in Brazil, and as I had seen in Chiapas, Papua, and elsewhere before, is expressed most often of all by those who live on the land – those whose rural lives are despised or misunderstood by the city-based advocates of the global market dream. Those whose voices, as ever, are ignored.

In reality, it is globalisation which denies rural people choice. It is the missionaries of the market who support an economic system which destroys rural lifestyles and gives people like the MST settlers I met in Brazil no choice but to leave the land they feel at home on and break their backs in the cities, keeping the machine turning. It is globalisation, with its false consumer paradise dangled before all the world's people like a carrot on a string, that is the unattainable dream. And it is globalisation that prevents choice; prevents millions from choosing to stay on the land, providing for their families, living securely on the soil. If you don't believe me, ask the people of the MST; they know where they want to be, and they know who is preventing them from being there.

This is not a debate that is confined to Brazil. Every country on Earth is undergoing vast rural upheavals as a result of globalisation, and all over the world, rural people are fighting back. Across the Americas, landless people, farmers and rural inhabitants, undergoing the same pressures with the same results as in Brazil, are linking up through the Latin American Congress of Rural Organizations (CLOC), in which the MST is a key player. Like the MST, CLOC, which represents millions, is campaigning against the neoliberal policies that are destroying farmers everywhere. In Bolivia, which recently set up its own version of the MST, the indigenous leader of the coca farmers, Evo Morales, came within a whisker of the country's presidency in 2002, riding a tide of anti-neoliberal resentment.

In India, the National Alliance of People's Movements, the Karnataka State Farmers' Association and other groups, representing tens of millions of farmers, are marching against free trade, blockading World Bank meetings, demolishing fast-food outlets and burning Monsanto crops. The Peasant Movement of the Philippines represents 800,000 peasants, landless people and fisherfolk campaigning against the free-trade model. South Africa set up its own Landless People's Movement in 2001, a few months before I visited the country. Farmers in Korea, Japan and Bangladesh are linking up their struggles, and such links are being made all over the world. The tide of rural resistance is increasingly global.

If globalisation is looked at in its historical context, it could be said that what is currently being experienced all over the world is the final act of something that began in the West hundreds of years ago: enclosure. In Britain, and then in other industrialising countries, acts of parliament, economic change and landlord pressure enclosed common land, forced peasants into the new cities, destroyed small farms and consolidated land ownership – a process that made the free-trade project of the nineteenth century possible. The same is now happening all over the world.

So, though, is the struggle against it – for in the rich countries too, farmers fight back. The French Confédération Paysanne, led by the new folk hero José Bové, attacks McDonald's and '*mal bouffe*' (junk food). Canada's National Farmers' Union campaigns against genetically modified crops. Small farmers in the USA protest against NAFTA and the WTO. And increasingly, these currents of rural resistance from north and south link up through the world's first international small farmers' union, Vía Campesina, of which the MST was a founder, to campaign against, and develop alternatives to, the economic model that is destroying the last of the free farmers.

The MST, in other words, is far from alone; in fact, it is part of what is increasingly becoming a global peasants' revolt – a rural uprising against the free-trade economy. As in Brazil, this struggle is throwing up alternative systems, ideas and values: a model of grounded, small-farm agriculture, local traditions, ecological farming, food sovereignty and broad-based social progress that is anathema to everything that globalisation stands for.

It remains to be seen whether Brazil's new president – the Workers' Party leader 'Lula' da Silva, elected in November 2002 – will be willing to make the kind of great leaps that the MST is calling for; or whether the markets will let him. What I have seen in Brazil, though, has convinced me of one thing: these people – the farmers, the landless, the rural classes, here and everywhere – will not go away. Why would they? It is not just wages, jobs and money that are at risk as the global market destroys farming as we know it – it is a way of life that has always been with us; the culture of the land and the people who work it.

This new peasants' revolt can only get bigger, for these people – millions upon millions of them – have no place at all in globalisation's Brave New World. Free trade wants them dead. They have other ideas.

8 **california dreaming**

'I hope that we shall crush in its birth the aristocracy of our monied corporations, which dare already to challenge our government to a trial of strength, and bid defiance to the laws of our country.'

THOMAS JEFFERSON, 1816

'There can be no effective control of corporations while their political activity remains. To put an end to it will be neither a short nor an easy task, but it can be done.'

THEODORE ROOSEVELT, 1910

November 1864. Abraham Lincoln, sixteenth president of the United States of America, is writing a letter to Colonel William Elkins, one of the millions of Federal soldiers who are helping to win the American Civil War for Lincoln's United States. In five months' time their victory will be officially confirmed with the Confederate surrender. Six days later, Lincoln will be dead. An assassin's bullet will deprive America of the man who abolished slavery, and deprive Lincoln of the grim satisfaction of seeing the fears he outlined in his letter to Elkins – fears about the shape and structure of the post-war nation – begin to become reality.

'We may congratulate ourselves,' he had written, 'that this cruel war is nearing its end. It has cost a vast amount of treasure and blood . . . it has indeed been a trying hour for the Republic; but I see in the near future a crisis approaching that unnerves me and causes me to tremble for the safety of my country. As a result of the war, corporations have been enthroned, and an era of corruption in high places will follow, and the money power of the country will endeavour to prolong its reign by working upon the prejudices of the people until all wealth is aggregated in a few hands, and the Republic is destroyed. I feel at this moment more anxiety for the safety of my country than ever before, even in the midst of war. God grant that my suspicions may prove groundless.'[1]

January 2001. George W. Bush, forty-third president of the United States of America, has just taken office, despite losing the popular vote. At over $193 million, his election campaign has been the most expensive in American history. It has also been a heavy, but potentially lucrative, corporate investment. Most of the money Bush has spent on campaigning has been handed to him by giant corporations and industrial interests: nearly $2 million from oil and gas companies; half a million from electrical utilities; $4 million from real estate; $1.3 million from the car lobby; $1.3 million from the banks; $1.6 million from the insurers; $5 million from lawyers; almost half a million from drugs companies; almost $3 million from securities and investments, $1.1 million from the computing sector . . . the list goes on and on.[2] Now, in the newly spring-cleaned corridors of power, it's payback time.

In Washington, Bush, a millionaire oilman, has gathered together some of the richest and most influential corporate movers and shakers in America. There is the former chief executive of the Halliburton Energy corporation, the world's largest oilfield services company. A supporter of oil drilling in the Arctic National Wildlife Refuge and an opponent of international measures to prevent global warming, his personal wealth lies somewhere between $22 million and $104 million. There is the former Chief Executive of the drugs company GD Searle, another millionaire (worth between $62 million and $115 million) who has also served on the boards of several other companies, from Kellogg's to Tribune newspapers. There is the former board member of Gulfstream Aerospace and America Online (worth between $10 million and $50 million). There is the former Chairman and Chief Executive of oil and gas company Tom Brown, Inc. (between $10 million and $47 million); the former board member of Calgene, Inc., producers of genetically modified foods; the former lawyer for Delta Petroleum; the former board member of Chevron oil and the Transamerica Corporation . . .[3]

These people are the progenies of some of the biggest business interests in America. It would be regarded as a coup for any corporation to get such close access to the president of the world's most powerful nation, so their presence in Washington now must be regarded as the coup to end them all. Their names are Dick Cheney, Donald Rumsfeld, Colin Powell, Donald Evans, Ann Veneman, Gale Norton and Condoleezza Rice, and Bush has just appointed them Vice-President, Defense Secretary, Secretary of State, Commerce Secretary, Agriculture Secretary, Interior Secretary and National Security Advisor respectively. For the next four years, the safety of Lincoln's Republic will be in their hands.

February 2002. I am sitting on a cliff top in Humboldt County, northern California, watching wild, white waves break over the jagged black headlands that stretch away for miles on each side of me. Redwood trees stud the coast. Down on the rocks, a hundred feet below, groups of sea lions bask in the salt spray.

'It's about legitimacy,' says Paul Cienfuegos, blinking in the wind. Cienfuegos is in his forties, with a large, unruly black beard, milk-bottle glasses, thick cords and a woolly hat perched on top of a mass of black hair. He has driven me to one of his favourite spots in his rattling car to talk to me about corporate authority in modern America, and what he's doing to challenge it.

'In this county, for example, there has been massive civil disobedience against clearcut logging for years. Beautiful old growth forests being chopped down by logging corporations. I spent four years campaigning against that. I campaigned against the nuclear industry, the weapons industry, chemical farming. And it took me a long time to understand, slowly, that I was actually fighting the symptoms of something, not the root cause.' A huge wave crashes on to the rocks below with a roar.

'I realised,' he goes on, 'that the real problem was that somehow these logging corporations had ended up with the authority to decide what would happen to our forests. Well, where did they get that? Who gave it them? And I saw that this was a fundamentally different issue – it was about governance rather than trees. And all these light bulbs began going on in my head.' He looks at me, to check that I'm getting the point.

'We had a revolution in this country,' he goes on. 'For all its flaws, and despite the fact that it was a revolution by and for white, male property-owners, it threw up some radical ideas that became the founding principles of the United States. And the most important one was that sovereign power lies with the people, and that our governing institutions are given permission by We,

the People, to govern on our behalf. That is the absolutely fundamental basis of our democracy.' It's an idea, he says, that all
Americans today pay lip service to – but one that isn't functioning.

'This was an extraordinary revolutionary idea,' he emphasises,
'but what happened to it? Today, we find ourselves in a situation
where corporations have utterly usurped that authority, to the
extent that people in this country almost do not question it any
more. Wealth has enabled corporate leaders, through lobbying
and buying elections and all the rest of it, to change fundamental
laws that give them actual *rights*. Rights which fundamentally
change the relationship between human beings and these institutions called corporations. And that's all they are – legally
subordinate institutions, legal fictions. That's what corporations
were supposed to be, in the intentions of the Founding Fathers of
the United States; institutions, created to perform certain functions on behalf of the people. They were never intended to be as
powerful as they are today. Now, these legal fictions have broken
out of the bonds that democracy set for them, and they are challenging our authority to govern.' He looks out to sea, squinting in
the light.

'Now,' he says, 'we don't just try and stop one clearcut at a
time, one toxic waste spill, one downsizing – we try and challenge
the very *authority* of corporations to do *any* of those things. The
anti-globalisation movement talks a lot about the problems of corporate power: this argument, though, is not just about corporate
power. It's about corporate *authority* – it's an important distinc-
tion. *By what authority* do they buy up our political system, pollute
our rivers, rewrite our laws, dominate our culture? In a supposed
democracy, the people are the authority; now we are expected to
ask corporations nicely to behave themselves; to *persuade* them to
be "responsible" and "sustainable"; to negotiate with them. These
are all the wrong questions, the wrong approaches. Why should we
negotiate with these *things*? Where did they get the power to represent themselves as equals, or even masters, of the people? The
real, crucial question is *by what authority* do these corporations

wield any of this power, do any of these things? By what authority do they even *exist*?' The waves are still battering against the rocks. Paul is on a roll.

'We are challenging that authority,' he says. 'And we are going to take it back.'

A few miles up the coast, in the clapboard-and-whitewash town of Eureka, is Paul Cienfuegos's office; a generous word for what is, in fact, a small corner of a small flat owned by Kaitlin Sopoci-Belknap, co-director with Paul of the organisation he founded in 1996: Democracy Unlimited of Humboldt County. I came to Humboldt seeking answers to some of the questions posed by the dominance of private corporations in modern life. Back at the World Social Forum, I'd heard some ideas for regulating the power and influence of multinational corporations at international level. Now I wanted to see how people could impose such limits on the ground, in their own communities, and what difference it would make. I'd heard it was starting to happen, perhaps ironically, in the US – the birthplace of the modern corporation. But how, and could it provide a model for other people in other places? Paul Cienfuegos is first on my list of people to ask.

Right now, he's rummaging through boxes, folders and teetering piles of papers stacked up in Kaitlin's lounge, searching for documents he thinks I should read. He doesn't seem to be quite sure where to look.

'We're kind of between offices right now,' he explains, still rummaging. I console myself with the thought that past revolutions have begun in less auspicious circumstances. Probably.

'Hopefully not for too long,' says Kaitlin, sighing. She is in her early twenties, and has only been working with Paul for eight months. I get the impression that she's the organised one.

'Would you like a drink?' she says. 'I think I have tea.'

Despite the temporary chaos, it's possible that operations like Democracy Unlimited could represent the future of anti-corporate activism in America. Cienfuegos won't use those words: they are not anti-corporate, he says; they are pro-democracy. Corporations have their place, but it's subservient to the people's will, it's a long way from the public realm, and it's nowhere near the political arena. Whatever you call it, the sort of work that Democracy Unlimited is carrying out may yet come to connect with a large and potentially powerful section of the American people; a people who, like most others in 'developed' countries all over the world, are becoming keenly aware of the sickness inside their body politic.

The work that Paul and Kaitlin and others like them carry out in Humboldt County takes several forms. One of Democracy Unlimited's primary aims, says Paul, is to 'begin a national conversation about the role of corporations within our democracy'. To this end, they run study groups in which local people come together to 'read, think and talk about stuff they don't know anything about'. That, says Paul, 'is how this all starts – just reading stuff, thinking about it, adjusting your approach. It's how I started. In many ways, re-thinking the entire relationship between corporations and people is mindwarp stuff.' He laughs.

'Reading and learning about this stuff fundamentally alters your consciousness in a way that most anti-globalisation activists think they get, but they don't,' he says. 'It's a leap. When you think about this in a fundamental way, your language changes and the way you look at things changes. It's like moving from thinking that the world is flat, and if you go past a certain point you fall off, to thinking that the world is a sphere – that's a fundamental shift, a thought-form shift, a paradigm shift. This one is as big as that, and yet it's only about governance; it's about moving from "The corporation is the primary actor in society, and we are merely stakeholders – workers or consumers", to "We, the people, are the source of all authority, and we have the power to decide what role these institutions play in our lives and our communities".'

This is not just talk though; not even just ideas. In a small corner of Humboldt County, now, it's the law. In 1998, after a few years of running discussion groups, touring with workshops on 'first steps toward dismantling corporate rule', distributing newsletters and generally trying to stir up community interest, Paul and a group of allies decided to see if anything could be done to institutionalise their new take on corporate authority. Democracy Unlimited set up a spin-off organisation, Citizens Concerned About Corporations (CCAC), based in the nearby town of Arcata, where Paul was then living. Its purpose was to rewrite local law to try to reassert some of the people's powers over the private corporations operating in their town.

Its weapon was the innocuously named 'Measure F', a local ballot initiative. Ballot initiatives are a curious remnant of America's constitutional past which allow ordinary citizens to propose new laws. Any person or organisation can propose one – if they collect enough signatures in support, the proposed measure is put on the 'ballot' for citizens to vote on at the time of the next election. If a majority vote for it, it becomes law. Only twenty-four of the USA's fifty states allow ballot initiatives; California is one of them, and CCAC was about to use it to its advantage.

Cienfuegos and colleagues drafted a ballot initiative for the Arcata local elections in 1998. Measure F, or, to give it its full name, the 'Arcata Advisory Initiative on Democracy and Corporations', called on the city council to sponsor two mass meetings for Arcata citizens entitled 'Can we have democracy when large corporations wield so much power and wealth under law?', and to establish an official committee, policies and pro-grammes to 'ensure democratic control over corporations conducting business within the city, in whatever ways are necessary to ensure the health and well-being of our community and its environment'. In a flurry of activity, they collected the 1,110 sig-natures they needed, got the measure on to the ballot, initiated a local debate about it and began to win widespread local support. On 3 November 1998, the people of Arcata went to the polls and voted, by 60 per cent to 40 per cent, in favour of Measure F. The first ballot initiative in US history on the subject of dismantling corporate rule had become law.

'It was fantastic,' says Paul. 'People really began to ask themselves what role corporations played in their lives, why local shops were disappearing, whether it was right for corporations to pay politicians, why they had so little say in the role that corporations played in their town. For a while, all the talk in the bars and the shops was about Measure F, and about corporations in Arcata. Arcata is still a small town, but there are more than fifty giant corporations doing business there; Measure F simply said the people should be allowed basic authority over their activities. It struck a chord.' The city's mayor and many of its councillors supported the measure. Messages of support began to come in from other parts of the country. Cienfuegos was asked to give talks all over the US, and groups of people came together in other towns to plan their own versions of Measure F.

The two town hall meetings were held, and took the debate further. Today, the 'Measure F Committee' created by the new law is pushing forward that debate, discussing ways and means to reassert public control over corporate activity. It is currently drafting a local law proposing a cap on the number of chain restaurants in Arcata, and is trawling other states and counties to look at potential ways to reassert authority over corporations. All this, says Paul, is 'helping people regain their sovereign attitude – something that has really been lost in America. People are starting to believe again that power really *does* reside with the people, and that they can actually *use* it.'

If it seems that Paul Cienfuegos and his fellow campaigners are exaggerating the threat posed by the power and influence of corporations, a brief look at the history of the USA might suggest otherwise. In many ways, that history is the story of a conflict between private corporations and public institutions for the right to govern America.

The corporation came to North America with the original British settlers.[4] Corporations had existed in Britain since Norman times, but were usually non-commercial bodies – churches, schools, hospitals – which were 'incorporated' by the Crown to allow them to carry out certain tasks: by forming a corporation, the workings of such bodies could be simplified and legalised. Individual owners of corporations were not allowed to profit from their activities, and the Crown could revoke the charter it had issued them if they acted outside the strict limits it had set out.

Things began to change with the growth of Empire. Corporations – the Russian Company, the African Company, the Spanish Company and others – were chartered to seek out and control trade with other parts of the world. In 1600, Queen Elizabeth I issued a Royal Charter to the East India Company, which would later take advantage of its growing and unprecedented power to break free of its legal obligations and become the world's first profit-making multinational corporation. Originally chartered to trade in India, the British East India Company became so powerful that it ended up governing most of India – running its own army, building infrastructure, controlling the food supply and dealing brutally with anybody who came between the corporation and its pursuit of resources and monopolies.

Meanwhile, in North America, the British government's taxes, political heavy-handedness and refusal to allow its American colonies a political voice were tied up with the power and influence of the Crown corporations. The infamous Boston tea party, a precursor to revolution, was sparked by a tea tax imposed upon the residents of the colonies to help the East India Company pay its debts. It was the corporation's tea that the Bostonians cast into the harbour.

After the revolution of 1776, the new nation set about drawing up the first constitution in the world in which ultimate authority lay with the people (though 'the people' at the time consisted of white male property-owners). Mindful of how corporations had colluded with the British government in the oppression of the colonies, the new government ensured that the few private companies that existed were kept on a very short lead. The power to

grant corporate charters was given only to elected state legisla-
tures, and such charters were a privilege, not a right. They were
issued for a limited period and for a specific purpose. Corporations were restricted in their activities, land holdings and
sometimes profits, and could not be based outside the state in
which they were chartered. They were banned from involvement
in politics, and stockholders and directors were held personally
responsible for debts incurred or crimes committed by their institutions. Their charters could be revoked at any time if they
transgressed.

Even this wasn't enough for many Americans, who were wary of
any institutions being given enough to potentially 'enslave' the
people again. 'We believe,' wrote a group of independent mechanics, opposing the creation of a new carriage corporation in
Massachusetts, 'that incorporated bodies tend to crush all [small]
enterprise and compel us to work out our days in the service of
others.'

But this tight lead around corporate activity was to be loosened,
and finally snapped, in the nineteenth century, with the coming of
both the industrial revolution and civil war. The American Civil
War unleashed a great struggle for control between corporations
and governing institutions. Corporate leaders, empowered by the
wartime need for increased and streamlined production and the
post-war demands of national reconstruction, grew richer and
more self-confident. Railway corporations in particular, which
operated a monopoly over this new and vital means of transport,
became hugely powerful in just a few years. Emboldened by such
new-found influence, corporate leaders began to call for more
power, more authority and – something which the Founding
Fathers would have found chilling – legal rights.

After the war, Lincoln's fears that corporations would be
'enthroned' began to be realised – and the means of their coron-
ation was to be the courts. A series of court cases, brought by
corporations with the specific intent of bending the law to their
advantage, saw judges granting more powers to corporations by

way of generous or downright suspicious interpretations of the constitution. The most notorious court decision came in 1886 when the innocuously named *Santa Clara County vs Southern Pacific Railroad* case was interpreted to mean that a corporation was a 'natural person' under the constitution. As such, corporate lawyers began to argue, a whole slew of constitutional rights designed to ensure human freedoms should now apply to corporations too.

The consequences of this decision were enormous, and they resonate to this day. A further raft of court cases confirmed the new concept of 'corporate personhood', and corporations began to claim constitutional rights. The Supreme Court ruled that the fourteenth amendment to the constitution, written to guarantee equal rights to freed slaves, now gave a corporation – legally a 'person', after all – the right not to have its 'privileges or immunities' 'abridged'. No state, says the amendment, shall 'deprive any person of life, liberty or property without due process of law . . .' Soon, judges all over the country were using the decision to strike down local, state and federal laws designed to protect people from corporate abuses and underlining that, in the eyes of the law, a corporation had as many rights as a freed slave – or any other American.

Of the 307 cases brought before the courts under the fourteenth amendment between 1890 and 1910, just 19 dealt with the rights of African-Americans; the other 288 were brought by corporations. By 1876, just twelve years after Abraham Lincoln had written to Colonel Elkins, another US President, Rutherford Hayes, was lamenting the coming-to-pass of Lincoln's prophecy. 'This is a government of the people, by the people and for the people no longer,' he said. 'It is a government of corporations, by corporations and for corporations.'[5]

After the Santa Clara case, there was no stopping the emboldened corporations. Over the next century, the courts granted corporate 'persons' the right under the fourth amendment ('The right of the people to be secure in their persons, houses, papers, and effects, against unreasonable searches and seizures') to avoid government inspections without a warrant. The fourteenth amendment was used again to strike down 'discriminatory' corporate taxes. Under the first amendment ('Congress shall make no law . . . abridging the freedom of speech') corporations successfully claimed that advertising, making contributions to political candidates and spending money to influence elections could be equated with 'free speech'. Enacting laws to prevent any of this was thus deemed an unconstitutional infringement of the free-speech rights of corporate 'persons'. In 1976, the Supreme Court ruled that placing any limits on the amount of money corporations could donate to a political campaign would unconstitutionally limit corporate free speech.

Legally, much to the corporations' glee, all this made perfect sense. Meanwhile, in the real world, the effects on America's famed democracy were increasingly disastrous. Today, the results are clear. Economic and political life in the United States is dominated by fictitious corporate 'persons' wielding more power and influence than any real person could hope for. Corporations fund elections, own most of the media, control much of the regulatory industry set up to police them and tower over the national economy. They enjoy the support – political and often financial – of the state while circumventing many of its laws. They rake in enormous profits while taking care to incur minimum costs, whether it be through scouring the world for the cheapest labour or offloading the costs of cleaning up their pollution on to society as a whole. Their directors are protected by law from any liability for debts or crimes committed by their companies. In short: power – and profit – without responsibility.

The people, meanwhile – or that section of the people who can afford it, in this most unequal of industrialised nations – are compensated for the buying-up of their freedoms with an array of consumer goods that would have made the Founding Fathers faint with astonishment. The chances of them engaging in a national debate on the implications of all this are slim while the vast majority of the (corporate-owned) media and virtually all (corporate-funded) politicians maintain a virtual information blackout on the issue which the government of North Korea could probably learn from.

In many ways, it seems, the American people are back where they were in 1776: their lives and their government run in the interests of giant, unaccountable profit-seeking entities which have claimed the people's rights for their own – and are slowly suffocating the meaning of their revolution.

'Corporate personhood,' says Jeff Milchen, thoughtfully. 'It's a big issue. Most people have never heard of it, but in my experience, when they do, they can't stop thinking about it.' He's telling *me*. The more I've discovered about the power of corporations in the USA, the more overwhelmed I've become. I knew that corporations were influential in American life in a way they are probably not anywhere else on Earth – but it seems I didn't know the half of it. Now I'm wondering whether Paul Cienfuegos's ideal – of resubordinating corporations to the will of the people (whatever that is) – can ever be realised. Can little stabs like Measure F hope to tackle this behemoth? Or will it take another revolution to reassert the people's will?

Jeff Milchen thinks it might; but he has a different kind of revolution in mind. Jeff lives in a small wooden house in Boulder, Colorado, with his partner and co-worker, Jennifer Rockne, and two large, mad, endearing dogs. Like Paul Cienfuegos, Jeff and Jennifer have an ambitious vision for America's future and, like Paul, they are doing something about it. When you talk to them, you hear the same arguments, even some of the same language; Jeff, it seems, was one of Paul's inspirations. You also hear the same sense of history – and the same appeal to resurrect the original, hard-won rights of the American people. Jeff's organisation, ReclaimDemocracy.org, also busies itself locally to try to translate this sort of talk into some kind of reality.

'We kind of look to the original role of corporations as a blue-print,' says Jeff. We're sitting in his living room, drinking beer. Jeff is slim and articulate, with black hair and a small beard which, unlike Paul's, is under strict control. Jennifer has long brown hair, glasses, and a quick and easily deployed laugh.

'What we had in this country over two hundred years ago makes an awful lot of sense,' continues Jeff. 'Strict charters, no political involvement, citizen oversight, all that stuff – it kept cor-porations in a place that citizens wanted them to be – subservient, not dominant. Corporations should be kept in this little box, and not let out. Reclaim Democracy grew out of this attempt to create such a long-term campaign. Our work is about creating the demand for long-term, systemic political change – rewriting the relationship between people and these hugely dominant economic interests called corporations.'

What I want to know from Jeff is how this is supposed to happen. In twenty-first-century corporate America it seems a mil-lion miles away. Corporations are very big, very powerful and very dominant. Most people seem suspicious of them; most might even agree with Jeff about the problems they cause. But what are little organisations like Reclaim Democracy going to be able to do about it? Jennifer chuckles.

'The big question,' she says.

'That's part of the problem,' admits Jeff. 'What we're looking for is long-term systemic change, and it's tough to get people to focus on that. People react to the crisis of the day, from the attack on the World Trade Center to the deforestation going on in their state. It's not that these defensive battles are unimportant, but there needs to be more strategic, long-term thinking. If you look at history, though, there are precedents. One example is the movement to abolish slavery. Back in the 1820s, when the aboli-tionist movement began, there were some folks who said, well, it's not realistic to *abolish* slavery; it's a huge part of our economy, it's always been with us, people depend on it. We should pass laws to say that slaves must be treated humanely, we should have a slave-owners' code of conduct for them to buy into. Today, there are activists with similar approaches: they say we should look for "corporate social responsibility" or demand that the Environmental Protection Agency protects the environment for us; basically trying to get corporations to cause a little less harm, and try to regulate their behaviour. The approach is similar.' He takes a swig of beer.

'We reject this approach,' he says. 'We see the corporation as a machine – like all machines, it's designed to do a specific job: to maximise returns to shareholders at the expense of everything else; to grow in perpetuity, to externalise its costs on to society as a whole, to minimise the returns to its employees. To expect it to do otherwise is like expecting a toaster to . . . to, er, well, to do something completely different. You get the point: to expect a machine to be "socially responsible" is a great distraction.'

Jeff is making a fundamental point. Over the last few years, a drive to persuade corporations to be 'socially responsible' has taken off, supported by everyone from politicians to 'reformist' activists to corporate executives themselves, keen to embrace voluntary attempts at niceness rather than be forced by law to act differently. Yet people like Jeff and Paul reject this approach almost as strongly as they reject corporate authority itself. A 'legal fiction', as Paul Cienfuegos would have it, cannot make moral decisions; it cannot be 'responsible'. A corporation cannot be moral or immoral; it is amoral, a machine programmed to pursue the narrow agenda of financial profit. Trying to persuade it to behave itself, they stress, is not likely to get anyone very far.

'Ultimately,' says Jeff, 'the folks in the abolitionist movement decided they needed to take a strong stand – to say, simply, "slavery is unacceptable". When they did that – when they took civil disobedience, decided to ignore the law and seek to change the existing paradigm, that ultimately led to their success, and they changed the constitution, fundamentally. They completely transformed the paradigm, and the law, and they changed the course of US history.' Jeff is clearly an ambitious man.

'We want to engineer a similar paradigm shift,' he says, confirming my suspicion, 'and we want to persuade other people out there to do the same. To be bold, to say, simply, "Here's what's right, here's what needs to be done, now we have to figure out how to get there."'

Figuring out how to get there is, of course, the tricky bit. Reclaim Democracy has decided that the starting point is a local base. Boulder's would-be paradigm shifters, like Humboldt County's, are feeling their way as they go, because no one has provided them with a roadmap. Even so, as Jeff and Jennifer explain to me over dinner, the distance travelled in just a few years is already impressive.

'If you're working on this thirty-, forty-year timeline, as we are,' says Jeff, 'it's about slowly changing the attitudes of a huge proportion of the public. It's not enough just to work in your little activist segment, you have to work with everyday folk, across the political spectrum. This stuff appeals to people on the right as much as on the left.' Jeff and Jennifer have various ways of working to make this happen. Jeff writes articles for anyone who will take them, and gives talks across the country. Then there are the various national efforts that emanate from this little house on the edge of the Rockies: campaigns to get corporations out of schools, to open up national presidential debates to candidates who aren't from the two main corporate-funded parties (there is a bumper sticker on Jeff's rarely used car which says 'Unrepentant Nader Voter'), to introduce laws that would allow for the winding-up of corporations that commit serious crimes.

Then, of course, there is the law. Like the good citizens of Arcata, the law is one of the avenues down which the paradigm shifters of Boulder have travelled. One of Reclaim Democracy's initiatives, put together with local business owners and other citizens in 2000, was the 'Community Vitality Act'. Like Humboldt County's effort, it sought to strike a blow for people's right to determine the shape of their own community. The Act would have required the city council to create a 'local purchasing preference', ensuring that city money was spent first with locally owned businesses; ensure that city-owned commercial property was leased to locally owned businesses; and – the most controversial clause – introduce a cap on the number of chainstores in Boulder.

'All we were saying,' says Jeff, 'was "this far and no further". At the moment we have hundreds of chain operations in this community, but we also have loads of small and community businesses – the balance is OK, so we said, right, at this point let's put on a cap, see if people agree that we should stop things here. That created a huge amount of controversy and interest in the community . . .'

'It was fun!' laughs Jennifer. 'One man took out a full-page ad in one of the papers explaining why the Act was a bad idea. We really enjoyed that. The level of debate it got going was huge.'

'That *was* fun,' admits Jeff. 'It's nice to have the other side protesting about your agenda for a change, instead of the other way round. It was a proactive vision and it created just an incredible amount of public interest. One of the city council members who's been there for twenty-five years said it was by far the most public communication they'd ever received on an issue. It really struck a nerve.'

The debate engendered by Boulder's Community Vitality Act, like that kicked off by Measure F in Arcata, strikes me as a fascinating demonstration of how much passion can be inflamed by even a mild incursion into corporate power. The Act, after all, was hardly the kind of thing designed to bring the corporate edifice crashing down. It also seems to show how popular such an incursion can be among the public. The debate, as in Arcata, was also at least half of the point: 'At even the most basic level, it made people think about how they spent their dollars, and about who was making decisions about the shape of their community,' says Jeff.

In the end, the Community Vitality Act failed to get off the ground. 'The city council dissected it,' says Jennifer. 'But they also decided to see what they could do to incorporate it into the city's five-year comprehensive plan . . . so something may come of it.' Even if it doesn't, Boulder is thinking hard now about the issues that Jeff, Jennifer and their allies have raised. Down in the town centre, you can see the evidence.

You can also see what Jeff and Jennifer are up against. The next morning, Jeff takes me down to Pearl Street, Boulder's main shopping area. In less than a decade, according to locals, it has been transformed. Locally owned shops have closed, chains have proliferated; as a result, less money comes back into the community for every dollar spent, people have to travel further for basic goods, corporations have increasing control over local shopping habits and the place is beginning – though only beginning – to look like everywhere else. In this, Boulder is merely following the route that is being travelled by most of small-town America. Since 1990, for example, more than 11,000 independent pharmacies have closed across the country. The market share of independent bookshops has fallen from 58 per cent in 1972 to 15 per cent today. Five corporations now account for a third of all grocery sales; two corporations for a third of all hardware sales; two for a quarter of all book sales. Blockbuster video accounts for one in every three videos rented; Wal-Mart controls 7 per cent of nationwide consumer spending.[6] And the consolidation goes on.

Jeff and I walk down Pearl Street as blue stormclouds gather over the mountains on the western horizon. We pass a Sunglass Hut, a hip and overpriced clothes shop, a café, a bar, a café, a boutique, a café, the Body Shop, Ben & Jerry's, Häagen-Dazs, a café. A plague of coffee shops seems to have descended from the mountains. Several of them are Starbucks, playing their usual game of competing with each other to see who can wipe out the most local competition. On the plus side, the local cafés have fought back with white chocolate mocha, of which I take it upon myself over the next few days to drink as much as possible. It's tough, but I feel duty-bound to support the local economy.

'Five years ago,' says Jeff, 'this was full of shops that people could buy *useful* stuff in.' He looks despondently along the street towards the branch of Banana Republic on the corner. 'But then, five years ago there was open farmland between Boulder and Denver. Now it's all strip malls. We're becoming a suburb.' He's not exaggerating. I travelled here from San Francisco to Denver on an Amtrak train through stunning scenery: the peaks of the Sierra Nevada; the bleached sands of the Utah desert; the thin sliver of land which carries the train tracks across the water to lonely Salt Lake City; tunnels and cuttings hewn through the pine-swathed Rocky Mountains; men fishing in the gorges of the Colorado River hundreds of feet below. Then I got to Denver and switched to a bus, which took me through a five-mile tarmac-and-neon avenue of Taco Bells, Wal-Marts, McDonald's and Home Depots to Boulder. I was in a bad mood until the next morning.

Jeff being Jeff, though, he is not about to take this kind of thing lying down, and in 1998, with a small group of local business people, he founded an organisation to do something about it. The Boulder Independent Business Alliance (BIBA) emerged from the work he was doing with Reclaim Democracy, and represented another way of practically limiting the influence of corporations in the town. BIBA started with a handful of members and now has 150, from bookshops to cafés, bars to video shops; even a local bank. Walk down Pearl Street and look closely at the shop windows: dozens of them bear stickers sporting the BIBA logo. The local businesses are fighting back.

'We wanted,' Jeff explains, 'to try to create a model of local and independent businesses that can halt and hopefully eventually reverse the process of national and transnational chains driving out independent and community-based businesses; hopefully it will be something that other communities around the world can look to for inspiration. What was interesting was that creating BIBA meant working with pretty mainstream people; ordinary folk, business owners, not "activists". And what was interesting is that it appealed to so many different people. Questioning the idea of a national chain being able to open up a branch wherever they want without the local community having a say appeals to people whatever their politics. These kind of ideas really catch on among so many different people. Virtually everyone will say, "Hell, yeah, we have the right to say no to corporations – they don't have rights to do this to us. How did we get the idea that we don't have a right to define how our community looks?" That's it – click.'

BIBA did click, and it is still growing. Its members form co-operative buyers' groups to get better deals, work with the city council to promote local businesses and campaign to keep out more chains, produce a directory of local businesses and discount cards for people who shop locally. Four years on, it has two full-time staff, and Jeff has pulled out of running it to take his idea national. BIBA was, as far as he knows, the first independent business alliance in the US. Inspired by it, others have sprung up across the country. When I arrived in town, Jeff had just received the official papers confirming the existence of the next step in his project to rejuvenate small-town America: AMIBA, the American Independent Business Alliance.

'I like to keep busy,' he explains.

Jeff provided the impetus behind BIBA, but David Bolduc provided the money. Bolduc owns the Boulder Bookstore on Pearl Street. He is tall and slow-talking. He has the obligatory paradigm-shifter's beard. I've come to seek him out among the floor displays and the special-offer bins.

'A lot of book chains started to come into Boulder six or seven years ago,' he says, 'which was a catalyst for me. Some of us got together and said, "What can we do? What makes us different to them?" The obvious answer is that we're local, but we had to work out why that mattered, and what it actually meant. I think that a town, a place, a region has some kind of identity that people like – that they're proud of where they live, they want to keep it that way, or at least they want to define how it changes, and on whose terms. But frankly, if I hadn't gone out there myself, and put my money into this, and if others like Jeff hadn't done the same, nothing would have happened. It doesn't happen by itself. If people value something about their local area, they have to get out and do something about it themselves, because no one else will.'

The Boulder Bookstore has been around for twenty-eight years. The local branch of Borders – one of the two biggest book chains in the US – has been around for less than five. Since the creation of BIBA, and the debate over the Community Vitality Act, though, something odd has happened – Bolduc's takings, despite the presence of the chain, have increased.

'The idea of a nation of shopkeepers,' he says to me, as he walks me round the store pointing out various books that he really thinks I ought to buy, 'was historically a very important part of the original American vision; a nation of independent small property-owners and local traders. In a town like Boulder you can talk about these things, and people get it; people talk about it with you. BIBA and the debate about the Community Vitality Act have made a real difference to local attitudes. Borders opened down the street about five years ago, and it doesn't seem to have affected my trade at all. Possibly it has even helped me. I can't think of another town in which that could happen. And it's just a rumour, but I heard that the Boulder branch of Borders is one of the worst-performing in the country.' He considers the ramifications of this for a second.

'You know,' he says, deadpan, 'that makes me feel terrible.'

'At some stage,' says Jan Edwards, 'you have to do more than go on marches and make puppets. I mean, it's great fun, but at some stage, if you really want to make change, someone's got to sit down and read the stupid court cases.' She sighs. 'I just can't believe it has to be me.'

I had to hire a car to find Jan. There's no other way to get to the light, airy timber house, surrounded by woods of pine and birch, where she lives with her husband, Bill Meyer, back up on the wild coast of northern California. Paul Cienfuegos told me I had to visit Jan and Bill, who turn out to be a couple of charming forty-some-things who call themselves anarchists, and who have caught the corporate paradigm-shifting bug. Jan has black hair, and is on crutches – she broke her ankle recently. Bill has a beard. So does his friend, Doug Hammerstrom, who is also there when I arrive. Doug looks a bit like Donald Sutherland, and wears a blue T-shirt with frogs on. I am late, but nobody minds. This is California, after all.

'Would you like a cookie?' says Jan. 'I just baked them. They're still hot.' It seems rude to refuse, so I have a cookie, and a glass of milk to go with it. Call me a bourgeois counter-revolutionary, I think, but this is my kind of anarchism.

Bill, Jan and Doug are also members of the growing but scat-tered tribe of Americans who are worried about the place of corporations in society. Friends of Paul Cienfuegos and Jeff Milchen and others like them, they too can be heard comparing their work to abolitionism, comparing corporations to toasters and using the word 'paradigm' with their heads held high. They can also be heard discussing legal technicalities, constitutional niceties and how to change the law. Jan, Bill and Doug, and espe-cially Jan, are the sort of spirited amateurs who have been almost accidentally sparking off societal change for centuries, in the face of expert derision. Jan says that this thought is what keeps her going.

'I've found stuff in the constitution that even lawyers hadn't worked out,' she says, as we all sit round Jan and Bill's big wooden table, the birch trees swaying gently through the windows. 'Loopholes and stuff. I'm much less educated than either of these people,' she says, indicating Bill and Doug.

'In the formal academic sense,' interjects Bill, hurriedly.

'Right, well, I'm not a lawyer. Actually I used to work in the-atre, but that means I don't look at things in the same way. It can be helpful. I got into all this when I heard someone on the radio talking about corporate personhood. I looked into it, I got out-raged, I put an ad in the paper to see if anyone else was outraged and Doug answered. Actually, he was pretty much the only one who answered.'

'Was I?' says Doug. He sounds surprised.

'Well, pretty much. So we started to get people together for meetings to see if there was anything we could do to challenge this corporate personhood stuff around here. I'd been worried about corporations for a long time, and wondering what could really be done to control their activities. I realised at this time that we couldn't tackle them because they were *us* – they were people, for God's sake, they had the same rights as us! No wonder we could-n't tackle them. So we thought we might try and get a law on the local ballot to revoke corporate personhood, but we found that we couldn't – it's not legal to vote to take away the rights of a person!' She laughs.

'And a good thing too,' says Bill, 'otherwise there are certain people who would like to take away the rights of certain sections of the community pretty damn quick . . .'

'And I somewhat favoured not trying to make a new law anyway,' says Doug. 'I didn't think people were ready for that yet. I rather favoured something symbolic. And that was kind of what we ended up with.'

'Although it's not entirely symbolic,' chides Bill. 'Even though it wasn't made into a law, it is the official position of the city – the city agrees that corporations should not have personhood rights.'

What the three of them are talking about is the Resolution of the City of Point Arena on Corporate Personhood, which was passed by the city, thanks to Bill, Jan, Doug and a handful of others, in April 2000. Following the now-familiar pattern of intro-ducing a local proposal, kicking off a heated debate and then, just, making it official, they persuaded the council of the nearby town of Point Arena to pass a resolution stating that, in the city's view, corporations were not, after all, 'persons' under the law. They quoted the opinion of a Supreme Court judge who had said the same thing in 1938. The resolution, like Arcata's Measure F, also resolved that the city council would 'encourage public discussion on the role of corporations in public life and urge other cities to foster similar public discussion'.

Point Arena's resolution was the first to renounce corporate personhood anywhere in the US, and it doesn't look like being the last; other cities across the country are currently considering similar moves. Though Bill calls the resolution 'basically toothless', it was, as ever, an education tool for a local community who had no idea that corporations were 'persons' or why it mattered that they were.

Jan, who has been rummaging around in a file, hands me a piece of paper.

'Here's a list we did of what would actually change if we didn't have corporate personhood,' she says. 'We' turns out to be the venerable campaigning group the Women's International League for Peace and Freedom (unfortunate acronym: WILPF), founded in the early twentieth century to campaign for women's rights, whose US branch has adopted the abolition of corporate personhood as one of its national campaigns. WILPF is mobilising to get fifty cities in the US to adopt resolutions like Point Arena's by 2005, and to make corporate personhood an issue in the 2004 presidential election; though Osama bin Laden may have scuppered any chances of getting it on to the national agenda for a while.

Revoking corporate personhood, claims Jan's list, would allow local, state and federal government to do things which corporations currently claim are a violation of their constitutional rights. Prohibit political activity by business, for example; revoke corporate charters by popular referendum; allow government agencies to inspect corporate premises with no notice; ban advertising for dangerous products like guns or cigarettes (currently protected as 'free speech'); prevent damaging mergers or limit the size and scope of corporations. The potential, she says, is enormous.

And Jan is an optimist. She has spent the last few years researching corporate personhood in depth (I've seen enough to know that it's one of those issues that turns people into obsessives once it gets hold of them). She's read court cases, dissected the constitution, written essays, compiled histories; and she thinks the battle to remove corporate personhood, though it will be a long one, is winnable. It exists at all, she points out, because of a string of Supreme Court judges' interpretations of the constitution. But it was another Supreme Court interpretation of the same constitution that decided women couldn't vote; another again that decided racial segregation was constitutional. Both were overturned as a result of mass popular campaigns, says Jan; this could be too.

'It would make a difference,' she says. 'It just *would*. OK, we have international laws, too; WTO agreements, NAFTA, and all of these enshrine corporate power as well. But if it can start to be rolled back in the USA, which in many ways is the home of the modern corporation, then that starts something incredibly important. Sure, all we've done here in one sense is pass this little local resolution. But everything starts somewhere. I like to see Point Arena as a weak point in the shell of corporate America; a crack that we can start to lever open. Anarchism begins at home!' She grins, widely. 'Help yourself to another cookie.'

If Point Arena – and Humboldt County, and Boulder – really are weak points in the armour of corporate America, they are not the only ones. In fact, the chinks seem to be growing more numerous. In the few weeks I spent in the US, I found a few others myself. In Santa Cruz, another Californian coastal town, this time south of San Francisco, I met Lois Robins, a determined woman in her seventies who has gathered together another group of optimists to try to change state law. I sat in on a meeting in her living room, in which a handful of locals were discussing a plan to introduce a new law to crack down on corporate crime. They had cheekily stolen their language from the plague of right-wing politicians who, in recent years, have popularised the idea of 'three strikes and you're out' laws for criminals – get caught committing the same crime three times and you go away for life, or something similarly over the top. Lois and her gang want a 'three strikes and you're out' law for corporate crime.

Under their proposed law, if a corporation based in California commits a 'major violation of the law' three times in a ten-year period, then its charter will be revoked, and it will be closed down. It strikes me that if such a law had been in existence in Texas, Enron would have probably been shut down a long time ago. Corporate crime, explained Lois, costs the public far more than individual crime, and is far less likely ever to be punished. 'If you get stopped by a cop,' said one of her co-conspirators, Len, to me, 'he can radio in your name and licence plate and get details of everything you've done down to the last traffic violation. But if some corporation is spilling toxins into the bay and you want to find out if they've ever done it before, you have to go rooting through file drawers for months. There's no database of corporate crimes, and very little monitoring. They have the legal advantages of people without the legal responsibilities.'

Lois, Len and Co. will need to gather 175,000 signatures in support of their idea just to get it on to the Californian ballot; for this, says Lois, they will need a lot of money and time, and that's before they've even thought about promoting it. Even if it never happens, though, the concept has inspired others. In Sacramento, California's state capital, Nancy Price and Ben Sher told me that they liked the idea, even if they weren't sure of its practicality. Nancy and Ben run the local chapter of the Alliance for Democracy, a national organisation founded in 1996 which describes itself as a 'new populist movement' aiming to build popular support for ending 'the domination of our economy, our government, our culture, our media and the environment by large corporations'.[7] There are over thirty chapters around the country, including one in Point Arena run by Jan and Bill. The Alliance for Democracy, like everyone else I met, though focused on American politics and corporations in US life, also sees itself as part of a global movement, and a global trend. Alliance for Democracy representatives were at the Johannesburg Earth Summit in 2002, reporting back on corporations elsewhere and staging debates about reining in corporate power at global level; debates that people like Jeff Milchen and Paul Cienfuegos hope that their fundamental re-think of the relationship between people and corporations can help to influence.

Nearly 3,000 miles away, in Cape Cod, Massachusetts, I met Mary Zepernick and Virginia Rasmussen, both of whom work for the organisation that has inspired all the campaigners I met in the USA. POCLAD – the Programme on Corporations, Law and Democracy – is the thinktank that provided much of the intellectual engine-room work that people like Paul Cienfuegos and Jeff Milchen are building upon. Virginia describes part of its work as 'training the trainers'. Mary sees it as a project to finish the work that the American revolution began: bringing about real democracy. 'That was the promise,' she says, 'but it's never been realised. POCLAD is about, simply, contesting corporations' authority to govern: it's not even anti-corporate.' All over the US, this 'democratic conversation' is going on at ever louder levels.

I've been intrigued, even excited, by a lot of what I've seen across the USA. It really does seem possible to at least begin challenging corporate power at a local level, and to engage people in debate about democracy, authority and private power. It's something that could happen, in different ways, anywhere on Earth. But there are still hard questions to be asked and there are, it seems to me, flaws in this model of campaigning. Most of the laws and resolutions passed so far, for example, are primarily symbolic. Even if they weren't, how would a corporation react? It would quite probably react to, say, Lois Robins's Californian 'three strikes' initiative by moving its base out of California so as not to get caught. However strong a local law is, it's not going to be enough in itself. Then there is the international network of trade rules, mostly drawn up under corporate influence, and mostly favouring multinationals. Even without the 'corporate personhood' that so many American campaigners are keen to abolish, the WTO, NAFTA and a host of other agreements, official and informal, would still bind America, and the globe, into a corporate free-trade model. Global trade relies on giant corporations. To hem them in would be to alter that trade model dramatically: a good idea, most of the campaigners seem to agree; but a tough one to implement, and one with wide implications.

But it also seems to me that all of this, while true, is to miss the point slightly. For the value of everything that Jeff, Paul, Lois, Bill, Doug, Jan, Mary, Virginia and many others all across the USA are doing is not so much in the specific tiny law changes, resolutions, business alliances and all the rest, but in the public discussions that go with them, and the support they build up as they go. As I was told so many times, this is a long-term campaign to delegitimise corporate authority – to build a head of steam that will bring about change. It may or may not work – even if it does, it may become something quite different from what today's campaigners imagine. One thing does seem certain though: building a popular base will be its keystone. Without popular support, nothing of any significance will change. With it, anything seems possible.

And who knows: it may happen. It wouldn't be the first time, for the USA has a hidden but strong populist tradition. The last time it bubbled to the surface and took on corporate power on a national scale was probably in the late nineteenth century, when a 'Farmers' Alliance' movement sprang up across the country, dedicated to destroying industrial and agricultural monopolies, breaking the power of rich financiers in the countryside and bringing democracy back to local level, in a country increasingly dominated by newly empowered corporate 'persons'. At its height, the Farmers' Alliance had 1.5 million members, with a parallel organisation, the Colored Farmers' National Alliance, boasting another 2 million African-American farmers committed to an aim that seems almost contemporary: 'To secure our people from the onerous and shameful abuses that the industrial classes are now suffering at the hands of arrogant capitalists and powerful corporations.'

In the 1890s, the Farmers' Alliance linked up with disenchanted Democrats and others to form the most influential third party in American history – the Populist Party, dedicated to political reform, reining in corporations and protecting farming. In the 1890 elections, the Populists saw dozens of senators and representatives elected; in 1892, their presidential candidate drew over a million votes.[8]

The party itself eventually fell apart, but many of its ideas lived – and live – on. Many people I met claimed inspiration from the Populists. If anything like it were to happen again the shock waves, emanating from the world's economic powerhouse, would surely be global.

Today, with an American populace apparently persuaded by terrorist attacks and a longing for national unity to draw together behind the most venal corporate administration in decades, such a popular movement against corporate involvement in democracy might seem further away than ever. But it may not be as far as it looks. The initiatives I saw in California and Colorado, for example, are not the only stirrings of local resistance to corporate control across the republic. The harder you look, in fact, the more you see.

In 1993, the small town of Greenfield, Massachusetts went to the polls to vote against a planned Wal-Mart superstore being built in their town. The man who masterminded the campaign, former journalist Al Norman, has since founded a national movement, Sprawl-Busters, dedicated to empowering communities across the country to prevent mega-retail chains from cannibalising their communities. Over thirty towns have rejected Wal-Marts and other 'big box' chains as a result. Carmel and Solvang, two towns in California, have banned all chain restaurants. Palm Beach, Florida, and Santa Cruz, California, have enacted laws limiting chain operations. Plymouth, Massachusetts, prohibits 'box stores' from part of the town. And nine entire states have adopted laws prohibiting corporations from engaging in agriculture. There will undoubtedly be more.

And it's not all local: increasingly, the discontent is national. In 1999, for example, something remarkable happened. An 89-year-old woman, Doris Haddock – or 'Granny D' as she was soon to become known – began a walk across the United States to protest against corporate involvement in politics. Despite her age, her emphysema and her arthritis, the five-foot grandmother trekked 3,200 miles from California to Washington DC to campaign for legislation to get corporate money out of politics. She gave speeches in towns and cities along the way, drawing thousands of people. Congresspeople walked part of the way with her and everywhere, people expressed support for her aims. An ABC News opinion poll, conducted in September 2000, was typical of many others: it found that 63 per cent of Americans believed that 'large corporations have too much power for the good of the country'.[9] When she arrived in Washington, thousands came out to greet her. She told them, as she had told others, that her aim was to 'defeat utterly those forces of greed and corruption that have come between us and our self-governance'.[10]

Corporations, says Granny D, are 'hogs at the public trough'. Tens of thousands appeared to agree. In March 2001, as Congress debated a controversial bill designed to put an end to at least some of the corporate money that US politics is awash with, Granny D walked continually around the outside of the Capitol building for seven days. Much to the Bush administration's chagrin, the bill was passed.

What is fascinating, and peculiarly American, about all of this is that it is based on an appeal to patriotism – to the original ideas of the revolution. Freedom, self-government, liberty and democracy: government by, for and of The People. An appeal like this can, and does, unite right and left, young and old, in a struggle for a new kind of American democracy, based on the best of the democratic spirit of 1776. As it does so, it uses the tools of that democracy – local laws, ballot initiatives and the like – to try to fundamentally alter, or perhaps repair, the relationship between citizens and corporations. To reposition The People as the authority and the corporations as supplicants, rather than, as is so often the case now, the other way around. Could a new populist movement arise in America? If it does, it will surely grow from these seeds, planted in the heartland of corporate rule, and nurtured by its supposed beneficiaries.

9 **the gathering storm**

'First they ignore you. Then they laugh at you. Then they attack you. Then you win.'

MAHATMA GANDHI

'From what we now see, nothing of reform in the political world ought to be held improbable. It is an age of revolutions, in which everything may be looked for.'

THOMAS PAINE, 1791

Wednesday, 12 June 1381 was a sunny day. On Blackheath, an old stretch of common land five miles south-east of medieval London, birds were singing. It was the eve of the feast day of Corpus Christi, and on the grasslands a vast crowd of English peasants was gathered. Some of them were listening to a sermon by a priest named John Ball. Ball was preaching more than the gospels – he was speaking of revolution, advising the assembled masses to 'get rid of all the Lords, Archbishops, Abbots and Priors',[1] to abolish feudalism and serfdom, to take the lands of Crown and Church and hand them out to the people.

Around him, peasants from Kent, Essex and beyond were sharpening daggers and stringing bows. There were over 100,000 of them, angry, exhausted and out of patience. These were the peasants, the serfs, the villeins; virtual slaves on the bottom rung of the feudal ladder. Now they had risen up against their masters.

It was an unprecedented and utterly unexpected revolt. But it was not without reason. For decades the peasants had been held down by laws restricting their wages, extreme punishments for minor crimes, the corruption and greed of Church and gentry and a studied lack of interest in their woes from King and government. The last straw had been a 'poll tax' levied on them by a cash-strapped parliament. In May 1381, peasants in Essex began attacking tax collectors. From there, things spiralled rapidly through Kent, Norfolk, Lincolnshire and other counties. Within days, armies of peasants were marching through town and country stringing up lawyers and tax collectors and burning the great houses of clergy and gentry. Together, they began to move towards London.

By the time the rebels reached the outskirts of the capital they had a leader – 'one Watt Teghler of Maidstone' – they had weapons and vast numbers, and they had swept all before them.

Their initial grievances had developed into a radical analysis of the state they were in – one fed by the revolutionary preachings of John Ball and the self-belief of Watt Tyler. Now they wanted more than tax relief and justice – they wanted an end to serfdom, a breaking-up of the Church, a sweeping shift in social relations and economic organisation.

Now, on Blackheath, the commons had come for the King. The peasant army was demanding an audience with the newly crowned monarch, Richard II, only fourteen years of age. They had demands to make – and they trusted him to meet them. The rebels, for all their talk of radical change, for all their dislike of grasping gentry and corrupt ministers, trusted their King. The system was rotten, they knew – but the King had the power to restore it. He was appointed by God to be their rightful master. They knew that if they could put their case to him, he would listen, he would see reason – and he would turn the system the right way up again.

But the King didn't come. Outraged, the peasants stormed London, breaking through the gates and raining fire on the streets of the walled city. For three days they burned the houses of the rich, invaded churches and legal temples, killed clergy, lawyers, gentry and royal advisers, released prisoners. They dragged the Archbishop of Canterbury from his prayers and beheaded him. Then they surrounded the boy-King and his trembling ministers in the Tower of London and refused to leave until he listened.

But the mob outside Richard's palace had come not to bury him but to save him – to save him from corrupt advisers and the mistakes of his ministers, from a system that wasn't working. They wanted, in the end, not quite revolution but reform. They wanted a better, fairer England, and they trusted their King to deliver it. That was, after all, what feudalism was supposed to be about: the nobility meeting their obligations to the lower orders. That was the deal. They believed that the King would stick to it. It was to be their undoing.

The King agreed to meet the rebels at Smithfield, on the edge of the city. Watt Tyler rode across the cornfields to meet him. 'Why will you not go back to your own country?' asked Richard. They would not go back, said Tyler, until the King had given them what they wanted. They wanted the removal of harsh criminal laws designed to repress the poor; the end of outlawry; the abolition of all lords and all bishops except for the King himself and one Archbishop. They wanted all Church land and goods to be divided up among the people and all land owned by lords and barons to become common. Finally they wanted an end to serfdom – for 'all men to be free'.

The King's response was simple: he agreed. The rebels had his word, he said, that their demands would be met. The system would be reformed and the King would do the reforming. After all, it was in everyone's interests that the powerful meet their responsibilities. Now, said the King, Tyler should take his people back home.

Tyler was taken aback. There seemed little he could do but agree. He called for a drink and was given a flagon of ale, which he drank 'in a very rude and villainous manner before the King'. One of Richard's valets insulted him for his behaviour. A fight broke out. Tyler had a small dagger. The King's men had concealed swords. Within seconds, one of them had run him through. Watt Tyler was dead.

When they saw what had happened, the peasants panicked. With their leader dead they were directionless. Some drew their bows and began to fire upon the royal party. Without blinking, the fourteen-year-old King rode straight towards the assembled commoners. Tyler, he shouted, had betrayed them; he was a traitor. Now they had a new leader – Richard himself. 'I will be your King, your captain and your leader,' he cried.[2] And they believed him. The crowd fell to their knees in gratitude, begging their master's forgiveness for doubting him. The rebellion was over.

The hundred thousand returned home and prepared for the better life that their King had promised. But Richard kept none of his pledges. Instead, he sent soldiers to arrest the ringleaders and hang them. Months of bloody reprisal swept through Kent and Essex. What had looked, just days before, like the irresistible rise of the marginalised against the elite, had dwindled to nothing. 'This storm,' wrote one historian, 'assumed vast dimensions, spread over the whole horizon, swept down on the countryside with the violence of a typhoon, threatened universal destruction and then suddenly passed away as inexplicably as it had arisen.'[3] The weather had changed. Feudalism was saved.

Here in the early twenty-first century, I am sitting at my desk thinking about where I have been and what I have seen. I am thinking about a new revolt of the marginalised; a new storm gathering out there, beyond the radar screens of the powerful. It seems a long way from Blackheath, bishops and barons – a long way, too, from where I'm sitting, in front of a computer screen in the depths of an English winter. From here, without an effort of the imagination, it can seem equally unlikely to overwhelm the way the world works. But I think it could happen. In fact, I think it is happening already.

What I have seen, on five continents, is a rapidly rising popular movement, led by the poor in the 'developing' lands and now developing in the rich world too. It is a movement of people who feel cut off. Some cut off by faceless economic forces from the wealth that others revel in. Some cut off by illegitimate private power from a role in their own governance. Some cut off by trade laws drawn up half a world away from their own land, their traditional resources, their way of life. Some cut off by an all-pervasive consumerism from any meaning other than money and any goal other than growth.

For these people – millions upon millions of them – globalisation is exclusion. It is a system, a process, which cuts more and more people off every year; a system which grows by excluding increasing numbers of people from what they need, desire or value. It is this exclusion which has created this movement, and which is swelling its numbers as the anger spreads and the resistance continues to mount.

A new march on the capital has begun. And the more I think about it, the more I see comparisons between 1381 and 2003; lessons that can perhaps be learned from the storm that was weathered – just – by King Richard II and that which is currently being nervously confronted by the new rulers of the world. Perhaps they are lessons that this movement is already learning.

Reliance on a leader, for example, can be fatal: once Tyler is dead, where do you turn? Spontaneous uprisings can be stunningly effective: they can also disappear again with remarkable speed if they are not well organised, focused and in it for the long haul. When a king, or a corporation, promises to work with you for the general good, listen to the alarm bells. When you march on the city, you don't plead – you demand. It's the only way to make them sit up and listen.

The most important lesson, though, is surely the oldest one of all – that power is never given, it is always taken. You can gather in vast numbers, you can storm their palaces, you can tear the capital apart, you can call for striking change – but if you hope to achieve that change by expecting an inherently unjust system, one which thrives on inequality, to deliver the goods, you are likely to be very disappointed.

If this sounds like revolutionary talk I make no apologies. I wrote at the beginning of this book that this was a revolution, and it wasn't just a figure of speech. Perhaps not a revolution in the sense that recent history has taught us to understand it: not a series of power-grabs by red-starred guerrillas or 'People's Parties' equipped with Big Ideas for a New Utopia. But a revolution nonetheless. When will it happen? It is happening already. It is going on in Soweto and Porto Alegre, Jayapura and La Garrucha, Itapeva and Point Arena. It is growing in speed, size and ambition. Even as I sit here at my desk, I hear whispers of it – I hear the grinding of the machine, and the spanners being employed in response. Things are moving out there. This has only just begun.

Here is a randomly plucked selection of events that took place just in the time it took me to write this chapter:

Exhibit A: CONSUMER CHOICE

In Ecuador, a new left-wing president, Lucio Gutierrez, won the presidency, beating his billionaire businessman rival comprehensively, and adding another country to the increasing number of Latin American states which are experiencing an anti-neoliberal backlash. In the months leading up to his election, thousands of people took to the streets of the capital, Quito, to protest about the proposed Free Trade Area of the Americas, a White House-driven plan to extend NAFTA to every country on the continent. In early November 2002, tens of thousands of indigenous people and others flooded into Quito, chanting, '*Sí a la vida, No al ALCA*' ('Yes to life, No to the FTAA').

Exhibit B: RACE TO THE BOTTOM (OF THE ATLANTIC)

The *Prestige*, a 25-year-old oil tanker, ran aground, broke in two and sank in the Atlantic with 70,000 tonnes of oil on board, coating the north-west coast of Spain with thousands of tonnes of crude. The ship, noted the *Observer*, was 'chartered by the Swiss-based subsidiary of a Russian conglomerate registered in the Bahamas, owned by a Greek through Liberia and given a certificate of seaworthiness by the Americans. When it refuelled, it stood off the port of Gibraltar to avoid the chance of inspection. Every aspect of its operations was calculated to avoid tax, ownership obligations and regulatory scrutiny.'[4]

Exhibit C: EUROPEAN UNION

Twenty-five thousand people gathered in Florence, Italy, for the European Social Forum, and 750,000 people took to the streets of the same city to loudly reject a likely attack on Iraq. Organisers of the World Social Forum, to be held again in Porto Alegre, announced that they were expecting at least 100,000 people in 2003 – almost twice the previous year's attendance.

Exhibit D: WEALTH CREATION

Jean-Pierre Garnier, chief executive of GlaxoSmithKline, one of the world's leading pharmaceutical corporations, demanded a pay rise. Garnier, who lives in Philadelphia, explained that his current package, worth around £7 million, was not enough. He demanded a new deal worth an estimated £24 million to keep him motivated. GlaxoSmithKline recently experienced a 25 per cent decline in profits.

Exhibit E: TRIED IT, DIDN'T LIKE IT

In Argentina unemployed workers, jobless as a result of the country's dire economic state, have begun re-opening bankrupt factories themselves, running them as co-ops. They are part of a virtually unreported popular rebellion taking place across the country. In late 2001, Argentina's economy spectacularly collapsed. Vast debts, decades of IMF-imposed privatisation, austerity and spending cuts and a collapse in 'market confidence' destroyed, within hours, the lives of millions of people in a country held up for years as a neoliberal success story. Today, people across Buenos Aires and elsewhere are forming street-level 'popular assemblies' to run their own neighbourhoods and economic affairs, and refusing to listen to the strictures of either markets or politicians. *Que se vayan todos* – 'away with them all' – has become a popular rallying-cry in a nation which did everything the globalisers told it to and paid the price.

Exhibit F: YOU CAN'T BUCK THE MARKET

Morgan Stanley, one of the US's leading investment banks, advised its clients not to invest in companies with active unions or decent pension schemes. 'Look for the union label . . . and run the other way,' the bank recommended, explaining with disarming frankness that 'rigidity in labour costs, processes and pension requirements, while perhaps beneficial to employees, may prove toxic to shareholders'.[5]

Exhibit G: WHO ASKED YOU?

The World Economic Forum released the results of a global survey it had carried out on the subject of 'trust'. The ambitious project collected the views of 36,000 people in forty-seven countries on six continents, which were said to represent the views of 1.4 billion people. Two-thirds of those questioned did not believe that their country was 'governed by the will of the people'. Over half of those questioned trusted neither their national parliament nor large corporations to 'operate in society's best interests'. The World Trade Organization, World Bank and IMF were trusted less than the UN, NGOs or even the armed forces. 'Trust in many key institutions has fallen to critical proportions,' fretted the Forum.[6]

Perhaps you can hear it from where you're sitting now: that low, distant rumble, growing steadily louder as you focus on it. It's the sound of change, and it's coming your way – our way – whether we like it or not. The world is not going to go on like this: with the richest 20 per cent of us rolling in 86 per cent of the wealth, the poorest 20 per cent scraping by on 1.3 per cent. It cannot and will not, and the rise of this movement is just one sign of how that change is likely to make itself felt.

Before I set out on my travels, I had two questions foremost in my mind. What, in summary, does this movement stand for? And how can we build a new world based on those principles? Now, after all I've seen, I think that I can begin to answer them.

What do we stand for?

This is an enormous and chaotically diverse movement, full of passionate and intensely argumentative people. It's impossible to sum up everything that every person or group stands for, particularly as some of them contradict each other. It is possible, though, to draw up a list of principles and values which run through most of this movement.

This is a movement which stands for redistribution – redistribution of both wealth and power. It stands for equity – a world in which everyone gets their share, of material wealth, of representation, of influence. It stands for autonomy, and for genuine democracy, both participatory and representative. It stands for a model of organising which rejects, in many though not all cases, traditional hierarchies, and similarly rejects the old left-wing model of leader and followers, vanguard and masses. It stands for DIY politics – a willingness and a desire to take action yourself, to take to the streets, to act rather than to ask. It stands for economic independence, anti-consumerism and a redefinition of the very concepts of 'growth' and 'development'. It seeks a world where there are strict limits to market values and private power, where life is not commodified, where the commons are redefined and reclaimed, where ecology and economy go hand in hand. It stands for a rejection of top-down models and all-encompassing 'Big Ideas'. And it stands, perhaps above all, for a reclamation and a redefinition of power itself.

In my eight months of travelling I had a lot of revelations, a lot of epiphanies: enough to last me for years to come. I discovered things I didn't know, abandoned a few beliefs I'd held, confirmed others, took on some new ones. But my biggest revelation, the biggest connection I made, the most important understanding was also, in many ways, the simplest: that this is really all about one thing. *Power*.

This, above all, is what connects all the movements I visited. The battles they are all fighting are not, fundamentally, about trade, treaties, agriculture, consumerism or corporations at all. These are all manifestations of a strikingly old-fashioned power struggle – a struggle for which 'globalisation' is only the latest word. It's a timeless, international battle to decide who runs the show; who wields that power and how, and by what authority do they do so? And what I discovered as I travelled was that virtually everything, everywhere came down to two thrillingly simple questions:

1. Who's in charge?
2. Why?

When this is understood, much else begins to fall into place. It becomes easier to see why this movement came first from the south, from the poor countries, those left behind by the system and its beneficiaries. It becomes clear, too, why those who believe this should not be a real resistance movement at all, but rather a coalition of polite negotiators working to 'make globalisation work better', or to persuade corporations to 'behave responsibly' are wide of the mark. This is a movement designed and built to contest power – to question, and to claim, legitimacy. And that is exactly what it is doing.

It also becomes easier to understand why this movement insists on trying, as it goes, to redefine what power means, and how it is used. Increasingly, it seeks to do two things with power. First, to wrestle it from increasingly remote and illegitimate elites, and spread it around at ground level. Secondly, to redefine what it is – to try to decentralise it, rather than, as so many past radicals have done, to try to seize it from one elite and hand it to another.

It is also a movement which understands that as power is concentrated further in corporations, stock exchanges, dealing rooms, presidential palaces and summit venues, the result is a steady and inexorable requisitioning of public goods for private gain. Power, in other words, is being used to exclude and to enclose. If this is at heart a power struggle it is a struggle, too, against that enclosure: against the theft of the public by the private. It is a struggle to reclaim space.

In Chiapas, the Zapatistas declare autonomous zones, reclaiming their political and physical space from the clutches of Mexico's 'bad government'. The citizens of Cochabamba fight the enclosure of their common water resources. Protesters in Genoa try to take back the streets that the Red Zone has enclosed. Sowetans reconnect their own electricity. The Reverend Billy wails in public about the theft of community space by chainstores. The MST scales the fences around enclosed land and claims it for the poor. The people of Boulder stake a claim to their streets on behalf of local traders. Everywhere, a struggle for power: everywhere a fight for space.

This movement, then, is an unprecedented, international gathering of political resistance, built to contest power and seeking a very different world order based on very different values from those on which the globalisation project rests. Those values can, I think, be boiled down to their essence and reduced to five key principles: democracy, diversity, decentralisation, sovereignty and access. If I list them, now, along with their polar opposites, you can see why:

What We Want	What We Get
DEMOCRACY Political and economic. More, and genuine, decision-making power at local level, over everything from resource use to education and 'development' decisions. Removal of market control over governance.	DICTATORSHIP Of markets, corporations and their allies and supplicants in national governments. Managerial political elites, with 'left' and 'right' increasingly indistinguishable, and societies guided by market values.
DIVERSITY Cultural, geographical, ecological, political and economic – a world with many worlds in it.	MONOCULTURE From crops to clothes to ideas: a global mall, the disappearance of difference, the bleaching of the human rainbow in the name of the global market.
DECENTRALISATION From food-growing to planning decisions, everything to be done at the lowest level possible; redefining power, spreading it around, locking it down.	CONCENTRATION Of ownership and thus of power. Decisions made at the highest level by bought-up politicians, unelected trade representatives and overpaid brokers.
SOVEREIGNTY Self-determination, autonomy, liberty – people actively and independently deciding their own fate, and that of their community and nation.	DEPENDENCE A world of consumers rather than citizens, reliant on distant corporations, governments and advanced technology to provide for their needs.
ACCESS Access to common land, resources, public services and a genuine civic domain; defined areas of life into which market values do not intrude.	ENCLOSURE Private control of resources, from land to electricity to gene lines; a world in which private interests buy up the world and sell it back to us, at mark-up.

What do we do?

If these are the key principles of this movement, then, what would a world based on them look like? Again, it's possible to pull together some answers, and to lay out at least the beginnings of a strategy. I've lost count of the number of times I've said, in these pages, that this movement has no manifesto; and that in many ways this is a good thing. It means there is no 'one way' for the world to go; it means that 'one no, many yeses' can be a basis for a set of practical principles, rather than just a slogan. I don't plan to change my mind now, and what follows is not a watertight, prescriptive plan or, needless to say, a new Big Idea. But it is one way in which we could get where we want to go; and it's a way based on ideas and principles that I've seen coming out of today's movement.

Globalisation creates exclusion, division and dependence. At every level it comes between people and their self-governance, people and their resources, people and their communities, people and nature, people and control of their economies, people and real human values. Change, then, has to come in two stages. The first task is to tear down those institutions, laws, ideas and systems which come between us and what we need and desire; to topple the menhirs of money that block out the sun. Only when the obstacles are gone will the second stage – building new worlds, new values, new systems, on a new paradigm – be able to properly take shape.

Two stages, then:

Stage One: Clearing the Ground

Neoliberalism, corporate power, mass-marketed materialism, the unthinking pursuit of narrowly defined 'growth' – these are cancers eating away at people and planet alike. They are the barriers that stand between us and the world we want to see. We need to sweep away these barriers and build up strong systems, checks and balances to ensure they are not erected again. We need, in other words, to reshape politics and economics on different principles: those that favour people rather than power, measure 'growth' in very different ways, and value systemically what people value individually.

This is no time for half-measures or gradual reforms. We need to clear the decks and start again. Here are just a few global proposals that would help make it happen:

ABOLISH THE WTO, IMF AND WORLD BANK

The whole of the post-war 'Bretton Woods' settlement is rotten; captured by corporate interests and making the world worse rather than better. All three institutions should be scrapped and new ones created, based on very different values. A good starting-point would be the suggestions laid out by the International Forum on Globalisation at the World Social Forum. Get rid of the Bank and the Fund, abolish the 'structural adjustment' principles that require countries to destroy their social services in the name of 'efficient' markets and replace them instead with democratic institutions under UN auspices, designed to wipe out Third World debt, limit international financial flows and ensure that the poor get their share of the world's resources. As for the WTO: let's replace it with an organisation whose purpose is to regulate trade strictly in the interests of environmental protection, poverty reduction and equity of access. The UK Green MEP Caroline Lucas, for example, has suggested replacing the WTO agreements with a 'General Agreement on Sustainable Trade', which would re-focus the global trading framework. Rather than basing development on WTO-style rules, which promote trade above all, a GAST would allow governments to promote local and national industries once more, abolish TRIPS and its like, promote sustainable farming and local economic activity, lock environmental protection into the global economic framework and generally turn the world's economy the right way up again.

TIE DOWN GLOBAL FINANCE

'I sympathise,' said the economist John Maynard Keynes in 1933, 'with those who would minimise, rather than with those who would maximise, economic entanglement among nations. Ideas, knowledge, science, hospitality, travel – these are the things which should of their nature be international. But let goods be homespun whenever it is reasonably and conveniently possible and, above all, let finance be primarily national.' Keynes was one of the founders of the World Bank and IMF, in the days when they were intended to be progressive rather than destructive institutions, and he understood only too well that when finance capital gets out of hand it eats human needs alive. Today, international banking systems and open flows of invest-ment are holding elected governments to ransom. Elected to bring about systemic change in your country? If the markets don't like it, they will destroy your economy in hours. This is at odds with every principle of democracy – if that word is to mean anything again, finance has to be reined in. Taxes on international financial speculation, re-regulating international banks and re-introducing exchange controls have all been sug-gested as methods of doing so. A new new world order should be one based on the real needs of real people in real places, not the instant gratification of traders, investors and shareholders, divorced from any responsibility for the real-world effects of their decisions.

RE-PROGRAMME CORPORATIONS

A corporation is a machine programmed to do two things: make profits and keep growing. Today, the machines have broken free of the boundaries set by their masters and are increasingly destroying anything that gets in the way of those goals – the environment, human rights, cultural differences, non-market values – like mad robots in a 1950s B-movie. Rafts of new regulations and voluntary commitments to 'corporate social responsibility' are nowhere near enough to tackle this problem. Corporations need to be re-invented; re-programmed, like those robots, with radical new rules designed to make them servants, not masters. The original model of corporate organisation in the USA can provide something of an idea for what these rules could be. Charters issued for specific purposes and up for regular renewal. Corporations forced to pay progressive taxes and remain accountable in one country. Bans on corporate involvement in politics. Directors and shareholders to have personal financial and legal liability for any crimes or misdemeanours committed by the corporation. To these, we could add other strictures: new laws requiring corporations to 'internalise' the costs they currently externalise on to society. For example, forcing oil companies to take financial and legal responsibility for their role in creating climate change; requiring forestry companies to add the massive cost of biodiversity loss to their balance sheets; making car firms, rather than society as a whole, pay for cleaning up air pollution, dealing with congestion and patching people up after road accidents. Local communities should have the right to decide how and if corporations operate in their area. We should impose strict controls on corporate media ownership and ban government subsidies and tax breaks to corporations. All of this, taken together, would change the world overnight.

RE-CREATE THE UNITED NATIONS

Strengthening and democratising the UN – not a simple or easy process, but probably a vital one – could provide a fair means by which the above measures could be achieved. Governments already agree to vast numbers of international laws, on everything from protecting labour rights to preventing climate change, which the UN, with scarce resources and an inadequate budget, is expected to administer. Usually, its efforts are undermined by the WTO, corporations, investors and governments themselves, who give the immediate demands of trade and commerce priority over more long-term goals like protecting biological diversity or preventing exploitation of the weak. So let's strengthen the UN, fund it properly and give it what the WTO already has – the power to back up its laws and punish those who break them. Let's bring regulation of trade and finance under UN auspices, creating a raft of new institutions like those suggested above. They, and all international agreements, should be based on a set of key principles: that all global economic activity should protect the environment, enhance equity, reduce poverty and be accountable to the people it affects, and that laws designed to protect the environment, democracy and human rights should always take priority over trade. To do all of this would require a radical democratisation of the UN – granting poor countries as much say as rich ones, basing influence on population rather than wealth and refusing corporations or commercial interests any say in global decision-making.

RE-THINK THE COMMONS

Let's also institutionalise a radical re-thinking of the relationship between private and public goods. Globalisation's tendency is to privatise everything possible and turn it into a commodity; a process which adds numbers to balance sheets but denudes what life is really about. So here's another task for that reformed UN: to define, protect and enhance the commons. Let's ring-fence public goods and public places and ban the monopolisation of public resources by private interests. Let's champion the civic and the public realm once again, and ensure through international law that certain institutions and goods are free from private incursion and market values for ever. Common land, as defined by communities. Public services – education, health care, public broadcasting, museums, libraries and more. Life itself, from gene lines to crop varieties. Water, space, the atmosphere – everything which provides a common good for people as a whole, should be bound in by strict rules guaranteeing public access and preventing private incursion.

A GLOBAL CONVERSATION

Finally, let's set the stage for a global conversation about where the world is going and what we want from it. What is democracy and how can it be made to work? What do we mean by 'growth' or 'development'? Are we happy about the direction in which the world is going? Are there universal human values, and if so, how do we turn them into actions? How can we balance local needs and global requirements? What more can be done to redistribute wealth and power on a global level, and ensure it stays that way? How are decisions made, and do we want to change it? The world is moving further and faster than at any time for centuries – possibly ever – and nobody, even those in power, seems to quite understand where. It's time we instituted a global democratic conversation about it; a conversation in which, for once, the poor are heard as loudly as the rich and people, not special interests, make the running.

Stage Two: Sowing the Seeds

This, measured by the standards of the age, is an ambitious list. But it's a minimum requirement for the kind of world this movement wants to see. It would go a long way towards clearing away the major obstacles which currently prevent people and communities defining their own relationship between themselves and the world they live in, and taking back their own sovereignty. It would open up a space in which genuine alternatives could flourish – a space in which those many yeses could come into fruition.

Globalisation is about taking control away from people. To turn the world into a market and its people into consumers, it's necessary to create economic and mental dependence. Ideas like those above are about moving us from dependence to sovereignty – real control by people, according to their needs. They are about hacking away the undergrowth and exposing the shoots of the new to a long-hidden burst of light.

But they're just a start. What happens then is up to us. Better worlds don't just create themselves, and with the obstacles gone and illegitimate power locked down, the rest comes from below. This means that people need to act personally, at local and international levels, to make change happen: join organisations, set up our own, fight for our own communities, lobby those in power, get together with others to make things happen (the Appendix, 'Action Stations', includes just a few places to start). If we want a world with many worlds in it, no one can say quite what the results will be – every place will develop in its own way, within a global community of equals. Some ideas for rebirth are fairly universal, however. Real local democracy, for instance, with meaningful devolution of powers to community level, including control over resources and land-use, would return governance to the people it is supposed to belong to. A systemic bias in favour of local business and trade, communities' rights to define economic activity in their area, political parties who actually disagreed with each other and were able to offer genuine national alternatives without being crushed by the markets – all these, and many more that we probably can't yet imagine, could flower in a re-worked world. A thousand systems would be free to bloom.

None of this is prescriptive. Plenty of people, within the movement as well as outside it, will undoubtedly disagree with at least some of it. Stage one and stage two will not operate in isolation; they can happen in tandem; they already are. But what is clear – as clear to me now as it was when I wrote my very first word – is that none of this – nothing – will happen at all, unless we make it happen. There will be no real change unless there is a worldwide popular movement with mass support and growing numbers able to demand it. This is already happening, but it needs to keep growing – in size and strength and reach and popularity. Power is never given up lightly, and serious change will not come about through asking politely. Demands, backed up by numbers, are the only thing that will make it happen.

There is more to it, though, even than this – for even making demands, however forcibly and visibly you do it, is not enough. This is something people were aware of everywhere I went. None of them had any intention of sitting around politely drumming their fingers while their elected representatives came up with the goods. This is a movement that, through practice and principle, is doing for itself what others won't do for it. It takes back space, reconnects wires, declares autonomy, creates its own alternatives without asking anyone's permission. That is its great strength. It's not a parade of lobbyists, it's a massing of people who are already making change happen where they live, in their own way. And while they call for those great systemic changes that will allow their visions to become a wider reality, they go ahead at local level and create those realities themselves. As they do, they re-create their own sovereignty, become what they demand – emerge from the consumer chrysalis to become citizens once again. After that, there is no going back. It is transformation.

Everywhere I go I have seen this: people who won't wait, can't wait: people creating their own worlds without asking permission. And as this movement grows and spreads, and as more people understand that democracy does not mean marking a piece of paper every five years, but defining your own community and creating your own world, this will grow. As it does, and as the numbers involved do too, there may be no choice for those at the top but to begin making changes themselves; real ones. In the meantime, though, change is already being constructed – from the bottom, not from the top. It may not be very long before the world's governors have to confront a very uncomfortable question indeed: how many people need to opt out of your system before it stops being a system at all?

We are at a unique moment in history. It is more fragile than it seems. What we thought was democracy is stalling, private power is becoming entrenched, old systems are failing to meet new needs. It may be that when historians look back on this moment, and this movement, they will see the beginnings of a new democratic revolution – a new stage in democracy's journey. It may be that people will look back on today's belief that 'democracy' means choosing a ruling elite from two gatherings of remote figures in suits as a historical anachronism, as hard to understand as support for slavery or absolute monarchy. It may be that today's model of 'democracy' is just a staging-post on the long road towards the real thing. It may be that this movement will help us all to travel further in that direction.

There are words of warning to be heeded, though. A fragile world could succumb, too, to the siren call of the far right, that trusted repository of easy solutions when destabilising change comes too fast. Governments could crack down, as they are beginning to do, on peaceful and legitimate dissidents, under the all-encompassing banner of 'anti-terrorism'. Or that terrorism itself, often feeding too on the insecurities created by globalisation, could prove more powerful and long-lasting than most hope, and drown out peaceful calls for a just transformation.

Then there is this movement itself: it is far from complete and far from perfect. Will it unite around one call for change, adopt a manifesto, elect representatives to put its cause on the world stage? If it does, will it survive as anything new and meaningful? Will it split and split again, and will those splits matter? Will it remain democratic? Will it develop a clearer identity in the eyes of the world? Can it sustain its momentum? Can it pull more people in, and keep developing, as it has so far done so successfully? Hard questions. We don't yet know the answers.

But I can't help being optimistic, and my optimism comes from the answers I find to a few simple questions. Has a movement this big ever existed before? Has such a diversity of forces, uncontrolled, decentralised, egalitarian, ever existed on a global scale? Has a movement led by the poor, the disenfranchised, the south, ever existed at all, without being hijacked by intellectual demagogues or party politicians in a way that this movement looks unlikely, because of both its principles and its organising methods, ever to do? How have we achieved so much in such a short time? Do the world's people want to listen? Are we going in the right direction? Are we gaining in momentum? I get the right answer to every one of these questions, and every one of those answers help to answer another: can the world afford to ignore this any more?

Above all, I have come to see that a belief in real, lasting change is the first step to bringing it about. Everywhere we turn we are told that globalisation is irreversible, that history has ended, that capitalism is triumphant, that everything about the way the world is currently set up is essential and unavoidable if we want 'growth', 'progress' and 'development'. This sort of talk is supposed to be 'realistic'. It's nothing of the sort: it's a failure of the imagination dressed up as a political opinion.

For if there is one thing that history teaches us it is that systems change – they always have, and they always will. Empires fall, values shift, power dissolves and most of the time the impetus comes from below. Back in 1381, imprisoned in the Tower of London by baying mobs of his own people, Richard II, despairing at this unexpected and all-powerful fury, feared that 'the heritage and realm of England were near lost'.[7] His luck held – just. But this is history's lesson: that radical change, far from being the exception, is almost the norm; that nothing is inevitable, that systems can be, and often are, swept away by their own, often shockingly sudden, illegitimacy in the eyes of their people. It happened to the Romanovs, then it happened to the Soviets. An army of peaceful peasants evicted the British from India, the Berlin Wall was torn down without a shot being fired, Nelson Mandela walked from Robben Island into the presidential palace and no one could have predicted any of them just a few years before they happened. So why not this? Why not now?

I'm not old enough to remember when ascendant Marxists trumpeted the historical inevitability of global communism, but now I hear, all over the world, precisely the same argument being used for precisely the opposite system. The claim is equally false. Nothing is inevitable in history. All this will change, because it will have to, and when it does, the changes should be big, bold, beautiful. Our job is to make it happen – and to be radical and visionary as we do so. Why can't we abolish the WTO, the World Bank, the IMF? Why can't we redistribute land, end debt, devolve power downwards? Why can't we feed the world, why can't we abolish poverty? Why can't we redefine power, lock corporations and markets back where they belong, make democracy do what we were always promised it would, whether the current elites like it or not? We can: the resources are there; so is the ability. What is missing is a willingness to use them. What is missing is vision, bravery, political will, a willingness to confront those who benefit from injustice – and if this movement has any purpose at all it is surely to provide them.

That is our job: to be bold. Not to tinker about at the margins, 'greening' corporations, waffling about 'sustainability', proposing voluntary targets, issuing policy papers, settling for better-than-nothing, politely gathering the crumbs from the table. Our job, now, is to call for everything we want, as loudly as we can – and to keep calling until we get it. Who knows – we might even surprise ourselves. We will certainly surprise the world. And if not us, then who? If not now – then when?

APPENDIX:
ACTION STATIONS

If this book has inspired you to act on any of the issues it has raised, to get involved in any of the campaigns or to support any of the organisations featured, then it has done its job. The following brief list gives web-based contacts for some of the key sources of information and action covered in the book, and also includes a few ideas for other places to go if you want to find out more about the issues or get in touch with those campaigning around them. It is, of course, only a start – the rest is up to you.

1: 'to open a crack in history'

The EZLN – all the Zapatistas' communiqués and publications online:
www.ezln.org

Global Exchange – campaigns, resources, links and other Chiapas information:
www.globalexchange.org/campaigns/mexico/chiapas/

Indymedia Chiapas – the latest news on the EZLN and Chiapas situations:
www.chiapas.indymedia.org/

2: the belly of the beast

Peoples' Global Action – forthcoming protests, days of action, directories of other groups and actions all over the world:
www.agp.org

3: apartheid: the sequel

Alternative Information and Development Centre – actions, campaigns and news from the South African struggle. Also the contact point for the Soweto Electricity Crisis Committee:
www.aidc.org.za

Johannesburg Anti-Privatisation Forum – news and solidarity actions:
www.apf.org.za/

4: the church of stop shopping

The Reverend Billy – tips, scripts and advice on how to campaign entertainingly against chainstores in your town:
http://revbilly.com

The Biotic Baking Brigade – how to pie, where to pie, pie-ers in your area – and some great recipes:
www.asis.com/~agit-prop/bbb/

Adbusters – culture-jamming resources and links, plus ideas for celebrating Buy Nothing Day where you live:
www.adbusters.org/home/

Indymedia – non-corporate news from around the world, plus access to national and local Indymedia sites:
http://indymedia.org

Mediachannel – news from, criticism of and action to challenge the corporate media beast, plus a directory of 1,000 similar organisations around the world:
www.mediachannel.org

5: the penis gourd revolution

West Papua News Online – latest news from the resistance struggle, and how you can help the fight for freedom. Every single extra voice raised in support of the Papuans makes a big difference to them; please do anything you can:
www.westpapua.net

The Presidium Council – homepage and contacts for the PDP, plus links to OPM, Demmak and other grass-roots campaigners and requests for international help:
www.westpapua.org.uk/pdp/

OPM Support Group – UK-based actions and news in support of the Papuan cause:
www.eco-action.org/opm/
e-mail: opmsg@eco-action.org

6: the end of the beginning

World Social Forum – website for the Porto Alegre event, plus other social forums around the world:
www.forumsocialmundial.org.br/home

International Forum on Globalization – resources, books and publications on globalisation:
www.ifg.org

Global Trade Watch – Public Citizen's useful resource page on trade and globalisation:
www.citizen.org/trade

7: land and freedom

The MST – latest news, and how to help the Brazilian struggle for land:
www.mstbrazil.org

Food First – good resources on land and landlessness, plus national and international campaigns on land and food issues:
www.foodfirst.org

8: california dreaming

Democracy Unlimited of Humboldt County and **Reclaim Democracy** – US-focused information and campaigns on corporate power and accountability:
www.monitor.net/democracyunlimited/
http://reclaimdemocracy.org

POCLAD – resources and information on corporate power in the US:
http://poclad.org

and some more . . .

Closer to home, the following are just a few organisations providing ideas and organising actions and campaigns around the issues covered in this book.

World Development Movement – campaigns against unjust globalisation at national level:
www.wdm.org.uk

Green Party – news, campaigns and alternatives to globalisation:
www.greenparty.org.uk

Schnews – excellent freesheet with irreverent news and forthcoming campaigns on the UK direct-action scene:
http://schnews.org.uk

Corporate Watch – research into and campaigns against corporations and the economic structure that sustains them:
www.corporatewatch.org.uk

New Economics Foundation – thinktank developing alternatives to the current economic model:
www.neweconomics.org

Common Ground – inspiring organisation campaigning for local distinctiveness and providing resources and ideas to help you do so:
www.commonground.org.uk

REFERENCES

1: 'to open a crack in history'

1   The fullest account in English of the 1 January uprising can be found in John Ross's excellent book *Rebellion from the Roots: Indian Uprising in Chiapas* (Monroe, ME: Common Courage Press, 1995), from which my account partly draws. Other partial accounts can be found in Tom Hayden (ed.), *The Zapatista Reader* (New York: Thunder's Mouth Press, 2002); Elaine Katzenberger (ed.), *First World, Ha, Ha, Ha!* (San Francisco: City Lights, 1995); and Subcomandante Marcos, *Our Word is Our Weapon* (New York: Seven Stories Press, 2001).

2   'Notes on the Economy in Chiapas in 1999', originally published in *La Jornada*, Chiapas, 6 October 1999: see http://flag.blackened.net and www.struggle.ws/mexico/reports/chiapas_econ_99.html.

3   Bill Weinberg, *Homage to Chiapas* (London: Verso, 2000).

4   Philip Howard and Thomas Homer-Dixon, *Environmental Scarcity and Violent Conflict: The Case of Chiapas, Mexico*, Project on Environment, Population and Security, American Association for the Advancement of Science, University of Toronto, January 1996.

5   'Notes on the Economy in Chiapas in 1999', op. cit.

6   *A Storm and a Prophecy*, communiqué by Subcomandante Marcos, August 1992.

7   Weinberg, op. cit.

8   George A. Collier with Elizabeth Lowery Quaratiello, *Basta! Land and the Zapatista Rebellion in Chiapas* (Chicago: Food First Books, 1999).

9   Eduardo Galeano, *Open Veins of Latin America*, quoted in Weinberg, op. cit.

10   *Private Rights, Public Problems: A Guide to NAFTA's Controversial Chapter on Investor Rights* (Winnipeg: International Institute for Sustainable Development, 2001).

11 'Down on the Farm: NAFTA's Seven-Year War on Farmers and Ranchers in the US, Canada and Mexico', Public Citizen's Global Trade Watch, USA, June 2001. See www.citizen.org.

12 Quoted in *The Zapatistas: A Rough Guide* (Bristol: Chiapaslink, 2000).

13 Quoted in John Ross, *The War Against Oblivion: Zapatista Chronicles, 1994–2000* (Monroe, ME: Common Courage Press, 2000).

14 Quoted in Ross, *Rebellion from the Roots*, op. cit.

15 *The Retreat is Making Us Almost Scratch the Sky*, communiqué by Subcomandante Marcos, February 1995.

16 *The Majority Disguised as the Untolerated Minority*, communiqué by Subcomandante Marcos, May 1994.

part 1: one no

2: the belly of the beast

1 Press release from the 'Anti-Statist Black Bloc', Independent Media Center of Philadelphia, 9 August 2000: see www.phillyimc.org.

2 This, and more along the same lines, can be found in 'Black Blocs for Dummies' on the web at www.infoshop.org/blackbloc.html. To be fair, not all Black Bloc-ers are this gung-ho.

3 The website of Peoples' Global Action lists such events around the world on the many global days of action since 1998: www.nadir.org/nadir/initiativ/agp/en/index.html.

4 Christopher Lockwood, 'Swiss thwart forum protest', *Daily Telegraph* online, 30 January 2000.

5 *Vital Signs 2001*, Worldwatch Institute, New York, USA.

6 *Human Development Report 1999*, United Nations Development Programme.

7 *World Development Report 2000/2001: Attacking Poverty*, The World Bank.

8 *Human Development Report 2001*, United Nations Development Programme.

9 *World Development Report 2000/2001*, op. cit.

10 *Human Development Report 2001*, op. cit.

11 Susan George, 'A Short History of Neoliberalism', speech given at the Conference on Economic Sovereignty in a Globalising World, Bangkok, 24–26 March 1999.

12 David Jenkins, *Market Whys and Wherefores*, quoted in James Bruges, *The Little Earth Book* (Bristol: Alasdair Sawday Publishing, 2000).

13 *Human Development Report 2001*, op. cit.

14 *Invisible Government: The World Trade Organization – Global Government for the New Millennium?* (San Francisco: International Forum on Globalization, 1999).

15 'Network guerrillas', *Financial Times*, 30 April 1998.

16 Jimmy Langman, 'Neoliberal policies: big loser in Bolivian elections', Americas Program of the Interhemispheric Resource Center, 5 July 2002.

17 An excellent account of the Cochabamba 'Water War', by local journalist Jim Schultz, can be found on the Democracy Center's website: www.democracyctr.org/waterwar/index.htm.

3: apartheid: the sequel

1 'Eskom v. Soweto: The battle for power', *Focus* magazine, South Africa, March 2002.

2 Patrick Bond, *Elite Transition: From Apartheid to Neoliberalism in South Africa* (London: Pluto Press, 2000).

3 'Structure of the South African Economy: Challenges for Transformation', South African Communist Party, paper presented at the SACP Special Strategy Conference, September 1999.

4 Bond, op. cit.

5 *The Reconstruction and Development Programme*, 1994. Full text available at www.polity.org.za.

6 Patrick Bond, *Against Global Apartheid: South Africa Meets the World Bank, IMF and International Finance* (Cape Town: University of Cape Town Press, 2001).

7 Jon Jeter, 'South Africa weighs a welfare state', *Washington Post* Foreign Service, 9 July 2002.

8 *Focus* magazine, 2002, quoted by Patrick Bond, personal correspondence.

9 David A. McDonald, *The Bell Tolls for Thee: Cost Recovery, Cutoffs, and the Affordability of Municipal Services in South Africa*, Queens University, Canada/Municipal Services Project, March 2002. See www.hst.org.za/local/lgh/docs/MSPreport.doc.

10 Pravasan Pillay and Richard Pithouse, 'The Durban march on the UN Conference on Racism: An eyewitness report', *New Internationalist* online, September 2001. See www.newint.org.

11   Ashwin Desai, *The Poors of Chatsworth* (Johannesburg: Madiba, 2001.

12   Ashwin Desai, *The Poors of Chatsworth* (Johannesburg: Madiba, 2001).

13   Thomas Friedman, *The Lexus and the Olive Tree* (New York: Farrar, Straus & Giroux, 2000).

4: the church of stop shopping

1   Facts compiled by Shape Up America (www.shapeup.org) – and the New Road Map Foundation (www.ecofuture.org).

2   Kalle Lasn, *Culture Jam: The Uncooling of America* (New York: Eagle Brook, 1999).

3   New Road Map Foundation, op. cit.

4   Allan Casey, 'Make your school an ad-free zone', *Adbusters*, No. 28, 2000.

5   David Bollier, 'The Grotesque, Smirking Gargoyle: The Commercialising of America's Consciousness', August 2002: see www.tompaine.com.

6   Sharon Beder, 'Marketing to Children', edited from a conference paper presented in Sydney in 1998. Available at:
    www.uow.edu.au/arts/sts/sbeder/children.html.

7   Bollier, op. cit.

8   Todd Halvorson and Yuri Karash, 'Russia takes the lead in space-age advertising', www.space.com, 31 May 2002.

9   New Road Map Foundation, op. cit.

10   David G. Blanchflower and Andrew J. Oswald, 'Well-being Over Time in Britain and the USA', paper, Dartmouth College and Warwick University, 1999.

11   Lasn, op. cit.

12   Quoted in Edward Goldsmith, 'Development as Colonialism', in Mander and Goldsmith (eds), *The Case Against the Global Economy* (San Francisco: Sierra Club Books, 1996).

13   'Is globalisation doomed?', *The Economist*, 27 September 2001.

14   Katharine Ainger, 'Empires of the senseless', *New Internationalist*, April 2001.

15   See www.billboardliberation.com.

16   A recommended gallery of recent and classic subverts can be found at www.subvertise.org.

17   *Adbusters*, No. 40, 2002.

18   See www.fanclubbers.org.

19   Katharine Ainger, 'From the streets of Prague', *New Internationalist* online: see www.newint.org/streets/prague.htm.

20   See www.rtmark.com.

21   Quoted in 'Filtering the news', *New Internationalist*, April 2001.

22   Lasn, op. cit.

23   Quoted in Kim Masters, *The Keys to the Kingdom: How Michael Eisner Lost His Grip* (New York: Morrow, 2000).

24   Neil Hickey, 'Unshackling big media', *Columbia Journalism Review*: see www.cjr.com.

25   Quoted in Ainger, 'Empires of the senseless', op. cit.

26   Ibid.

27   Matthew Arnison, 'Open publishing is the same as free software', June 2002: see www.cat.org.au/maffew/cat/openpub.html.

5: the penis gourd revolution

1   This estimate is widely quoted by human-rights campaigners, including John Rumbiak, head of West Papua's leading human-rights organisation, ELS-HAM.

2   The imprisoned Swiss journalist, Oswald Iten, wrote of his experience, and of the torture he witnessed, in the Swiss newspaper *Neue Zürcher Zeitung* on 22 December 2000.

3   Throughout this chapter, people referred to by first names only have had their identities disguised, for obvious reasons.

4   According to the AFL-CIO union's 'Executive PayWatch'. See www.aflcio.org.

5   Many of these facts and figures can be found in Project Underground's 1998 report *Risky Business: The Grasberg Gold Mine – An Independent Annual Report on PT Freeport Indonesia* (available on the web at www.moles.org). Others can be found in Abigail Abrash and Danny Kennedy, 'Repressive Mining in West Papua', in *Moving Mountains: Communities Confront Mining and Globalisation* (London: Zed Books, 2001); on Freeport McMoran's website (www.fcx.com) and in the company's 2001 annual report.

6   John McBeth, 'Bull's eye', *Far Eastern Economic Review*, 4 December 1997, quoted in *Risky Business*, ibid.

7   *Van Zorge Report* on Indonesia, 1 May 2001.

8   President Harry S. Truman, Inaugural Address, 20 January 1949.

9   Emily Rosenberg, *Spreading the American Dream: American Economic and Cultural Expansion, 1890–1945* (New York: Hill & Wang, 1982).
10 'Trifungisi: The Role of the Indonesian Military in Business', paper presented by Lesley McCulloch to the International Conference on Soldiers in Business, Jakarta, 17–19 October 2000. Available at www.bicc.de.
11 Ibid.
12 *Risky Business*, op. cit., p. 7.

part 2: many yeses

6: the end of the beginning

1   Philippe Legrain, *Open World: The Truth About Globalisation* (London: Abacus, 2002).
2   'A different manifesto', *The Economist*, 27 September 2001.
3   Stanley Fischer, 'What I learned at the IMF', *Newsweek*, December 2001–February 2002.
4   See the World Economic Forum's website, www.weforum.org.
5   Adam Smith, *The Wealth of Nations*, Book 1, Chapter 10.
6   'World Social Forum Charter of Principles', available on the WSF website at www.forumsocialmundial.org.br/home.asp.
7   John Madeley, *Hungry for Trade: How the Poor Pay for Free Trade* (London: Zed Books, 2000).
8   Noted in Michael Moore's film *Bowling for Columbine* (2002).
9   John Rees, 'The battle after Seattle', *Socialist Review*, Issue 237, January 2000.
10 'Goblin', 'Letter to a British socialist on anti-capitalist movements', 26 May 2001. Available at www.commoner.org.uk.
11 Guy Taylor, personal correspondence, 18 September 2002.
12 Quoted in 'Monopolise resistance? How Globalise Resistance would hijack revolt', *Schnews*, September 2001.

7: land and freedom

1   National Institute of Colonisation and Land Reform (INCRA), quoted in *National Report on the Situation of Human Rights and Agrarian Reform in Brazil*, Global Justice Centre, Brazil, 17 May 2000.

2   See www.mstbrazil.org.

3   UN Population Fund, 2001.

4   Sue Branford and Jan Rocha, *Cutting the Wire: The Story of the Landless Movement in Brazil* (London: Latin American Bureau, 2002). This is easily the best and most comprehensive book on the MST in English.

5   Ibid.

6   Ibid.

7   Ibid.

8   Ibid.

9   National Institute of Colonisation and Land Reform (INCRA).

10 'A plot of their own', *Newsweek*, 21 January 2002.

11 Branford and Rocha, op. cit.

12 Geoffrey Lean and Sue Branford, 'GM-free nations fall to Monsanto', *Independent*, 31 March 2002.

8: california dreaming

1   Archer H. Shaw, *The Lincoln Encyclopaedia* (New York: Macmillan, 1950). Quoted in Rick Crawford, 'What Lincoln foresaw', at www.ratical.org/corporations/Lincoln.html.

2   Center for Responsive Policies, USA. See www.opensecrets.org/2000elect/select/AllCands.htm.

3   Personal wealth figures from Thomas B. Edsall, 'Bush has a cabinet full of wealth', *Washington Post*, 18 September 2002. Corporate–cabinet connections from Center for Responsive Policies, op. cit.

4   This brief history of the corporation is based primarily on two excellent sources: *Who's in Charge?* by Daniel Bennett, issued by POCLAD UK; and 'The Short History of Corporations' by Jeffrey Kaplan, published in *Terrain*, USA, 1999. Other sources include Richard Grossman and Frank T. Adams, *Taking Care of Business* (POCLAD USA, 1993), and the *Timeline of Personhood Rights and Powers*, compiled by Jan Edwards for WILPF, USA.

5   *Hear Ye, Hear Ye*, Democracy Unlimited of Humboldt County, 1999.

6   Stacy Mitchell, 'Homegrown Economics', *Orion Afield*, USA, 2001.

7   See www.afd-online.org.

8   From 'An Outline of American History' (http://odur.let.rug.nl/~usa/H/1994/chap8.htm) and 'The Short History of Corporations', op. cit.

9   ABC News, 13–17 September 2000. See www.pollingreport.com/
    bnews2.htm.

10 See http://grannyd.com.

9: the gathering storm

1   This account of the Peasants' Revolt, except where indicated, is taken
    from the *Anonimalle Chronicle*, generally accepted as the most reliable
    contemporary source, as reprinted in R. B. Dobson, *The Peasants' Revolt
    of 1381* (London: Macmillan, 1970).

2   From the account of Thomas Walsingham, in Dobson, op. cit.

3   Charles Oman, *The Great Revolt of 1381* (Oxford: OUP, 1969).

4   Will Hutton, 'Capitalism must put its house in order', *Observer*, 24
    November 2002.

5   Charlotte Denny, 'US bank in hot water after telling clients to pull out
    of unionised firms', *Guardian*, 25 November 2002.

6   'Voice of the People Survey 2002', World Economic Forum. See
    www.weforum.org.

7   Jean Froissart, *Chroniques X*, in Dobson, op. cit.

INDEX